"This is a wonderful book. Neil Broom plants the
seeds of a richer conception of biology, one found beyond the
unreasonable limits of materialistic reductionism—a new
biology that, with some careful nurturing,
should grow into a powerful new science of intelligent design."
PAUL NELSON, *SENIOR FELLOW, THE DISCOVERY INSTITUTE*

"Coming against popular ideas that 'science'
can do all things, Broom makes strong logical and critical
commentary on the reductionistic deflation
in scientific materialism and shows how the world is much richer
and more complex than scientific reductionism will permit."
JAMES E. LODER, *PRINCETON THEOLOGICAL SEMINARY*

How Blind Is
the Watchmaker?

Nature's Design
& the Limits
of Naturalistic
Science

NEIL BROOM

InterVarsity Press
Downers Grove, Illinois
Leicester, England

InterVarsity Press
P.O. Box 1400, Downers Grove, IL 60515-1426, USA
World Wide Web: www.ivpress.com
E-mail: mail@ivpress.com

Inter-Varsity Press, England
38 De Montfort Street, Leicester LE1 7GP, England

InterVarsity Press® is the book-publishing division of InterVarsity Christian Fellowship/USA®, a student movement active on campus at hundreds of universities, colleges and schools of nursing in the United States of America, and a member movement of the International Fellowship of Evangelical Students. For information about local and regional activities, write Public Relations Dept., InterVarsity Christian Fellowship/USA, 6400 Schroeder Rd., P.O. Box 7895, Madison, WI 53707-7895.

Inter-Varsity Press, England, is the book-publishing division of the Universities and Colleges Christian Fellowship (formerly the Inter-Varsity Fellowship), a student movement linking Christian Unions in universities and colleges throughout the United Kingdom and the Republic of Ireland, and a member movement of the International Fellowship of Evangelical Students. For information about local and national activities write to UCCF, 38 De Montfort Street, Leicester LE1 7GP

Cover photograph: K. Eward/Photo Researchers Inc.

ISBN 0-8308-2296-8
UK ISBN 0-85111-554-3

Printed in the United States of America ∞

Library of Congress Cataloging-in-Publication Data

Broom, Neil.
   How blind is the watchmaker?: nature's design & the limits of naturalistic science/
Neil Broom.
     p. cm.
  Originally published: Aldershot: Ashgate Pub., 1998.
  Includes bibliographical references and index.
  ISBN 0-8308-2296-8 (pbk.: alk. paper)
    1. Science—Philosophy.   2. Science—Social aspects.   3. Life—Origin—Philosophy.   4.
Materialism.   5. Religion and science.   I. Title.

  Q175.B792183 2001
  501—dc21

                                      00-054449

British Library Cataloguing in Publication Data

A catalogue record for this book is available from the British Library.

19	18	17	16	15	14	13	12	11	10	9	8	7	6	5	4	3	2	1
17	16	15	14	13	12	11	10	09	08	07	06	05	04	03	02	01		

Dedicated to
Ruth, Benjamin, Reuben, Elizabeth

Contents

Acknowledgments

This book could never have been written in solitary confinement. Rather, it was born out of discussions, arguments and debates with numerous people of wide-ranging philosophical, religious and nonreligious persuasions. One person deserves special mention—my good friend and fellow theist Robert Mann. Throughout the book's writing Robert has provided a rich resource of ideas that have helped shape many of the arguments I have sought to develop.

The editorial staff at IVP have been from the beginning a pleasure to deal with. In particular I wish to thank both Andy Le Peau and Drew Blankman for their editorial wisdom and their unflagging responsiveness to the many issues and questions I raised in the course of working on this new edition. It is a long journey for messages to wing their way across the Pacific from Auckland to Illinois but the quick and efficient attention given to my e-mails and faxes at the IVP end of things took much of the stress out of the task.

*   *   *

The original edition of this book was published by Ashgate, Aldershot, U.K., in their Avebury series in philosophy.

Foreword

Many critics of intelligent design find it inconceivable that someone properly exposed to Darwinian evolution could doubt it. They treat this theory as if it were one of Descartes's clear and distinct ideas that immediately impels assent. Rejecting Darwin's theory thus would require some hidden motivation—like wanting to shore up traditional morality or being a closet fundamentalist.

Critics who think they can dismiss intelligent design merely by assigning disreputable motives to its proponents need to examine their own motives. Why, for example, does Michael Shermer, publisher of *Skeptic* magazine, take such a hard line against intelligent design? Trained in psychology and the social sciences, Shermer endlessly psychologizes those who challenge his naturalistic worldview. But is he willing to psychologize himself? Look at his popular books (e.g., *Why People Believe Weird Things* and *How We Believe*), and you'll notice on the inside dust jacket a smiling Shermer with a bust of Darwin behind him, along with several books by and about Darwin. Shermer's devotion to Darwin and naturalism is as fervent as any religious devotee's.

Neil Broom has no hidden agenda in challenging Darwinism or the scientific naturalism that buttresses it. In *How Blind Is the Watchmaker?* Broom shows conclusively that intelligent design's opposition to Darwinism rests primarily on scientific grounds. He also explores cultural, theological and philosophical implications of intelligent design, but he does so only because Darwinism is, on its own terms, an oversold and overreaching scientific theory. Indeed, his scientific case against Darwinism is devastating.

The success of intelligent design neither stands nor falls on the motives of its practitioners; it hinges on the quality of insights it inspires. Yes, Broom is a

Christian theist. But he offers compelling arguments that need to be taken seriously on their own terms, regardless of one's religious or metaphysical beliefs. Broom's *How Blind Is the Watchmaker?* belongs among the informed critiques of Darwinism and origin-of-life studies that have consistently appeared since Darwin published his *Origin of Species,* keeping company with the works of Louis Agassiz, St. George Mivart, Richard Goldschmidt, Pierre Grassé, Gerald Kerkut, Michael Polanyi, Marcel Schützenberger and Michael Denton.

Criticism, however, is never enough. I'm fond of an insight by Napoleon III: one never destroys a thing until one replaces it. Although it is not a requirement of logic that scientific theories be rejected only when a better alternative is found, the sociology of science does seem to require it—to wit, scientific theories don't give way to criticism but to new, improved theories. Concerted criticism of Darwinism within the growing community of design theorists is therefore only the first step—it is the "thin end of the wedge," as Phillip Johnson calls it.

Nonetheless, critiques like *How Blind Is the Watchmaker?* constitute a necessary first step. In keeping with Thomas Kuhn's stages in scientific revolution, people will take seriously the need for an alternative theory only after their confidence in Darwinism—and especially in the power of natural selection—has been undermined. The next step is to develop a positive scientific research program as a positive alternative to naturalistic approaches to the origin and subsequent development of life. I have no doubt that Neil Broom, expert biophysicist that he is, will have much to contribute in this respect.

Intelligent design is only now beginning to gather momentum. When Broom originally published this book in England (Aldershot, U.K.: Ashgate, 1998), he included almost no references to American design theorists. What impresses me about this earlier edition is that Broom, despite moving outside the circles of the intelligent design community, had come almost point for point to the same conclusions. This demonstrates the robustness of his work as well as that of the design community, and suggests both have drunk at many of the same wells, notably the work of Michael Polanyi. (One of the great selling points of this book is that Broom updates Polanyi's pivotal work from the 1960s on life's irreducible structure.) In this updated edition Broom makes explicit connections to the work of American design theorists.

If there is one theme in *How Blind Is the Watchmaker?* it is freedom. Broom wants to free science from arbitrary constraints that stifle inquiry, undermine education and turn scientists into a secular priesthood. In such a setting intelligent design has been denied a fair hearing.

Broom's title alludes to Richard Dawkins's *The Blind Watchmaker: Why the Evidence of Evolution Reveals a Universe Without Design*. Broom rightly insists that science address not only evidence that suggests a universe without design (Dawkins's method) but also evidence that suggests a designed universe. Evidence is a two-edged sword: claims can be refuted *or* supported by evidence. Even if design ends up being rejected as an unfruitful explanation in science, the evidence for and against design must be fairly considered.

Many in the Christian academic world will find Broom's rejection of reductionism and scientism congenial. They will be less comfortable with Broom's call to take teleology in science seriously. This book is not an invitation for Christian academics and scientists to continue business as usual. Broom's is a far-reaching critique that announces a crisis in the basic concepts of science. To acknowledge and respond to this crisis is to liberate science from the suffocating power of scientific naturalism. To ignore it is to prolong what Mark Noll calls "the scandal of the evangelical mind." Would that the Christian academic community heed the call.

William A. Dembski

Preface

Modern science is without doubt the most powerful cultural force ever devised by the human mind. The sheer grandeur of its achievements and the extent to which these have influenced our daily lives have given it enormous prestige and authority. The so-called hard facts of science are served up routinely on television as "edutainment." The glitzy style of many of these programs and their deliberate avoidance of the vast array of problems that lie beyond the reach of science (and that, if addressed, would do little to help in the ratings war) tend to reinforce the lie that there is no problem too hard for science to solve.

Underlying much of the popular thinking of our age is the assumption that modern science, built on the philosophy of materialism, has enabled humankind to discover the truth about itself and its rightful place in the universe. Scientific materialism, it is widely held, offers us the sole pathway to objective knowledge—knowledge that is free from the distorting influences of religious myth and dogma, and all those imaginary constructs that shaped the worldviews of prescientific societies. Thus scientific materialism provides us with the stark truth about our existence. And this "truth" is simple: we humans are not the handiwork of a transcendent yet personal God; rather, we are merely one of a myriad of biological artifacts produced without purpose or design by the impersonal flow of a cold and unfriendly universe.

This book examines and confronts the view widely held in modern industrialized cultures that the materialist model of the universe is alone consistent with the facts revealed to us by modern science. As part of this general analysis we will explore possible reasons why the modern, scientifically conditioned mind appears so confident in holding to this godless view of the world and of human existence. We will ask whether this confidence is really supported by the findings derived from science itself. Could it be that in much of modern science an overriding set of assumptions actually stifles the obvious, permitting only a particular version of truth (one purged of all religious implications) to surface?

In writing this book I have mainly drawn on material derived from the biological sciences. There are two reasons for this.

First, although I was originally trained as a materials scientist and became involved in research investigating crystalline structures, some years later I changed research areas to explore the world of living materials. This is where I have lingered for the last two decades or so. My exposure to both nonliving and living systems, with their striking similarities but also their much more fundamental differences, has stirred me philosophically, and I have felt compelled to put pen to paper.

Second, in discussions with many fellow scientists I have observed that it is the biologist who often seems most inclined to adopt the hard-nosed materialist position. I find this perplexing, for in my view the living world tells a dramatically different story. Perhaps my observation serves to demonstrate that biology, of all the sciences, in some mysterious way comes closest to religion and therefore feels the threat of the transcendent most acutely.

My title—*How Blind Is the Watchmaker?*—is inspired by both older and more recent sources. The eighteenth-century theologian William Paley argued in his treatise on natural theology that the complexity of the living world pointed to a divine artificer—God![1] For Paley, if the living world could be likened to the complicated workings of a watch, then God was indeed the Grand Watchmaker. A great many contemporary scientists, with their strong naturalistic bias,[2] have dismissed the argument from design for the existence of God. Instead, they argue, the forces driving the unfolding of life are entirely material—the Watchmaker is only our personification of an impersonal set of processes acting without ultimate purpose or meaning. In this scheme of things the notion of God is irrelevant.

As this book began to take shape, I felt increasingly drawn into combative engagement with what I believe is the flimsily crafted but persuasively packaged myth of scientific materialism. While a relatively small number of contemporary materialists are the main focus of my challenge, many readers will appreciate that I have merely identified several of the louder and more influential voices that can be heard above the chorus of mainstream support for naturalism within the contemporary scientific community.

Finally, I should add that this book is not first of all a religious work. Yes, I do refer to God, and I am unashamedly a Christian. But my primary aim is to point the interested reader beyond the desert of scientific materialism to the splendor of a living world that functions poised, as it were, in the presence of a transcendent, nonmaterial dimension—a dimension that both nourishes and imparts meaning to the processes of life. Any science of life that fails to acknowledge this essential integrative aspect is, I believe, an impoverished science. Whether I have argued my case with sufficient conviction is left for the reader to judge.

---

[1]William Paley, *Natural Theology: Or Evidences of the Existence and Attributes of the Deity Collected from the Appearances of Nature* (London: SPCK, 1837), chap. 1.
[2]Throughout this book I use the terms *naturalism* and *materialism* more or less synonymously as referring to the belief that the entire workings of the cosmos can ultimately be reduced to the impersonal play of wholly material processes.

1

A New Shape of "Divinity"

The modern high-tech world is a towering monument standing as a tribute to the remarkable intellectual and creative potential of the human mind. But it is not just a monument; it is also an enormous power that is relentlessly reshaping and transforming almost every aspect of our daily lives. This power is derived from a mode of human thought and activity and from a way of investigating the natural world that had its birth some four centuries ago—the modern scientific method.[1]

The philosophy of materialism, or naturalism, largely dominates the modern scientific interpretation of the natural world. Put simply, this conceptual model states that the cosmos is to be explained in terms of material processes alone and that lifeless matter and energy are all that make up ultimate reality. In this view humankind, instead of occupying a special place, is just one of many equally insignificant cogs within the vast, impersonal cosmic machine.

Philosophical materialism sees humanity as an unplanned artifact, a fluke biological byproduct of a wholly material sequence of events. The re-

---

[1]The appendix of this book traces some of the key historical steps that led to the rise of modern science. Readers especially interested in this aspect of humanity's intellectual pilgrimage may find it helpful to read the appendix before continuing on here.

lentless grinding away of an unfeeling cosmos is the sole cause of our existence. Humans are merely one particular arrangement of molecules in a universe containing many other equally improbable arrangements. In this system of thought the play of entirely *impersonal* processes has ended up producing *persons*.

By contrast, the religious interpretation of the cosmos asserts that ultimate reality transcends the purely material, that the universe is expressive of a great mind—the mind of God. As the layers of complexity comprising the material world are progressively peeled away, we draw closer to a dimension that transcends the purely material.

Theism—one particular religious view—asserts even more than the existence of *Something* behind and beyond the material world; it also claims that the world is constantly sustained and nurtured by this transcendent dimension. (I am, of course, using the word *material* to include both nonliving and living things.) Logically it follows that if the material world really does depend for its existence on this higher influence, then any attempt by the materalist to construct a coherent science of the natural world while denying this nonmaterial dimension is doomed to failure.

In a nutshell this book is about the abject failure of scientific materialism to account for the phenomenon of life because of its unyielding belief that reality is, ultimately, lifeless matter.

Science Redefines Humanity

Scientific materialism represents a momentous shift in human thought. Herbert Simon, computer theorist, psychologist and Nobel prize winner, comments thus:

> The definition of man's uniqueness has always formed the kernel of his cosmological and ethical systems. With Copernicus and Galileo, he ceased to be the species located at the centre of the universe, attended by sun and stars. With Darwin, he ceased to be the species created and specially endowed by God with soul and reason. With Freud, he ceased to be the species whose behaviour was—potentially—governable by rational mind. As we begin to produce mechanisms that think and learn, he has ceased to be the species uniquely capable of complex, intelligent manipulation of his environment. What the computer and the progress in artificial intelligence challenge is an ethic that rests on man's apartness from the rest of nature. An alternative ethic, of course, views man as a part of nature, governed by natural law, subject to the forces of gravity and the demands of his body. The debate about

artificial intelligence and the simulation of man's thinking is, in considerable part, a confrontation of these two views of man's place in the universe.[2]

What Simon seems to be saying is that modern science has fundamentally redefined human significance within the cosmos. We should therefore ask what it is about science that qualifies it to offer such a radically different interpretation of our humanness. To answer this question we must first seek to understand the ethos and culture within which the practitioners of science operate.

The Inner Sanctum of Science

The sheer scale of science's achievements seems to engender a strong humanistic optimism within its ranks. Science is spectacularly successful in the way it works. A problem is confronted; a solution is found; a new insight is revealed; gradually a more coherent and complete picture begins to emerge; and finally there comes (quite often, anyway) a big breakthrough. After months and sometimes years of painstaking experimentation and detective work in which many fragments of evidence are systematically collected and analyzed, a new and unifying scientific principle is established.

At the center of all this action is the human achiever—the scientist, the person whose very name may become synonymous with the truth as revealed by science. Philosopher John Passmore comments, "Participation in the scientific enterprise generates, of itself, a confidence in human potentialities, contrasting, very strikingly, with the emphasis on human limitations, human failure, so characteristic of the greatest literature, the comic as much as the tragic."[3] Furthermore the scientist, when engaged in research, is able to set up a mini-universe and be a kind of master of ceremonies within it. The scientist can personally define the boundaries of a particular investigation, excluding those aspects that might be beyond his or her immediate capabilities as a scientist and thereby improving the chances of achieving a positive outcome.

The boundaries within which the scientist works often mean that the results obtained may have limited relevance to the real world we experience. Reality is often vastly more complex than anything the scientist can hope to

---

[2]Herbert Simon, "What Computers Mean for Man and Society," *Science* 195 (1977): 1186-91.
[3]John Passmore, *Science and Its Critics* (London: Duckworth, 1978), pp. 45-67.

Figure 1.1. The ultimate scientific accolade—a Nobel medal. (Copyright © The Nobel Foundation. Image used with permission.)

simulate in an experiment or represent in a model. Despite these limitations, scientists are nearly always able to see some kind of fruit for their labors—they commonly are seen to be achievers, solvers of mysteries, revealers of truth.

Scientists are also real people driven by motives that may not always be consistent with the selfless pursuit of truth. There is the human ego, attracted by the fame and fortune that often go with a dramatic discovery. There is the chance to have a satisfying and stimulating career. And for a chosen few there is the prospect of a Nobel prize or the like (see figure 1.1). This we might call the inner sanctum of the scientist's world.

Aristocrats and High Priests

Passmore has coined the word *aristoscience* to describe the most prestigious scientific disciplines—scientific disciplines that might, for example, examine a particular set of phenomena separated from their wider and more meaningful context in the actual world. Scientists analyze these phenomena in great depth in terms of their fundamental makeup and then describe or model them in the language of complex mathematics.

This method of breaking down a highly complex system or structure into simpler, more manageable portions and then reconstructing it in a virtual, mathematical form has proved enormously valuable to science. In particular it has enabled scientists to make predictions concerning the behavior of complex systems that are not easily investigated by actual experimentation. Models that attempt to predict climatic change associated with rising global temperatures clearly fall into this category. It is very difficult to conduct controlled experiments on the weather!

A fascinating example of how a sophisticated model can be created using the reduction-reconstruction method is shown in figure 1.2. It is in fact a "mathematical eye." A group of research engineers at the University of Auckland has developed this virtual three-dimensional eye that can move—its pupil can dilate and contract, and the eyelids blink. Even the eyelashes and surrounding facial skin are generated mathematically. This computer-based graphical realism is achieved by varying the parameters in the complex mathematical relationships used to formulate the model.

However, we must always remember that even the most sophisticated model will only provide a partial glimpse of how the actual living organ functions. The many layers of complexity that comprise the biological world will always surpass the scientists' ability to express this reality in the relatively crude language of mathematics. In the next chapter I will explore further this issue of biological complexity using the familiar example of plant photosynthesis. Then in chapter five we will return to the topic of scientific models to examine not only their strengths but also their potential to mislead us into thinking that a rigorous understanding of biological reality is achievable with the tools of science.

While I do not claim membership in the elite club of aristoscientists, my own area of research— joint-tissue biomechanics[4] and arthritis research—illustrates rather nicely another fundamental limitation of science. In reality it is a person's whole joint that malfunctions, becoming painful, diseased or arthritic. But whole joints are extremely difficult, if not impossible, to investigate in a rigorous scientific sense. However, by removing some part of the joint structure (in my own laboratory we are concerned with the disease-prone cartilage and underlying bone tissues), it is possible to carry out detailed studies of these tissues and thus gain some understanding of their individual properties.

Figure 1.2. The "mathematical eye." This realistic eye model has been generated mathematically using sophisticated computer graphics. (Images courtesy of Mark Sagar, Gordon Mallinson and Peter Hunter, University of Auckland.)

So one approach, which might attempt to examine the whole joint, has its feet planted firmly in the real world but would yield results having limited scientific respectability. A second approach involves the scientist taking bits of tissue out of their

---

[4]Biomechanics, as the name suggests, is an interdisciplinary area of research which seeks to apply the principles of mechanical analysis to the tissues and organs of the living body.

meaningful place within the complete functioning joint and devising a rather artificial set of tests or experiments in the laboratory (a kind of mini-universe) so that sciehtifically respectable, quantitative results can be ob-

tained. This second approach may have its head in the clouds but stands a much greater chance of gracing the pages of important scientific journals. And if it does, it will further enhance the scientist's reputation, add to his or her list of research publications and improve prospects of promotion and job security.

There is another, perhaps less obvious but more disturbing consequence of this kind of science. Although real-world problems may not always be solved, the scientist is perceived by society to be the solver of mysteries, the person with the power to unravel, manipulate and control the forces of nature. Theologian-philosopher Langdon Gilkey draws an interesting parallel between the religious priest (see figure 1.3) and the aristoscientist:

Figure 1.3. Who are the "knowers" of ultimate truth in a culture dominated by science? Has the scientist's white coat replaced the high-priestly robe? (Photograph by the author. Courtesy of St. Paul's Anglican Church, Auckland.)

> Greater knowledge always means greater power. Thus, whether this be their intention or not, the 'knowers' in any society bequeath to their culture ever-new powers to transform its life. It is for this reason that knowers, religious or scientific, are valued as well as revered by their society, the priest's robes and the scientist's white coat signifying much the same social role as the knower of significant secrets and so the doer of all-important deeds.[5]

But Gilkey goes even further than this. He sees science, by its power to control the mysterious forces of nature, as usurping the traditional role of religion in society.

> Whenever knowledge and control have such a sacral character—that is, whenever they promise salvation from what we take to be our most funda-

---

[5]Langdon Gilkey, *Society and the Sacred: Towards a Theology of Culture in Decline* (New York: Crossroad, 1981), p. 76.

mental ills—they dominate the culture that forms itself around them. As religion had dominated the civilization of the medieval period, so science has dominated ours. It has determined or shaped education, molded our sense of human excellence, grounded our hopes for the future, and established itself as the queen of all the other disciplines of learning.[6]

Science in our modern technological world has come to symbolize the power of the human mind to rise above all prior conditioning and arrive at objective truth. Edward Goldsmith sees the scientific community as a kind of secular priesthood with its "holy" writings expressed in an esoteric language often completely unintelligible to the layperson but creating an image of mystery and sanctity (see figure 1.4). He writes of those in the "sacred" community of aristoscientists:

> They have defined truth in such a way that they alone have access to it, for it must be established by a set of scientific rituals which only they can perform: only they possess the necessary scientific skills; only they are equipped with the requisite scientific technology; only they have access to the holy places where, in order to be valid, these rituals must be performed.[7]

Goldsmith's appraisal is provocative and perhaps somewhat extreme, but it does serve as a timely warning to science to tread carefully, to admit to its own fundamental limitations and not to yield to the temptation of pronouncing on matters that lie beyond its legitimate reach. The nature of science as a human activity means that it can never have the final say on the really big questions of life. We shall be returning to this important issue in due course.

Mechanistic Mongers of Gloom

In the secular industrialized world it is now widely held that the knowledge gained from science is pure, unembellished truth. This "truth" stands in contrast to the subjective view of truth derived, for example, from religion or from various forms of spiritual experience. Science alone, the materialist will argue, gives us the brute facts about the cosmos and about ourselves within the natural order of things. Science allows us to see things as they really are—or so we are told.

It is in this spirit of supposed scientific objectivity that Nobel laureate Jacques Monod insists we face up to the stark fact of human existence

---

[6]Ibid., p. 78.
[7]Edward Goldsmith, *The Way: An Ecological World View* (London: Rider, 1992), p. 80.

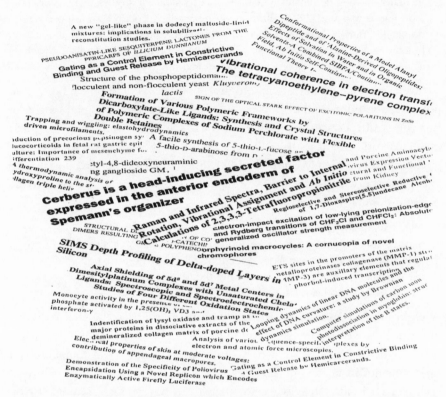

Figure 1.4. A montage of scientific esoterica—sample titles of research papers published in recent scientific periodicals. The technical language that is used is largely unintelligible to those outside the inner sanctum of science.

trapped within a cosmos that is ultimately meaningless and amoral: "Man must at last wake out of his millenary dream; and in doing so, wake to his total solitude, his fundamental isolation. Now does he at last realize that, like a gypsy, he lives on the boundary of an alien world. A world that is deaf to his music, just as indifferent to his hopes as it is to his suffering or his crimes."[8] And then Monod declares, "The ancient covenant is in pieces; man knows at last that he is alone in the universe's unfeeling immensity, out of which he emerged only by chance."[9] These haunting words serve to illustrate a philosophy that is widely articulated, particularly in our affluent technocracies where the fruits of modern science are so powerfully evi-

[8]Jacques Monod, *Chance and Necessity* (London: Collins, 1972), p. 160.
[9]Ibid., p. 166.

dent. It assumes that science has shown that life in all its diversity has been produced by a mechanistic, chance-driven process that, by its very definition, destroys any ultimate basis for meaning and purpose within the universe. The implication is that science, by virtue of its supposedly unique ability to reveal the hard facts concerning our existence, can provide answers to those questions that religion was once asked to address.

Within this materialistic framework of thought there is no God, there is no moral reference point, there is no higher purpose to be searched for and to be expressed in our lives. Rather, we need to face the "truth." We need to discard the fairy-tale idea of a divinity who has given humanity a sense of moral and eternal purpose. Then, it is argued, we will find clearly revealed only the relentless throb of a vast, impersonal, law-bound cosmic machine that, having no mind itself, certainly did not have us in mind.

In much the same humanistic spirit, astrophysicist and Nobel laureate Steven Weinberg illustrates this faith many scientists have in their supposed ability to convey to us the brute truth about human existence. In the epilogue to his book *The First Three Minutes* he writes:

> It is almost irresistible for humans to believe that we have some special relation to the universe, that human life is not just a more-or-less farcical outcome of a chain of accidents reaching back to the first three minutes, but that we were somehow built in from the beginning. As I write this I happen to be in an airplane at 30,000 feet, flying over Wyoming en route home from San Francisco to Boston. Below, the earth looks very soft and comfortable—fluffy clouds here and there, snow turning pink as the sun sets, roads stretching straight across the country from one town to another. It is very hard to realize that this all is just a tiny part of an overwhelmingly hostile universe. It is even harder to realize that this present universe has evolved from an unspeakably unfamiliar early condition, and faces a future extinction of endless cold or intolerable heat. The more the universe seems comprehensible, the more it also seems pointless. But if there is no solace in the fruits of our research, there is at least some consolation in the research itself. Men and women are not content to comfort themselves with tales of gods and giants, or to confine their thoughts to the daily affairs of life; they also build telescopes and satellites and accelerators, and sit at their desks for endless hours working out the meaning of the data they gather. The effort to understand the universe is one of the very few things that lifts human life a little above the level of farce, and gives it some of the grace of tragedy.[10]

But we must ask, Is the science that Steven Weinberg practices equipped

---

[10]Steven Weinberg, *The First Three Minutes* (New York: Basic, 1977), pp. 150-55.

to pronounce on the supposed pointlessness of the universe? If the universe really is so "overwhelmingly hostile," why are we proliferating at the rate of some 90 million persons per year? Evidence clearly confronting us in at least one tiny corner of the cosmos—namely, planet Earth—indicates that conditions are incredibly encouraging of life.

So has Weinberg's picture of an ultimately pointless cosmos and an equally farcical human existence within that cosmos,[11] or Monod's claim that we have emerged by chance out of the unfeeling immensity of the universe, actually been derived with any certainty from their own scientific investigations? I would argue, no. For to draw such far-reaching, pessimistic conclusions, one would need to have experienced the cosmos as a whole. It could never be derived, as Paul Roubiczek notes, "from the content of a particular experience."[12]

For human beings confined within one tiny part of the cosmos to assert that the cosmos is futile, however clever their scientific observations might be, is surely the height of creaturely arrogance. It expresses more their unerring faith in an ideology of materialism than a true insight into the ultimate nature and purpose of our existence. Human finitude will always prevent us from knowing all the facts about the universe without some form of transcendent, or "outside," revelation. Therefore, dogmatic pronouncements by scientists concerning the supposed meaninglessness of life arise more from their own materialistic presuppositions than from a spirit of genuine, scientific open-mindedness.

In fact, I would venture to say that even from our scientific understanding of the living world it can be reasonably argued that we have not emerged by chance and that life is not merely the outcome of some cosmic lottery. The universe is not as unfeeling and impersonal as many modern

---

[11]To Weinberg's credit he has admitted more recently that his remark "the more the universe seems comprehensible, the more it seems pointless" in the above passage was "rash." Weinberg then adds that he "did not mean that science teaches us that the universe is pointless, but rather that the universe itself suggests no point." But we might then ask, how does Weinberg himself inspect the universe for evidence of this supposed pointlessness? One must presume that either he has access to some higher form of revelation (but he is adamant that there is no "interested God" who might have revealed anything anyway), or he draws on his own science for this evidence—which really returns us full circle to his first "rash" comment. See Steven Weinberg, *Dreams of a Final Theory* (New York: Pantheon, 1983), pp. 241-61.

[12]Paul Roubiczek, *Ethical Values in an Age of Science* (Cambridge: Cambridge University Press, 1964), p. 104.

materialists would have us believe. In the ensuing chapters we will look closely at evidence derived from science suggesting rather strongly that there is a profoundly personal dimension that undergirds and imparts meaning and purpose to the natural world.

2

The Business of Science

This chapter will look at how the "business" of science is conducted. I will then ask, Are there aspects of the scientific method that place an inherent limitation on what can be achieved or discovered? The fundamental issue is whether the activity of science provides the only pure, disinterested and objective pathway to truth. Is the scientific method the sole means of arriving at the real? For example, can any science be in possession of such a complete view of reality as to be able to declare authoritatively that we are merely a fluke biological artifact produced by the vast, impersonal flow of the universe?

These questions concern the meaning of life itself. It is vitally important that we understand just how far science can take us down the pathway to a right understanding of such ultimate issues.

The Kind of Truth Science Reveals

The media, especially television, have played a crucial role in the promotion of science. But popularized science can have both high interest and high propaganda content. We are constantly bombarded with pronouncements declared to be "scientific" (and therefore true!), or we are told that "science has proved such and such," but rarely are the nonexperts told that science by its very nature is limited in what it can actually tell us. What then are the limitations of this human activity we call science?

First, science is not equipped to give us truth in an absolute sense. Science is not nearly as objective as many would have us believe. Science does not just look at the raw facts and then arrive at the pure, unsullied truth. Rather the scientist will always bring some kind of prior commitment or personal bias or partiality to bear on the process of observing. A scientist is not a completely open-minded, passive receiver of truth.

Karl Popper argues that, without theoretical interpretation, observation remains uninformative. He says:

> In science it is *observation* rather than perception which plays the decisive part. But observation is a process in which we play an intensively *active* part. An observation is a perception, but one which is planned and prepared. We do not 'have' an observation (as we may 'have' a sense experience) but we 'make' an observation. (A navigator even 'works' an observation.) An observation is always preceded by a particular interest, a question, or a problem—in short, by something theoretical.[1]

Popper comments further, "Science never starts from scratch; it can never be described as free from assumptions; for at every instant it presupposes a horizon of expectations—yesterday's horizon of expectations, as it were."[2] In other words, the scientist always subjectively interprets or processes the data that is obtained. Mary Midgley expresses the same sentiment more strongly. "Merely to pile up information indiscriminately," she says, "is an idiot's task."[3]

Edward Goldsmith argues that "observation or perception, which is supposed to be the source of all our knowledge, begins with the detection of data. It is active rather than passive, detecting rather than merely receiving and it is also highly selective. Instead of accumulating available data in a random fashion, as empiricists assume we do, we isolate those which appear relevant to our behaviour pattern (a minute percentage of the total) from those which do not . . . , those that our upbringing and experience within a particular culture have taught us to regard as relevant to our behaviour."[4] And this is equally true of the scientist in his laboratory. There may be elements of an experiment that are overlooked completely by one trained observer but that another "sees" as being loaded with significance. And it is this

[1] Karl Popper, *Objective Knowledge: An Evolutionary Approach* (Oxford: Oxford University Press, 1979), p. 342.
[2] Ibid., p. 346.
[3] Mary Midgley, *Evolution as a Religion: Strange Hopes and Stranger Fears* (London: Methuen, 1985), p. 3.
[4] Edward Goldsmith, *The Way: An Ecological World View* (London: Rider, 1992), p. 65.

personal insight that becomes crucial to the growth of a particular area of knowledge. The scientist always brings a background of personal beliefs, values and evaluative skills into the practice of his or her profession.

Michael Polanyi rejects the idea that a scientist is some kind of "truth-finding machine." Rather, the scientist appears acting

> as detective, policeman, judge, and jury all rolled into one. He apprehends certain clues as suspect, formulates the charge and examines the evidence both for and against it, admitting or rejecting such parts of it as he thinks fit, and finally pronounces judgement. While all the time, far from being neutral at heart, he is himself passionately interested in the outcome of the procedure. He must be, for otherwise he will never discover a problem at all and certainly not advance towards its solution.[5]

Polanyi attacks the whole idea of objective knowledge, that is, knowledge supposedly free of preconceived beliefs, as being absurd. He insists that if this is to be our ideal of the acquisition of objective knowledge, then "we must accept the virgin mind, bearing the imprint of no authority, as the model of intellectual integrity." But, as he points out, the assumption of such a virgin mind is one that

> must be allowed to mature until the age at which it reaches its full natural powers of intelligence, but would have to be kept unshaped until then by any kind of education. It must be taught no language, for speech can be acquired only a-critically, and the practice of speech in one particular language carries with it the acceptance of the particular theory of the universe postulated by that language.[6]

This entirely untutored maturing of the mind would, as Polanyi notes, "result in a state of imbecility." Truly objective scientific knowledge is therefore a myth. The essence of scientific knowledge embodies the passions, prejudices, ego and belief system of the scientist as a person. These will all have an influence on the process by which scientific truth is shaped.

Fragmented Knowledge

The second point to emphasize is that the scientific method works largely by a process we call abstraction. Let me explain.

In order to study a complex system the scientist is usually compelled to break it down into smaller, more manageable pieces so that precise obser-

---

[5]Michael Polanyi, *Science, Faith and Society* (Chicago: University of Chicago Press, 1966), p. 38.
[6]Michael Polanyi, *Personal Knowledge* (Chicago: University of Chicago Press, 1962), p. 295.

vation and measurement can be carried out. Recall that in the previous chapter I briefly mentioned as an illustration some of the difficulties encountered when one attempts to study scientifically the complex functioning of the body joints. One important aim of this kind of research has been to try to understand how the cartilage layer covering the bone ends in the joint is able to endure high levels of mechanical force without wearing out, often for the entire span of a person's life. And related to this is the important question of how forces transmitted through the joint might also be responsible for contributing to the development of the common and crippling disease osteoarthritis (see figure 2.1). Ideally the experimenter would like to obtain an "inside" view of the tissue structure at extremely high magnification while it is actually loaded in the living joint. But this kind of real-life observation is impossible to carry out for reasons that I will endeavor to explain.

To study the detailed structure of cartilage, an electron microscope is required. This sophisticated instrument uses a focused beam of electrons rather than the beam of light employed in the optical microscope. The advantage of the electron beam over that of light is that a much higher resolution of structural detail can be achieved. The technique requires a sample of cartilage to be shaved from the joint surface (destroying it as living tissue) and then put through a complicated sequence of chemical "embalming" and coating treatments that allow it to be examined under the high-voltage electron beam of the microscope (figure 2.2).

Figure 2.1. A portion of the patella, or kneecap in cross-section, showing severe osteoarthritic destruction of the white layer of cartilage on the upper left side. (Photograph by the author.)

So the final act of scientifically studying the cartilage is conducted on something far removed from the actual soft cartilage tissue found in the living joint. We cannot image the important structural features in this tissue and still retain its living, functioning state. This dissected or fragmented view of reality is all to often the price the scientist must pay in order to observe a complex system in any great detail.

Another major problem that the scientist in this area faces is how to measure the mechanical forces in the cartilage tissue while it is in its correct location in the living joint. Again the experimenter is faced with taking

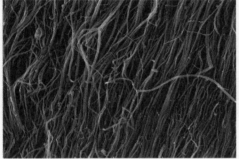

portions of the appropriate tissue out of the body of a dead animal or person and then subjecting these detached, or "abstracted," bits to rigorous testing and measurement. But each time we go through this scientific procedure we deprive these portions of tissue of their vital relationship within the living joint. So my detailed knowledge of some of the component parts of the whole joint, although scientifically respectable, in no way guarantees that I fully understand the living joint itself.

Figure 2.2. The detailed structure of cartilage when viewed at high magnification (approximately fifteen thousand times) using the scanning electron microscope. The rodlike elements consist of tiny protein fibers, or fibrils, that are largely responsible for imparting to cartilage tissue an exceptional degree of strength and flexibility. The upper photograph shows the structure in the healthy tissue in which the fibrils are knitted into a vaguely trellislike arrangement. In the lower photograph, obtained from a diseased sample of cartilage, the fibrils are strongly aligned without this effective knit between neighboring elements. (Photographs by the author.)

The fragmenting method of analysis I have described above, using the example of cartilage, is encountered to varying degrees in every branch of experimental science. And while achieving much, it can also create an overconfidence, a feeling that scientists have the ability to give us the complete picture. Paul Weiss rightly calls this "faith in the omnipotence of analytical decomposition."[7]

Images of complex structures, such as those of cartilage shown in figure 2.2, can be compelling but also potentially misleading. They are obtained using a highly sophisticated and expensive research instrument,

---

[7]Paul Weiss, *Within the Gates of Science and Beyond* (New York: Hafner, 1971), p. 214.

and this fact alone can all too easily add to the impression that a deep scientific mystery has been solved. The kind of images I have shown in figure 2.2 can certainly provide the scientist with important insights into the structure of cartilage. But is this what it really looks like? The reality may be vastly more complex, simply because we have had to destroy the cartilage as a piece of living tissue in order to view it under the electron beam of the microscope. Successful in-depth analysis is often at the expense of departing from reality.

Levels of Knowing

The scientific method is really just one way we humans acquire knowledge. This mode of knowing must be recognized with all its built-in limitations and prejudices. Philosopher Marjorie Grene suggests that the so-called objective knowledge science often claims to provide is rather an objectification of real things.[8] This is nicely illustrated with the example of the joint cartilage mentioned in the previous section. The cartilage tissue, as an integrated living system, is reduced to a nonliving and highly modified detached *object* so that it can be studied scientifically.

Consider another obvious example—a beautiful piece of music. We can analyze it physically as consisting of patterns of mechanical vibrations transmitted through the air. We can also study the music biochemically, physiologically and psychologically by analyzing the various mechanisms operating in the neuroanatomy and physiological functions of the listener (figure 2.3). But of course, with all this so-called objective and carefully quantified scientific knowledge, we have still left the music unexplained in the most meaningful sense—its subjective impression on our being as humans. We can enjoy and be deeply moved by a score of music without knowing a single thing about the physics of sound waves, their mechanical interaction with the complex structure of the ear, and the signal-processing activities of the brain.

Similarly, heat may be described physically as molecules in rapid motion, but this tells us nothing whatsoever about one of the most important physical experiences of the body—the sensation of heat. The reality of my feeling hot is simply not explained by a reductionist description of molecules in motion.

---

[8]Marjorie Grene, *The Knower and the Known* (London: Faber & Faber, 1966), p. 179.

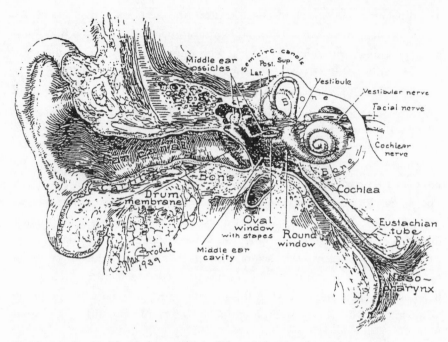

Figure 2.3. A scientific understanding of the mechanism by which sound waves are detected by the ear and then sent to the brain still leaves the music unexplained in its most fundamental sense. (Reproduced with permission from M. Brödel, *Three Unpublished Drawings of the Anatomy of the Human Ear* [Philadelphia: W. B. Saunders, 1946].)

Marjorie Grene puts in a nutshell this important idea that science yields a lower level of truth when she says, "Physics alone conveys no meaning, no utterance."[9] In the same way we cannot find a scientific definition of personal qualities such as intuitiveness, purposefulness, dogged commitment, honesty and sound judgment. And yet all of these are fundamental to the success of the scientific enterprise.

The Power of Scientific Analysis
Modern science has been singularly successful in providing us with a close-up, lower-level view of reality. Whether we focus our electron microscopes on the details of molecular reality or our radio telescopes on the vast dimensions of astronomical reality, we find that the tools of sci-

---

[9]Marjorie Grene, "Hierarchies in Biology," *American Scientist* 75 (1987): 506.

ence are superbly effective in analyzing the detailed cause-and-effect relationships in the cosmos that are governed by the material laws of nature.

There is a rich bounty of examples from science that could be used to illustrate the spectacular power of the analytical method. But for now let's consider the familiar example of photosynthesis. This is just one of the many truly remarkable life-supporting innovations that lie at the heart of the living world. The immensely sophisticated living machinery that is used to carry out photosynthesis in the plant world is the biological equivalent of "Russian nesting dolls." This machinery is literally made up of systems within systems within systems, starting

Figure 2.4. The leaf contains the plant's light-harvesting or photosynthetic machinery and is a splendid example of biological "nesting dolls." (Author's photograph)

at the level of the plant leaf (see figure 2.4) and extending right down to the subatomic world of the electron. So let me try to explain it in a little more detail.[10]

Photosynthesis takes place in seemingly insignificant microscopic bodies

---

[10]Some readers may find this section dealing with photosynthesis a little technical. For those unfamiliar with the terminology, this chapter contains other, less complex illustrations that make much the same point.

called chloroplasts (fig-
ure 2.5) that are present
in the cells within the interior of the leaf and that
account for its green
color. Within these chlo-
roplasts there are special
membranes stacked in
parallel layers known as
grana and visible only at
very high magnification
under the electron mi-
croscope (see figure
2.6). Embedded within
these membranes is the
very heart of the photo-
synthetic machinery—
complex clusters of pig-
mented molecules that
are able to collect sun-
light. These light-har-

Figure 2.5. Tiny cookie-shaped chloroplasts contained
within the honeycomblike cells of the plant as seen under
the light microscope at a magnification of approximately
one thousand times. Although seemingly insignificant in
appearance, each chloroplast is a wonderfully sophisticated energy harvesting and converting biological system
that is far from completely understood. To obtain this particular photograph, a thin sliver was pared from the
green stem of a common lilly plant with a sharp razor-
blade. This sliver was then sandwiched between two glass
slides to which a drop of water was added to enhance
optical clarity. (Photograph by the author.)

vesting units consist of a special chlorophyll molecule termed the "reaction

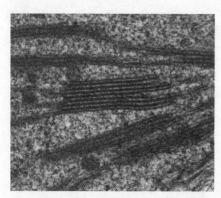

Figure 2.6. Part of a chloroplast viewed
at 160,000 times magnification under
the electron microscope to reveal the
stacked layers of membranes or grana.
(Image courtesy of the School of Biological Sciences, University of Auckland.)

center," surrounded by several hundred "antenna" pigment molecules that
include both chlorophyll and carotenoid molecules. Collectively this
combination of specialized light-react-
ing molecules is known as a "photosystem" (figure 2.7).

The chlorophylls absorb the light
of red and blue wavelengths while
reflecting the green portion of the
spectrum, whereas the carotenoid
molecules absorb the blue and green
wavelengths and reflect the yellow,
orange and red. Sunlight is absorbed
by the layer of antenna pigment mol-

ecules, which in turn transfer this energy to the reaction-center chlorophyll. The result is that an electron is boosted to a higher energy level.

There are known to be two distinct photosystems (identified as I and II) in the plant leaf, and these cooperate closely in the harvesting of the sun's energy. Both photosystems absorb the sunlight simultaneously, with electrons being raised to a higher energy level and then passed on to an electron-accepting molecule (figure 2.7). This loss of the negatively charged electron results in the reaction-center molecules in each photosystem becoming positively charged. The strong positive charge produced on photo-

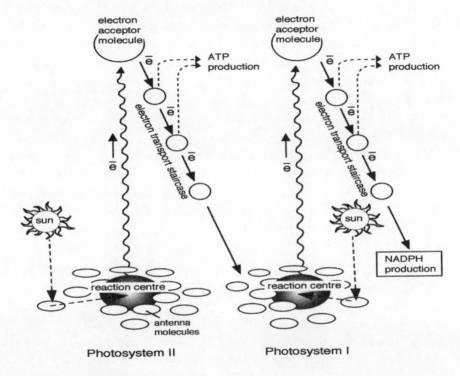

Figure 2.7. Schematic of the molecular "powerhouse" of the photosynthetic machinery. Note especially the electron transport system, or energy "staircase" down which the excited electrons cascade in controlled steps. (Image courtesy of Vivian Ward, University of Auckland.)

system II is able to pull replacement electrons from water molecules by splitting them into oxygen and positive hydrogen ions (that is, protons).[11]

---

[11]A proton is a hydrogen atom stripped of its electron, an ion with a single positive charge.

This oxygen is released into the atmosphere while the hydrogen ions or protons pass into the fluid space enclosed by the tiny membrane surfaces (more about these protons in a moment).

Let us now follow the journey of an electron that has left the reaction center of photosystem II (figure 2.7). After its reception by an acceptor molecule, it is passed down a voltage "staircase," or gradient of precisely arranged molecules called the electron transport system, ending up in the positively charged reaction center of photosystem I where it makes up for the electron deficit also created by the excitation process.

The original electron that was excited from photosystem I is received by its own acceptor molecule and then passes down another electron transport system. The energy given up by the electron in its passage down this "staircase" is used to form an energy-transacting molecule biologists abbreviate as NADPH, which drives important energy-storing reactions elsewhere in the cell.

The action of both photosystems produces a buildup of protons with a higher concentration on one side of the special membranes in the grana than on the other. It is this proton gradient that is used to power the production of another important energy-transacting molecule called ATP (see figure 2.7). Both molecules, NADPH and ATP, although they cannot be stored in the cell's energy bank, are used by the cell to produce energy-rich sugars that can be transported as required to different parts of the cellular factory, or stored as starch. This ability of the cell to store sugar and then transport it to where it is needed is essential for the plant's growth and survival. It is crucial for the many parts of the plant where photosynthesis cannot take place—for example, in the roots and the stem. During the night hours, when the photosynthetic machinery is unable to function, each cell, still requiring a maintenance supply of energy, draws on this storehouse of sugar.

This vastly incomplete description of just some of the principal mechanisms known to be involved in photosynthesis serves to illustrate just how successful modern science has been in providing a detailed understanding, at a molecular level, of the physical and chemical processes that are utilized in the living world. A casual browse through any modern biology textbook will provide ample evidence for the quite staggering achievements of the scientific method.

However, despite this remarkable success story, the most fundamental aspects of the living world remain largely unexplained by the insights that modern scientific analysis is able to provide. The living organism—even simplistically described as a purposeful, achieving, wanting-to-survive set of coherent, interrelated systems-within-systems—defies ultimate scientific explanation. This must surely cause us to question the frequent claim that the scientific method is the only objective pathway to truth.

The Faltering Power of Science

Continuing with our example of the plant's photosynthetic machinery, we find that modern mechanistic science is strangely silent on how this sophisticated biological system might have originated. Textbooks typically describe the chloroplast as having evolved from some simpler organism employing a metabolic system that might have been able to produce the first oxygen from an oxygenless early earth atmosphere.[12] Apart from rather vague comments like these, there is little serious discussion of the chloroplast's origin.

Photosynthesis is in fact the ultimate energy source of almost all living things known to us today, and its origin is just part of the much more fundamental question of how life began in the first place. While chapters four and five deal with the origin-of-life issue in some detail, at this point I would suggest that any attempt to provide an explanation for the existence of a biological system such as the chloroplast based on the impersonal material laws of nature is doomed to failure. Let me explain what I mean by this rather dogmatic statement.

First, for all the detailed knowledge we now have of the molecular mechanisms operating in the chloroplast, this still constitutes what I have previously termed "lower-level knowledge." This understanding, while fairly rigorous, fails miserably when it is used in any attempt to provide a coherent, higher-level explanation for the existence of the chloroplast as a purposeful biological entity.

In order to provide a more practical illustration of what I mean by lower- versus higher-level explanations I have adapted an idea taken from the writings of the British neuroscientist Donald MacKay.[13] In figure 2.8 we

---

[12]Explanations in biology are often couched in terms of things having "evolved" from simpler systems, thereby giving the impression that no deeper explanation is required. But this kind of talk has no more explanatory power than is contained in the statement "the modern computer evolved from the Chinese abacus." It might be historically true but it tells us absolutely nothing about the crucial role of human creativity and ingenuity in this technological evolution.

[13]Donald M. MacKay, *Brains, Mind, Machines* (London: Collins, 1980), p. 18.

begin with a rather nondescript but highly magnified view of ink on paper at the bottom left side of the figure. Stepping back just a little, we discover that this blob is actually part of a greatly magnified letter z (see lower right). But when viewed at progressively greater distances, this letter z is seen to be part of the name Elizabeth (my daughter) in a birth entry in a portion of newspaper text, which in turn is used as a cutout to form the letter P in a quite different medium of representation. Finally we arrive at the highest level of meaning in which the command "STOP!" is seen.

Figure 2.8. Transcendence illustrated—levels of explanation. A lower-level description would legitimately describe these pictures as ink on paper. However, a higher level of explanation involves a meaningful message that transcends the physical and chemical processes involved in the staining of paper with ink. (Illustration by the author.)

Now we could argue that each picture is just ink on paper, and in one sense this is perfectly correct. Each picture is the result of a simple chemical interaction between the molecules of ink dye and the cellulose molecules in the wood fibers from which the newsprint is made. This is the lowest level of explanation and is analogous to what we might call the scientific description. But such a description tells us nothing about the higher-level meaning of the ink on paper despite the rigor of our chemical explanations. No amount of scientific description could have accounted for a message commanding the viewer to stop. This second level of explanation stands fundamentally above and beyond anything we can derive by application of the scientific method.

So it is with our earlier example of the chloroplast. At the lowest level we can describe many of the biochemical reactions taking place within its beautifully synchronized structure in terms of the known laws of physics and chemistry. However, its existence as a microscopic biological machine whose purpose is to exploit the sun's energy for the ongoing support and growth of the plant is left completely unexplained by these laws. The latter is a higher level of explanation and concerns the ultimate purpose of the chloroplast. This purpose can no more be accounted for by our knowledge of physics and chemistry than can the meaning of the command "STOP!" be understood by scientifically analyzing the way ink stains a sheet of newsprint.

Mechanistic science is spectacularly successful in its pursuit of lower-level knowledge, but the fundamental laws of nature that modern science has revealed and systematized cannot be used to answer questions that relate to higher-level understanding. We can see, for example, that science is unable to deal with the much deeper question of why the biological system we call the chloroplast even exists without trespassing into the nonmaterial or transcendent dimension of purpose and meaning. The great danger for science is surely its own sense of self-confidence gained from its truly remarkable success in providing these lower-level explanations. It has developed an almost unwavering belief in itself as the maker of truth.

Science is very good at analyzing and explaining the individual bits that are contained within the much larger picture we call reality. But questions concerning this larger picture must inevitably take us away from the measuring instruments and microscopes of the laboratory and into the scientifically unquantifiable realms of metaphysics and religion. Here many scientists may feel dwarflike and insecure, for the very tools they have been trained to use are simply not appropriate to address the big questions that deal with purpose, meaning and the transcendent. Science may then be tempted to conclude that, because it cannot by its own methods see any "big picture," there is no big picture to be found. When this happens, it is guilty of straying from its legitimate mission.

In a somewhat related context nineteenth-century churchman John Henry Cardinal Newman argued that the exclusion of a theological professorship from the university is an intellectual absurdity. In contending that theology is a profoundly important branch of knowledge, Newman issued a timely warning:

> If you drop any science out of the circle of knowledge, you cannot keep its place vacant for it; that science is forgotten; the other sciences close up, or, in other words, they exceed their proper bounds, and intrude where they have no right. . . . They would be sure to teach wrongly where they had no mission to teach at all.[14]

---

[14]John Henry Newman, *The Idea of a University* (New York: Holt, Rinehart & Winston, 1964), p. 55.

As the modern industrialized world abandons its spiritual roots, the voice of a lesser god is increasingly heeded with awe and reverence. That god is, of course, the god of naturalism, and its "theology" has a persuasive simplicity—the universe and all that it contains, including us humans, is the product of purely material processes and events. The mind of the maker is entirely dumb, the only cause being the impersonal laws of physics and chemistry.

Michael Polanyi rejects this absurd reductionist myth that attributes the emergence of humankind to the play of material forces alone: "The rise of man can be accounted for only by other principles than those known today to physics and chemistry. If this be vitalism, then vitalism is mere common sense, which can be ignored only by a truculently bigotted mechanistic outlook."[15]

The Nonscientific Ingredient in Science

There is another aspect of naturalistic science that is all too often ignored by some of its most loyal followers, and it is this: the practice of science relies on something outside of science itself. Scientific knowledge, indeed all knowledge, exists because of the human mind. We cannot separate what is known from the knower. Michael Polanyi stresses repeatedly in his writings that knowledge exists only because it is brought into being and upheld by minds and that science only exists in living scientists. If all men died knowledge would no longer exist, though the mere brute reality of the universe would continue.[16] Thus the reality experienced and understood by the activity of science is much wider than the facts revealed by the methods of science itself. Or put another way, it is not so much what scientists discover but rather that there are scientists who discover.

Science is in fact possible only within a larger framework of nonscientific concepts. For science to be successful, it must have a nonscientific base. Yet this invisible but vital ingredient is rarely acknowledged by the practitioners of science themselves. And what is this vital ingredient? It is this: every scientist must have the conviction that behind all the apparent contradictions and ambiguities of his or her discoveries there exists a coherent and meaningful picture that will eventually integrate and make sense of the individual pieces of knowledge revealed by the scientific method.

[15]Polanyi, *Personal Knowledge,* p. 390.
[16]Michael Polanyi, "The Unaccountable Element in Science," in *Knowing and Being: Essays by Michael Polanyi,* ed. M. Greene (London: Routledge & Kegan Paul, 1968).

Philosopher Alfred North Whitehead has suggested that this belief in the underlying rationality of nature was one of the great intellectual and spiritual legacies of the Middle Ages. He describes this contribution of medievalism to the rise of modern science as

> the inexpugnable belief that every detailed occurrence can be correlated with its antecedents in a perfectly definite manner, exemplifying general principles. Without this belief the incredible labours of scientists would be without hope. It is this instinctive conviction, vividly poised before the imagination, which is the motive power of research—that there is a secret, a secret which can be unveiled.[17]

But Whitehead goes even further in suggesting the ultimate source of this belief:

> It must come from the medieval insistence on the rationality of God, conceived as with the personal energy of Jehovah and with the rationality of a Greek philosopher. Every detail was supervised and ordered: the search into nature could only result in the vindication of the faith in rationality. Remember that I am not talking of the explicit beliefs of a few individuals. What I mean is the impress on the European mind arising from the unquestioned faith of centuries.[18]

And so it is that in reality no scientist, whatever his or her beliefs might be, ever investigates the workings of the natural world within the framework of "faith" expressed by Bertrand Russell in one of his essays: "The world in which we live can be understood as a result of muddle and accident."[19] In fact, if every scientist were to walk into his or her laboratory each morning with the conviction that all of nature was a consequence of "muddle and accident" and thus ultimately devoid of rationality and meaning, science as a serious profession would cease.

Doing science is a bit like solving a complex jigsaw puzzle (figure 2.9). There must always be the belief that behind the apparent confusion represented in all the scattered and jumbled pieces a more meaningful picture will one day emerge. Few of us would be interested in trying to assemble a complicated jigsaw puzzle if we knew that someone had capriciously scrambled together a whole lot of separate puzzles. Science works because its practitio-

---

[17]Alfred North Whitehead, *Science and the Modern World* (Cambridge: Cambridge University Press, 1927), p. 15.

[18]Ibid., p. 16.

[19]Bertrand Russell, "Do We Survive Death?" in *Why I Am Not a Christian and Other Essays on Religion and Related Subjects,* ed. Paul Edwards (London: Allen & Unwin, 1957), p. 74.

ners are implicit believers in a universe that should make sense. Polanyi sees "scientific inquiry to be a thrust of our human mind toward a more and more meaningful integration of clues." [20] "A mind responds in a striving manner to comprehend that which it believes to be comprehendable but which it does

Figure 2.9. A coherent universe: jigsaw puzzle analogy. The activity of science can be likened to solving a complicated puzzle—there is always the assumption that a coherent and meaningful picture can be assembled from the individual pieces. (Photograph by the author.)

not yet comprehend."[21] Polanyi is adamant that "modern science cannot properly be understood to tell us that the world is meaningless and pointless, that it is absurd. The supposition that it is absurd is a modern myth, created imaginatively from the clues produced by a profound misunderstanding of what science and knowledge are and what they require."[22]

I end this chapter with the thought-provoking words of philosopher William Barrett. In speaking of the extraordinary power of the human mind, which produced the grand edifice of modern science, he comments on what he describes as one of the great ironies of modern history:

---

[20]Michael Polanyi, "Order," in *Meaning,* ed. Michael Polanyi and Harry Prosch (Chicago: University of Chicago Press, 1975), p. 178.

[21]Ibid., p. 176.

[22]Ibid., p. 181.

The structure [that is, modern science] that most emphatically exhibits the power of mind nevertheless leads to the denigration of the human mind. The success of the physical sciences leads to the attitude of scientific materialism, according to which the mind becomes, in one way or another, merely the passive plaything of material forces. The offspring turns against its parent. We forget what we should have learned from Kant: that the imprint of mind is everywhere in the body of this science, and without the founding power of mind it would not exist.[23]

---

[23]William Barrett, *Death of the Soul* (Oxford: Oxford University Press, 1987), p. 75.

3

What Is Life?

In addressing the question "What is life?" I am conscious that in one sense this is an exceedingly arrogant question for any person to ask. For how can we claim to be able to explain life objectively when we ourselves are confined within the complex web of the living world? A related question might equally be asked: Do the findings of science point beyond the purely material to an essential transcendent dimension? Or expressed another way, Should any clear-thinking scientist be expected to show an interest in natural theology?[1]

In order to address the above questions we will examine a number of features of the living world that point to something beyond the purely material. In other words, we will examine the evidence available to us as "insiders" confined within the biological world.

Nature's Incredible Machinery

First, we can state something that I believe no serious scientist will dispute—life is mechanical. Living systems at one level of description are unquestionably marvelous mechanical contrivances.[2] The living cell operates in principle just like any man-made mechanical system with all the

---

[1]Natural theology can be defined as the attempt to investigate the existence and nature of God by studying the natural world without recourse to special revelation. For those interested in pursuing this subject further, William Dembski, in chapter three of his book *Intelligent Design* (Downers Grove, Ill.: InterVarsity Press, 1999), provides a helpful historical overview of the changing status of natural theology.

[2]This is not to say that they are *nothing but* mechanisms. But they clearly are, at the very least, mechanisms.

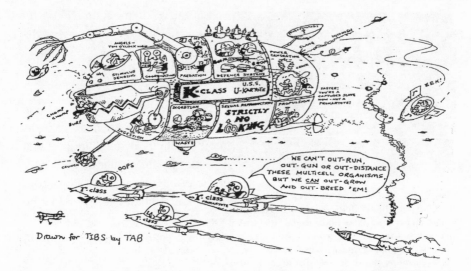

Figure 3.1. Life is mechanical. The cartoonist captures a vital aspect of the living organism—its obvious "mechanical" nature. (Reproduced from *Trends in Biochemical Science* 7, no. 128 [1982]. Used with permission of Elsevier Science and the artist, T. A. Bramley.)

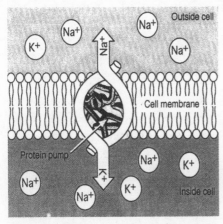

Figure 3.2. A conceptual representation of the sodium-potassium molecular pump found in nerve cells. The pump maintains a high concentration of sodium ions (Na^+) outside the cell membrane and a high concentration of potassium (K^+) inside; this being essential for nerve signal conduction. (Image by Vivian Ward, University of Auckland.)

appearances of having been carefully constructed according to principles of engineering design (figure 3.1).

The heart, lungs, kidneys and joints are all obvious examples of biological systems that perform a mechanical type of function in the living animal. Blood is repeatedly pumped and systematically filtered or cleansed of waste products, and the bones in the skeleton are hinged to provide low-friction articulations. But there is an equally impressive lineup of highly sophisticated "technologies" that operate at the microscopic and molecular levels. So let's take a brief look at some of these.

Lilliputian molecular pumps. One of the basic requirements of a living

Figure 3.3. *Upper:* **The tiny aquatic creature *Euglena* has a sickle-shaped flagellum at the upper end of its body that spins and propels it through the water. The author collected this specimen from a local sewage treatment pond. It was photographed alive at approximately one hundred times magnification in a "slowing-down medium" similar to wallpaper paste. (Photograph by the author. Flagellum image enhanced by Bryony James, University of Auckland.)** *Lower:* **Schematic drawing suggesting the likely structure of the molecular rotary "stepping motor" that spins *Euglena*'s flagellum. (Image by Vivian Ward, University of Auckland.)**

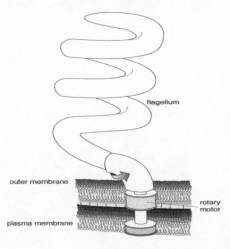

organism, be it the humble bacterium or the human body, is that the internal environment be maintained in a near-constant chemical state in the face of ever-changing external conditions. A frog bathing in a freshwater pond must have its internal salinity maintained at about forty to fifty times that of the pond. In the nonliving state this large concentration difference would be evened out by the tendency of the dissolved salts or chemical ions to migrate down this concentration gradient and out through the skin of the frog. However, embedded in the membranes of the frog's skin cells are arrays of tiny molecular machines that continuously pump the ions back inside the cells to maintain their correct internal salinity.

Every living cell utilizes these molecular pumps, and there are several different kinds. For example, in every red blood cell there are something like a million of these that simultaneously channel chloride ions out and bicarbonate ions into the cell. This process is crucial to the removal of carbon dioxide from the tissues into the bloodstream and out through the lungs.

In the specialized nerve cells at least two quite different chemical concentrations must be maintained simultaneously to allow for the transmission of nerve signals. Double-acting molecular pumps work continuously to maintain a high concentration of potassium ions inside and a high concentration of sodium ions outside the cell (see figure 3.2). All of these cellular pumps are powered via the energy-transacting molecule ATP described in the previous chapter.

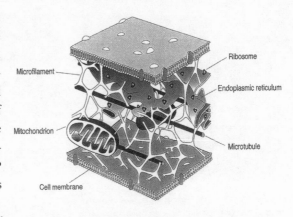

Figure 3.4. Schematic illustrating the three-dimensional construction of a cell with its fretwork of microtubules and microfilaments that make up the internal scaffold or cytoskeleton. (Image by Vivian Ward, University of Auckland.)

Rotary engines and corkscrew propellers. Many tiny aquatic organisms swim by using appendages called flagella (figure 3.3). Each flagellum is made from a special protein molecule that spins about its axis rather in the manner of a corkscrew propeller. At the site where the flagellum is attached to the encasing membrane of the animal there exists a highly complex, ultramicroscopic rotary motor, again constructed from a variety of proteins (figure 3.3). This molecular motor can spin the flagellum or filament at speeds of up to sixty revolutions per second. Although still poorly understood, this rotary motor appears to function as a biological equivalent of the electric stepping motor.

Molecular monkey bars. Within the cell there exists a complex, three-dimensional fretwork of extremely fine tubes or rods that form the cell's cytoskeleton (figure 3.4). These are constructed from pairs of protein molecules that are very similar in structure. Many thousands of these protein pairs, or "doublets," are closely packed to form the hollow, helically wound microtubules and microfilaments somewhat in the manner that kernels of corn are arranged on a cob (figure 3.5). They are involved in a whole variety of internal transport activities and are also used to bring about changes in cell shape. A special group of protein molecules function as "conveyor motors" on the cytoskeleton filaments and actually "walk" protein-laden containers and other cellular cargo from one part of the cell to another rather like a down-side-up version of a child swinging its way across a playground monkey bar (figure 3.5).

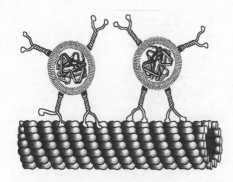

Figure 3.5. Tiny protein-based engines "walk" their cellular "cargo" along the delicate filaments crisscrossing the interior of the cell. (Image by Vivian Ward, University of Auckland, after scheme depicted in W. K. Purves, G. H. Orians and H. C. Heller, *Life: The Science of Biology* **(Sunderland: Sinauer, 1995.)**

The above examples are just some of a great number of clever mechanical systems found in the biological world.[3] At first glance they might appear to provide strong confirmation of the reductionist model of life. For if indeed life can be described as a machine, albeit a highly sophisticated one, then perhaps it can be accounted for wholly in terms of the impersonal laws of physics and chemistry. But this line of reasoning is conceptually flawed; in fact, quite the reverse is true. By describing a living system as mechanical, one is actually admitting that life cannot be explained in terms of the impersonal laws of physics and chemistry. It is therefore a strongly antireductionist pronouncement. To argue this case more convincingly it will be helpful to draw upon a number of important ideas developed several decades ago by the distinguished scientist and philosopher Michael Polanyi.

Polanyi's Concept of Hierarchical Structures

Michael Polanyi has written at some length to expose the fallacy he believes is at the heart of the reductionist view of life. He comments:

> There is a great deal of truth in the mechanical explanation of life. The organs of the body work much like machines, and they are subject to a hierarchy of controls, exercised by an ascending series of mechanical principles. Biologists pursuing the aim of explaining living functions in terms of machines have achieved astounding success. But this must not obscure the fact that these advances only add to the features of life which cannot be represented in terms of laws manifested in the realm of inanimate nature.[4]

Polanyi here is addressing two important and closely related issues.

---

[3]For an in-depth review of other highly sophisticated molecular machines that operate within the living cell, the interested reader is referred to a series of articles in the biological research journal *Cell* 92 (1998): 291-366.

[4]Michael Polanyi, *The Tacit Dimension* (London: Routledge & Kegan Paul, 1967), p. 42.

First, he is rightly acknowledging that the mechanical view of life has provided scientists with a working concept that has greatly advanced our understanding of the biological world. Second, Polanyi is equally adamant that the success of this mechanical model actually demonstrates that the living world cannot be reduced to the laws of physics and chemistry, or as he puts it, the laws of inanimate nature.

In two important articles Polanyi has shown by his principle of boundary control that the physical and chemical laws of inanimate nature cease explaining phenomena beyond their own limits.[5] The physical and chemical description of processes in nature may be exhaustive at one level and yet fail to explain higher levels of behavior. In other words, a rigorous knowledge of the laws of chemistry and physics is incapable of explaining the behavior of the complete system. Some higher, nonmaterial principle is required. Polanyi illustrates this hierarchical concept with the example of DNA, which is made up from a linear sequence of four different building blocks known as nucleic acid bases, forming a molecular code. However, before we look at the coding in DNA, there are some commonplace examples that may help illustrate this important principle.

Telegraphy provides us with a helpful analogy of the molecular code of DNA. Samuel F. B. Morse was an American portrait and historical artist of considerable repute in the early part of the nineteenth century. Morse was of the opinion that a method of rapid communication could have greatly reduced the extent of bloodshed in the 1812 war between America and England. He also had an intense interest in electricity, attended lectures on electromagnetism and saw "no reason why intelligence might not be instantaneously transmitted by electricity to any distance."[6] Morse went on to invent a crude telegraph system that worked by means of a suspended pencil making long or short marks on a piece of paper when moved by an electromagnet.

Although the invention of the Morse code is almost universally attributed to Morse, it was actually his coworker and eventual antagonist Alfred Vail who devised a mechanism capable of transmitting a sequence of dots, dashes and spaces over long distances and who saw in these characters a

---

[5]Michael Polanyi, "Life Transcending Physics and Chemistry," *Chemical and Engineering News*, August 21, 1967, pp. 54-56; and "Life's Irreducible Structure," *Science* 160 (1968): 1308-12.
[6]Quoted in G. P. Oslin, *The Story of Telecommunications* (Macon, Ga.: Mercer University Press, 1992), p. 16.

system by which an alphabet could be constructed. Different combinations of dots and dashes (or "bases") provided a means of representing the entire alphabet. By combining these elements in an appropriate sequence, a

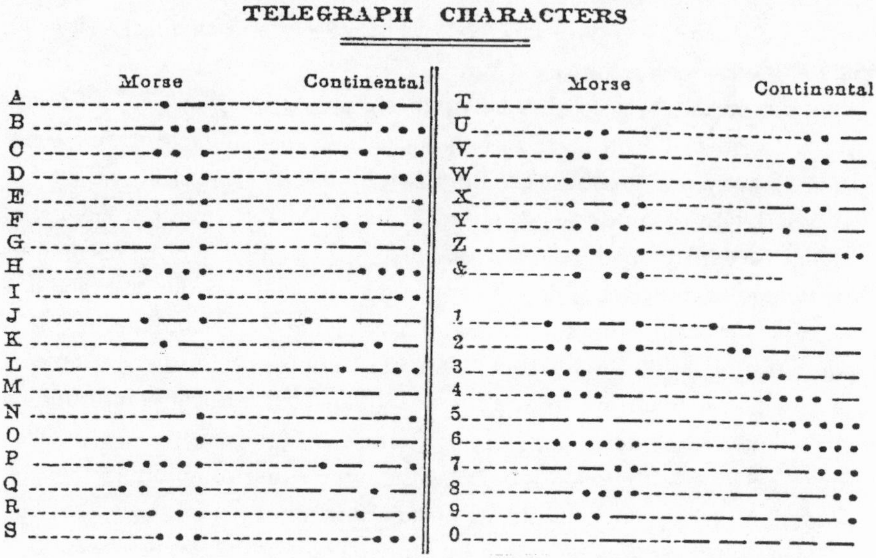

TELEGRAPH CHARACTERS

	Morse	Continental		Morse	Continental
A			T		
B			U		
C			V		
D			W		
E			X		
F			Y		
G			Z		
H			&		
I					
J			1		
K			2		
L			3		
M			4		
N			5		
O			6		
P			7		
Q			8		
R			9		
S			0		

Figure 3.6. The dot and dash "bases" used in Morse and Continental telegraphy. Note the slightly different "dialects" of these two coding alphabets. (Adapted from D. Mc-Nicol, *American Telegraphic Practice* [New York: McGraw-Hill, 1913].)

meaningful message could be delivered (figure 3.6).

The potential amount of information that can be carried by any form of code will have its maximum when the different base elements used to construct the code are equally available for placement in the encoding sequence. Any preference for certain base sequences will reduce the number of different combinations that can be achieved, thus causing the potential information content conveyed by the sequence to fall below the ideal maximum. Imagine for example if the sequence of dots and dashes in the Morse code were always arranged as a repeating sequence of alternating dots and dashes. This would produce a "message" made up of a string of *a*'s—decidedly uninformative. Morse code is a successful information-bearing code simply because the sequence of dots and dashes is truly free or indeterminate. There is no rule demanding that the dots and dashes must always alternate. The sequence specified is entirely in the hands of the person generating the message. Contrast this with the pattern of atoms in a crystal. Here the structure is highly ordered or fixed. Each atom or group of atoms in the crystal is positioned with monotonous regularity along each of the three directions in space. In terms of information content this arrangement is completely "dumb."

Precisely the same argument applies to the coding system employed in the modern compact disc (figure 3.7). The sequence of short and long microscopic pits that are arranged in a fine spiral on the disc's surface provide a coded message that is detected by a beam of light and then translated into musical notes by the stereo system. The precise order in which the pits are arranged is entirely dependent on what sort of correspondence has been established by the human code maker. There is no material requirement that a particular sequence of pits must prevail.

It is the same in any information-bearing system, whether it be the Morse code, ink on paper, a magnetic tape or a piece of sculpture emerging from a previously shapeless lump of stone. In the latter it is the artist's imagination and creativity, not the physical and chemical interactions prevailing within the mineral structure of the stone, that gives the sculpture its final, symbolic shape. These inter-

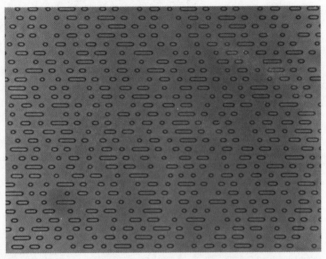

Figure 3.7. Inscription on a modern compact disc. The long and short optical coding "pits" are visible on its reflective surface when viewed at approximately twelve hundred times magnification under the light microscope. (Photograph by Steve Strover, University of Auckland.)

actions are, of course, exploited by the sculptor, but only in a secondary sense. The stone merely provides a physical medium through which an artistic vision can be expressed; it is never the *source* of that vision. This principle always applies in any system that conveys some meaningful message.

In the same way, DNA can operate as a coding structure only because the sequencing of its bases, referred to as A, G, C and T, is for the most part structurally unbiased.[7] The sequence making up a particular DNA strand is not dependent on any preferred bonding between the individual bases.

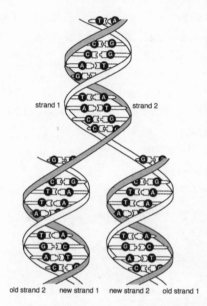

strand 1   strand 2

old strand 2   new strand 1   new strand 2   old strand 1

Figure 3.8. DNA code—a molecular equivalent of the Morse code. It functions as a linear code comprising a sequence of the bases A, G, C and T that are not constrained in any particular sequence along the code's length. However, a given sequence is normally found with another parallel sequence, the opposite bases always pairing up in a specific "lock and key" configuration as illustrated. This in no way reduces the amount of information the code can convey, but it is a crucial requirement if the DNA code is to be copied or replicated with a high degree of accuracy. (Image by Vivian Ward, University of Auckland.)

Each base is the molecular equivalent of the dot or dash in the Morse code and can be arranged in any linear combination without breaking the rules of chemical bonding (figure 3.8). The structure of DNA therefore contrasts with ordinary chemical molecules or crystals, whose structures reflect the most stable arrangement of their constituent atoms. In the latter the atoms take up a particular fixed pattern or arrangement in space because this arrangement represents the lowest energy or most stable state.

The chemical laws that bind each base, A, G, C or T, to its neighbor in DNA are lower-level, slavelike laws that must come under the control of a higher principle in a manner exactly analogous to the *intelligent* sequencing of dots and dashes required in Morse Code to create a *meaningful* message. And if it is accepted that the genetic information carried by the DNA has an important influence on the pattern of development and function of the living organism, then it is clear that on this basis alone life is inexplicable in terms of the lower-level laws of physics and chemistry. Some other, higher level of control that transcends the purely material laws is required.

---

[7]DNA will be discussed in considerably more detail in chapter five.

From Silica Tetrahedra to Stately Mansion

We can further develop this concept of transcendence, so evident in the operation of codes and especially of DNA, by considering a nonliving material as earthy as clay.

Oxygen and silicon are the two most abundant elements found in the earth's crust. Because of their particular atomic properties, these two elements will combine to form a stable three-dimensional tetrahedron, or pyramid, in which each silicon atom is surrounded by four oxygen atoms (figure 3.9). Nearly all the common minerals of the earth's crust are silicates formed principally from various combinations of these tetrahedral units in association with one or more other abundant elements such as aluminum, iron, calcium, sodium, potassium and magnesium. Clays are a

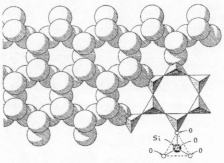

Figure 3.9. The silicate tetrahedron is the fundamental building block for the clay particle (see figure 3.10). (Reproduced from *Principles of Geology* by J. Gilluly, A. C. Waters, and A. O. Woodford © 1959 by J. Gilluly, A. C. Waters, and A. O. Woodford. Used with the permission of W. H. Freeman and Company.)

member of the family of silicate-based minerals (figure 3.10). When they are heated, or "fired," to a high temperature, the individual particles of silicate are fused into a highly stable and

mechanically strong material. We might choose to shape the damp clay into rectangular bricks (figure 3.11), fire them and finally assemble them into the meaningful shape of a humble cottage or a stately mansion (figure 3.12).

Now it could be argued that our stately mansion is really just an assembly of fused silica tetrahedra resulting from the special kind of chemical bonding that exists be-

Figure 3.10. Clay particles viewed at high magnification in the electron microscope. (Photograph by the author.)

tween the silicon and oxygen atoms. And in one limited, lower-level sense this is true. But nobody in their right mind would order a house to be built

by merely specifying that the special chemical bonding between silicon
and oxygen be exploited. Rather, from the moment the shape of the fired
brick is determined, there is an ever-increasing input of thought, planning
and creativity that is required in order
to have all those billions of tetrahedra
finally assembled into the appropriate
configuration of our stately mansion.
The fundamental atomic interactions
that produce the silica tetrahedron,
while important in determining the
physical properties of the brick material used to express our intended
goal, are simply powerless to achieve
this end. The essential ingredient is
intelligent, purposeful design.

Figure 3.11. The purposeful task of brick
making. (Reproduced with permission
from John Woodforde, *Bricks to Build a
House* [London: Routledge & Kegan
Paul, 1976].)

Aristotle established this important principle more than two thousand years ago. For him science was
in essence the search for causes or
explanations, and to this end he identified four categories of cause in his
philosophy of nature—material, efficient, final and formal.[8] Aristotle's
material and formal causes are
generally regarded as being descriptive rather than explanatory. The material cause is the
matter from which a particular
thing is made, whereas the formal cause is the shape of that
particular thing that distin-
guishes it from other things
made from the same matter. Aristotle's other two causes, efficient and final, are generally

Figure 3.12. A stately mansion—the final goal.
(Reproduced from E. Newton, *A Book of Coun-
try Houses* [London: Batsford, 1903].)

---

[8]For more on Aristotle's four causes, see Jonathan Barnes, *Aristotle* (Oxford: Oxford University
Press, 1982), chap. 12; John Morton, *Man, Science and God* (Glasgow: Collins, 1972), chap. 1.
While Morton employs Aristotle's terminology, his example of the bottle of claret is perhaps
more helpful to the modern reader.

considered to correspond more closely to the normal use of the word *cause*. His efficient cause is the agent who gives the original matter its particular shape so as to create something. The final cause is the purpose for which the thing is produced.

With regard to our stately mansion, Aristotle's material cause perhaps best describes the matter from which the bricks are made; that is, the silicon and oxygen atoms forming the tetrahedra are linked together in repeating arrangements to form a particle of clay. Efficient cause is seen at two levels. First, it is seen in the purposeful activity of the brick maker who shapes the clay and then uses heat to fuse the particles of clay into a terra-cotta body. Second, it is seen in the assembling of the bricks by the builder according to a specific plan into a stately mansion. Formal cause describes both the specific shape of each brick and the specific shape or design of the mansion. Final cause is embodied in both the intent of the brick maker—he shaped the clay in order to make the brick—and the intent of the architect who conceived the idea of designing a stately mansion to be lived in.

It is unfortunate that two of Aristotle's four categories have somewhat misleading names. But after more than two thousand years, it may be too much to expect any revision in the terminology. What is important to remember is that although efficient and final causes are not studied by science, it is these two alone that bring forth our stately mansion from those once-shapeless lumps of clay. So, in accounting for the existence of our stately mansion, there is an essential, personal dimension that both transcends and gathers up for its own ends the purely material clay structures so elegantly described by science. Much of this book is about the impossibility of avoiding this transcendent dimension (as scientific materialism attempts to do) when we study the world of living things.

Let the Scissors Speak
Any man-made machine illustrates nicely this important concept of transcendence in that it always works under the control of two distinct principles. The higher principle is that any such machine is always designed for a specific purpose or task, which is achieved by the machine's individual component parts interacting in accordance with distinct operational principles, or in Polanyi's words, "the devices of engineering."[9] The lower prin-

---

[9]Michael Polanyi, "Life Transcending Physics and Chemistry," *Chemical and Engineering News,* August 21, 1967, pp. 54-66.

ciple consists in the material processes on which the machine relies.

Consider a commonplace example: a pair of scissors. The laws of science can adequately describe the bonding forces between individual iron
and carbon atoms in the millions of crystal grains comprising the steel in
the scissors blades and therefore can account for the steel's strength and
hardness. But it is the higher principle of intelligent engineering design that
determines how the pair of scissors is constructed—the length and shape
of the blades and handles, the position of the pivot, and so on.

There is a fundamental asymmetry in the relationship between these two
principles. The pair of scissors is a "machine" by virtue of having been designed and constructed according to engineering principles of design. The
laws of physics are indifferent to these engineering principles. The forces
between the atoms in the microscopic grains of the steel would continue to
exist whether the steel is in the shape of a scissors blade, in a mangled and
discarded state in the scrap yard or melted down and remade into an entirely different object. We can therefore say that the impersonal material
laws serve the pair of scissors while they exist but that these laws cannot
determine the scissors' design and function.

But What About Biological Machines?

When we pass on to living organisms, we are similarly faced with machinelike systems, whether these be whole organs such as the heart, an individual cell, one of the many molecular machines contained within the cell
such as the sodium-potassium membrane pump (see figure 3.2) or the
rotary engines that drive the *Euglena*'s flagellum (see figure 3.3). Each of
these living mechanical systems involves an enormously complex sequence
of interactions among their component parts.

Michael Polanyi describes these living systems as functioning under the
principle of dual control. He describes the role of DNA as transmitting to
the developing organism information that results in organic differentiation;
that is, the living tissue is shaped into a new structure or organ. This structure serves as a set of meaningful boundaries within which the inanimate
processes of nature are harnessed by the biological system, thus enabling it
to perform its function. Note again a fundamental asymmetry: the inanimate molecular and chemical laws operate within the boundaries represented by the organism's structure, but this structure, whether it be an
individual cell, a heart, a lung or any other body organ, is not determined

by these laws. Paul Weiss expresses the same concept simply: "There is no phenomenon in a living system that is not molecular, but there is none that is only molecular either."[10]

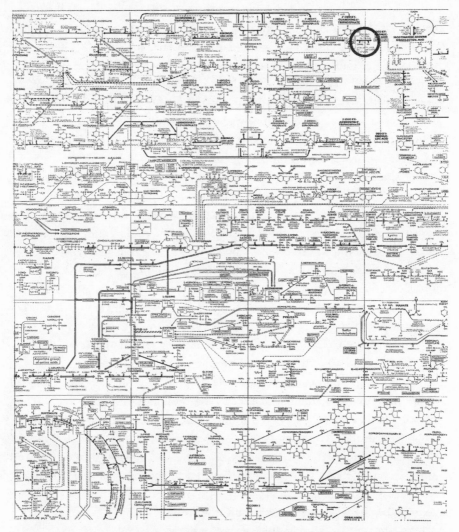

Figure 3.13. A part of the cell's biochemical circuitry. This diagram, while almost impossible to read at the magnification reproduced here, serves to convey just how sophisticated is the integrated biochemistry of the living cell. Note: the diagram does not represent the metabolic pathways of any actual cell but is a partial compendium of pathways known in various types of cells. (Image used with permission of Roche Diagnostics, GmbH, Germany.)

[10]Paul Weiss, *Within the Gates of Science and Beyond* (New York: Hafner, 1971), p. 270.

In fact, the processes of life involve levels of sophistication and complexity vastly greater than is suggested in the above. While DNA does provide a rich source of encoded information for the cell, it can do so only because the cell itself provides the appropriate context in which this information can be processed. Figure 3.13 constitutes the biological equivalent of an incredibly complex electronic circuit. In fact, the figure shows only a portion of the multitude of biochemical pathways that all act in beautifully orchestrated harmony within the living cell. The scale of complexity of this biochemical circuit is such that at the magnification reproduced it is virtually impossible to resolve with any clarity the individual pathways. I have presented it this way deliberately in order to convey some idea of the technological sophistication of the living cell.

The small circled region in the top right corner of figure 3.13 identifies that part of the circuit where DNA is copied, and it clearly represents just a tiny fraction of the total biochemical picture. What is important to appreciate is the sheer richness of the context within which individual nucleic acid bases are joined in correct sequence to form a replicated DNA strand, which can then be used as an information-bearing code. So DNA in isolation is essentially "dumb." In order to be able to function as a code it must be integrated within the richly structured and purposefully coordinated biochemical processes of the cell.

We then have to consider the specific tissues such as muscle, cartilage, skin, arteries and so forth that are therefore constructed from the integrated activity of many millions of these individual cells. From here we proceed on up through the hierarchical order to the multitude of organs comprising an individual animal. Finally, we come to the idea of a living animal itself, which in Aristotle's language is our final cause.

It is only within this multilevel world of increasing sophistication and purpose that we can appreciate the biological meaning of DNA. It is not "the master molecule." Rather, DNA is a molecule that has been given meaning because it has been placed under the control of a profoundly rich and coordinated system capable of exploiting its unique structure as an information-bearing code. To isolate a code from its context, whether it be the dots and dashes of Morse code or the nucleic acid bases of DNA, and then to pretend that it is primal, is to fundamentally misunderstand the real nature of information-bearing systems.

We can now challenge the widely held reductionist assertion, introduced at the beginning of this chapter, which states that because living systems are "mechanical" they are therefore explicable merely in terms of the impersonal laws of physics and chemistry. What we now understand about the hierarchical structure of living systems is surely incompatible with any such reductionist claim. For the very moment it asserts that life can be described as nothing more than a complex set of inanimate biochemical mechanisms, it falls prey to its own deficient logic. To admit to "mechanism" in the living world is to admit, as Michael Polanyi so clearly shows, to the need for boundary conditions that cannot be accounted for by these inanimate processes alone. To speak of a living organism as a biological machine is to admit, at the very least, that it cannot be reduced to the operation of impersonal material laws. By their very "mechanical" nature, biological systems require a higher level of control analogous, it would appear, to the operation of mind.

The biochemist Rupert Sheldrake draws attention to this widespread misconception about what is implied in the use of the term *machine* when it is applied to the living world. He writes with understandable disdain for the reductionist view of life:

> From the mechanistic point of view . . . there is no such thing as 'life', just complex patterns of mechanistic interaction taking place in accordance with the eternal laws of physics and chemistry. Biological organisms are complex mechanisms that have evolved through random genetic mutations and natural selection. Since the earth does not reproduce, does not have genes and has not (as far as we know) evolved as a result of natural selection, it is not alive. Even biological organisms, such as dolphins and bamboos, which we conventionally refer to as living, are not alive in the sense that they are animate. They are just complex, self-regulating mechanisms.[11]

Biochemist Michael Behe in his recent book *Darwin's Black Box* demonstrates clearly the irreducibly complex nature of various biological machines.[12] He also draws particular attention to the molecular motor that drives the flagellum, the tiny propeller that I discussed earlier in this chapter (see figure 3.3). The point that Behe makes repeatedly is that these highly sophisticated biological machines, because they require a number of closely integrated and matched components before they can function, are,

---

[11]Rupert Sheldrake, *The Rebirth of Nature* (London: Century, 1990), p. 125.
[12]Michael Behe, *Darwin's Black Box* (New York: Free Press, 1996); and "Intelligent Design Theory as a Tool for Analyzing Biochemical Systems," in *Mere Creation*, ed. William A. Dembski (Downers Grove, Ill.: InterVarsity Press, 1998), chap. 7.

in his words, "mammoth barriers to gradualistic, Darwinian evolution" and that they are best interpreted as being the result of deliberate intelligent design.[13]

Figure 3.14. Michael Polanyi (1891-1976), scientist and philosopher. (Reproduced from Michael Polanyi, *The Logic of Personal Knowledge* [London: Routledge and Kegan Paul, 1961]. Used with permission of J. C. Polanyi.)

There is little doubt that the materialist belief system has had an enormous influence on the conceptual mindset of many of those in the biological sciences. It would seem that Michael Polanyi's insights, if heeded, would do much to counter the widespread and often uncritical acceptance of this simplistic, reductionist ideology. Sadly, in my experience too few students of science, or even practicing scientists themselves, have heard the name of this distinguished twentieth-century thinker (figure 3.14), let alone read his works.

Disembodied Knowledge

We saw in an earlier section that the scientific method works mostly by a process of abstraction. The highly complex systems in nature are artificially broken down into more manageable portions that can be studied and analyzed by the tools of science. For example, higher organisms rely on the coordinated functioning of millions upon millions of individual living cells. But to study in any rigorous manner the biochemical processes that take place within these cells, and on which the living organism depends for its very existence, is virtually impossible while looking at the whole functioning organism.

We can observe a tomato plant to thrive as it is supplied with sunlight, water, nutrients and so on. But while this is a significant observation (every serious gardener wants his or her tomato plants to grow and bear fruit), it provides little insight into how a living plant actually works in a detailed biological sense. To achieve this insight the scientist must dismember the

[13]Behe, "Intelligent Design Theory."

plant. Individual cells or groups of cells might be removed from the plant and then be kept alive by special culture techniques that biologists are skilled at applying in their laboratories. All kinds of microscopic and metabolic studies can then be conducted on this elite,[14] scientifically manageable fragment of life (figure 3.15). But herein lies one of the fundamental limitations of the scientific method: the very eliteness of that living fragment means that it is alienated from its meaningful place within the complete, functioning organism. So in another sense it has a kind of refugee status in that it is no longer part of an integrated web of biological activities that are a true expression of the whole organism.

However, it must be emphasized that an enormous depth of understanding of the living world has been achieved by the method of abstraction. The fact that modern science has unraveled for us such a detailed understanding of the biochemical machinery of the living cell as illustrated in figure 3.13 is a tribute to the great analytical power of the scientific method.

It is usually assumed that once a detailed understanding of the isolated parts of a complex system has been obtained, we can then establish the fundamental relationships between individual objects or components and gradually advance toward a complete understanding of the total system. This is the confident claim of the scientific method in all its reductionist power. The eminent biologist Paul Weiss is highly critical of this whole intellectual process, particularly as it is applied to the biological sciences. He says:

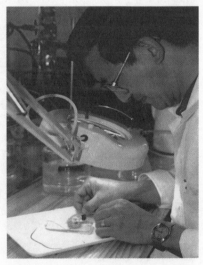

> The basic streak that runs through practically all of our biological thinking is still that science, given time, will succeed in describing and comprehending, by the consistent application of this synthetic method and without any further conceptual amendments, all that is

Figure 3.15. The scientist at work on an isolated fragment of tissue. (Courtesy of School of Biological Sciences, University of Auckland.)

---

[14]I use the term *elite* here because it conveys precisely the idea that it is only a select part of the whole plant that becomes the focus of the scientist's intense scrutiny and interest.

within the Universe in entities and properties and processes that is knowable to us, including the phenomena of life.[15]

Or beginning with only the detail, we assume we are able to construct the big picture. But recall the analogy used earlier in this chapter—we cannot predict the existence of our stately mansion from a knowledge of the silica tetrahedra.

DNA—a Pseudo-God

There is probably no more striking illustration of this supremely confident spirit of reductionism than is seen in the "aristoscience" of modern molecular genetics. An entire biological worldview has been assembled around the ultimate power of our genes. Our genes have become, in the dogma of modern reductionist biology, the "makers of men" (and women). Oxford zoologist Richard Dawkins in his popular book *The Selfish Gene* declares that our genes (he calls them replicators) "created us, body and mind; and their preservation is the ultimate rationale for our existence."[16] There is implicit within the modern reductionist worldview the belief that when we finally unravel the complexity of the gene we will understand the great mystery of life itself.

The popular press has played a crucial role in promoting the gene-is-supreme reductionist mentality as is vividly illustrated in the following headlines:

INFIDELITY—It May Be in Our Genes[17]

20TH CENTURY BLUES. Stress, anxiety, depression: the new science of evolutionary psychology finds the roots of modern maladies in our genes.[18]

BORN HAPPY (OR NOT). Happiness is more than just a state of mind . . . It is in the genes, too.[19]

BORN TO BE GAY?[20]

---

[15]Weiss, *Within the Gates*, p. 267.
[16]Richard Dawkins, *The Selfish Gene* (Oxford: Oxford University Press, 1989), p. 19. Dawkins's anthropomorphization of the gene is discussed in more detail in the next chapter.
[17]*Time*, August 15, 1994.
[18]*Time*, August 28, 1995.
[19]*New Zealand Herald*, August 8, 1996.
[20]*New Scientist*, September 28, 1996, p. 32.

WHAT MAKES THEM DO IT? People who crave thrills, new evidence indicates, may be prompted at least partly by their genes.[21]

YOUR GENES MAY BE FORCING YOU TO EAT TOO MUCH[22]

Almost every week, it seems, a new gene is announced to account mechanistically for yet another form of human behavior. In recent times we have been served up carbohydrate-craving genes, alcoholic genes and cocaine-addiction genes.

For our affluent, Westernized cultures, increasingly preoccupied with the pursuit of lifestyle themes popularly expressed through sexual adventurism, happiness pills, homosexuality, adrenalin-rush sports and bodily perfection, the implied or declared causal link between the shape of our DNA, the shape of our bodies and the shape of our behavior would appear almost irrefutable. And although such a view is a trite and ultimately demeaning commentary on the ethical foundations of human freedom, it is nonetheless one that fits compellingly within the framework of scientific materialism.

Canadian geneticist Richard Lewontin is an outspoken critic of the atomistic view of the gene so often seen in the popular presentation of science. Lewontin suggests that the reductionist endows the gene with a quality akin to some "modern form of grace." He questions the scientific and ethical motivation underlying the Human Genome Project, the aim of which is to sequence the entire 3 billion bases of the human genetic code. Obviously tongue-in-cheek, Lewontin says:

Genes make individuals and individuals make society, and so genes make society. . . . In this view, a culture is a sack of bits and pieces such as aesthetic preferences, mating preferences, work and leisure preferences. Dump out the sack and culture will be displayed before you. Thus, the hierarchy is complete. Genes make individuals, individuals have particular preferences and behaviours, the collection of preferences and behaviours makes a culture, and so genes make culture. That is why molecular biologists urge us to spend as much money as necessary to discover the sequence of the DNA of a human being. They say that when we know the sequence of the molecule that makes up all our genes, we will know what it is to be human. When we know what our DNA looks like, we will know . . . why some societies are powerful and rich and others are weak and poor, why one nation, one sex, one race dominates another. Indeed, we will know why there is such a thing

---

[21] *Time*, January 15, 1996.
[22] *Sunday Star-Times* (Auckland), January 18, 1998.

as a science of biology, which itself is one of the bits and pieces of culture lying at the bottom of the sack.[23]

Lewontin's basic contention is that the very idea of the gene being the molecular mastermind behind all living things is scientifically and conceptually flawed. So often in the popular presentation of the science of life the genes are portrayed as the "intelligent" molecules of life with the ability to make proteins and make copies of themselves. This kind of talk endows the gene with what Lewontin describes as "a mysterious, autonomous power that seems to place them above the more ordinary materials of the body."[24]

It is certainly true that the genes carry the vital coded information that is used by the functioning cell to construct the huge class of large molecules that form the basis of all living tissues—the proteins. Further, the DNA molecule possesses a number of quite remarkable features that are utilized by the living cell. (These are discussed in chapter five, where we examine current theories on the origin of life.) However, it is equally important to stress that genes *of themselves* make nothing, nor are they *of themselves* self-replicating. In order for a protein to be made, a whole sequence of exquisitely synchronized biochemical processes must take place within the complex machinery of the cell whereby the information encoded in the DNA sequence comprising the relevant gene is utilized. Similarly, when copies of the gene are made (a process known as replication), the cellular machinery is again harnessed in a highly orchestrated manner to achieve this end. In other words, these vital processes of life are mutually interdependent—the gene *and* the cellular machinery are essential.

If DNA can be considered to function as a source code somewhat in the manner in which a set of blueprints is used by a builder to construct a house, then some rather obvious conclusions need to be drawn. First, the blueprint is utilized as a guide that enables the builder to exploit his or her practical skills in a purposeful way so as to reach the intended goal anticipated in the blueprint. Second, while the blueprint functions as a vital source of information, it does not *act*. Rather, it is the builder who acts in a deliberate, intelligent and creative way by exploiting the infor-

---

[23]Richard C. Lewontin, *Biology as Ideology: The Doctrine of DNA* (New York: HarperCollins, 1992), p. 14.

[24]Ibid., p. 48. For another recent critique of this genetic "essentialism," see Dorothy Nelkin and Susan Lindee, *The DNA Mystique: The Gene as a Cultural Icon* (New York: W. H. Freeman, 1995).

mation contained in the blueprint.

In the same way, the gene is a crucial part of the living cell, but it is not the molecular mastermind of the living world. Concerning this widely held misconception that the gene is biology's commander-in-chief, Lewontin comments as follows: "Isolating the gene as the 'master molecule' is another unconscious ideological commitment, one that places brains above brawn, mental work as superior to mere physical work, information as higher than action."[25]

One of the most serious errors of modern materialistic science is its claim to be able to explain or account for the total picture because it has been successful in unraveling isolated parts of the whole. The scientific brilliance (witnessed, for example, in the work of Francis Crick, James Watson and Maurice Wilkins) that led to an understanding of both the three-dimensional structure of DNA as a molecular code and the mechanism by which it is replicated presented an almost irresistible temptation to science. Have we not at last, by human cunning alone, discovered the ultimate secret of life? In the euphoria that followed these dramatic discoveries of the 1950s, and that was repeatedly reinforced by the vast body of knowledge assembled by the "aristoscience" of modern molecular biology, there seems little doubt in the minds of many people today that the puzzle of life has been largely solved by the tools of modern science. Life has been successfully dissected into its component parts and laid out on the laboratory bench for all to see. Life, it would seem, has been emptied of its imagined mystery. But is this really true?

Returning for a moment to the gene, we need to remind ourselves that each individual step in the molecular process, whether it be the making of a particular protein or the replication of the gene itself, is not a result of the gene's isolated activity but arises from the functioning of an entire living cell or organism. We are compelled to think in terms of the behavior of an exceedingly complex and highly integrated system rather than the more easily understood but isolated portions within this system. This therefore requires us to address a fundamental question about the meaning of life.

What Does It Mean to Be Alive?

First, we must state emphatically that life is not just codified complexity.

---

[25]Lewontin, *Biology as Ideology,* p. 48.

Life is not simply a highly complex assembly of atoms or molecules in a particular informational configuration. The living state is certainly complex,

but that fact in itself does little to help us understand life. Although popular science often presents a picture of a continuum of gradual—and therefore supposedly effortless[26]—evolutionary development from "molecule to man" (see figure 4.1), this is quite misleading. I will attempt to explain why in what follows.

Paul Weiss uses two important words, *behavior* and *system,* in addressing the nature of life. He has this to say: "A living system that does not behave is dead; life is process, not substance. A living system is no more adequately characterized by an inventory of its material constituents, such as molecules,

Figure 3.16. The soap bubble, for all its delicate beauty, is a product of physical and chemical forces alone. (Courtesy of Gottfried Boehnke, University of Auckland.)

than the life of a city is described by the list of names and numbers in a telephone book."[27] In acknowledging that living systems are highly complex, Weiss argues that in contrast to a haphazard conglomeration, which may be exceedingly complex, the living system displays a distinct orderliness in the midst of this complexity. Thus, despite the enormous number of possible interactions and combinations that could occur in a complex system, "in the living system only an extremely restricted selection from that grab-bag of opportunities for chemical processes is being realized at any one moment—a selection which can be understood solely in its bearing on the concerted harmonious performance of a *task* by the complex as a whole."[28]

David Holbrook describes this superbly integrative behavior of the living

---

[26]I use the word *effortless* because it is commonly argued by the materialist that if exceedingly small and gradual steps of change are involved, then substantial increases in complexity are readily achieved over very long periods of time. In fact, I will seek to show in subsequent chapters that even where there is a gradual increase or evolution in complexity, this still requires the operation of a distinctly purposeful dimension.

[27]Weiss, *Within the Gates,* p. 267. Actually, Weiss's statement that "life is process" is open to question. We know that living cells can be frozen at very low temperatures to a state of suspended animation for years and then restarted by thawing. Perhaps we should call this "suspended process."

[28]Ibid., p. 268.

organism as if it were the product of "intelligent orchestration." [29] The living state is unquestionably task-oriented: it achieves; it can initiate novelty. In Holbrook's words again, "the living creature displays intentionality, it tries to become itself, to realise its potentialities, so that even the simplest life-forms manifest a kind of primal consciousness." [30]

The philosopher E. W. F. Tomlin has written extensively on what he calls "the concept of life." He describes bubbles and snow-flakes as objects resulting from the product of physical forces. These objects are part of a world of aggregates or statistical assemblages obedient to the laws of physics (figure 3.16). By contrast, living systems result from not

Figure 3.17. The orchestra as a metaphor of life. The organism is superbly "conducted." It plays out its living themes, movement by movement, with a profound sense of thematic (biological) destiny. (Image used with permission of CORBIS/TRANZ.)

only a composition of forces but also a unity of forces. Tomlin likens the living state to a musical melody (figure 3.17) that consists of a cycle of unified phases in which the first notes are as important as the last. This "organic melody" plays out its themes phase by phase and does so in anticipation of those to follow. The organism is poised. It can take measures against the future in a manner denied to an object, which cannot take measures at all. The

"We high altitude greywackees need to take full control of our lives - or else we'll simply add to that pile of rubble at the foot of the mountain."

Figure 3.18. Unfortunately for the materialist, material objects do not possess the attributes of persons. (Drawing by the author.)

[29]David Holbrook, *Evolution and the Humanities* (New York: St. Martin's, 1987), p. 127.
[30]Ibid., p. 126.

organism can provide for the future by reproduction or by self-repair following injury while all the time engaging in self-maintenance. Tomlin describes organisms as "existing in themselves," as "containing their own meaning," whereas an object is merely "possessed" by the external forces which have modeled it.[31]

A snowflake cannot resist melting when the temperature rises above zero. The stone, as it tumbles down the mountain stream (figure 3.18), succumbs inevitably to the forces of attrition and there are no measures it can take to compensate for this loss. Both the snowflake and the tumbling stone are totally at the mercy of the forces acting on them. The curiously shaped stones shown in figure 3.19 were not possessed of any desire to become the components of a primitive grain crusher. As a person with a particular idea, I imposed that function on these two stones. Contrast this complete lack of behavior of my two stones with that of the living organism: it can, within limits, challenge and creatively adapt to the external forces acting on it.

Leon Brillouin draws a similar and delightfully colorful comparison between the living and nonliving states. He says:

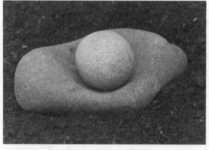

Figure 3.19. Primitive grain crusher. Despite the occasionally interesting and sometimes useful shape (here I have assembled something that could be described as a simple grain-crushing device), the well-worn stone has no sense of "personal destiny." It is rather a product of the relentless, impersonal forces of erosion acting largely at random on its material structure. (Photograph by the author.)

The living organism heals its own wounds, cures its sicknesses, and may rebuild large portions of its structure when they have been destroyed by some accident. This is the most striking and unexpected behaviour. Think of your own car, the day you had a flat tire, and imagine having simply to wait and smoke your cigar while the hole patched itself and the tire pumped itself to the proper pressure, and you could go on. This sounds incredible. It is, however, the way nature works when you "chip off" while shaving in the morning. There is no inert matter possessing a similar property of repair.[32]

---

[31]E. W. F. Tomlin, "The Concept of Life," *Heythrop Journal* 18, no. 3 (1977): 289-304.
[32]Leon Brillouin, "Life, Thermodynamics, and Cybernetics," in *Modern Systems Research for the Behavioral Scientist,* ed. Walter Buckley (Chicago: Aldine, 1968), p. 154.

So even at the simplest descriptive level there exists a fundamental qualitative difference between the world of nonliving objects and that of living organisms. And despite the enthusiastic claims of many modern materialists, there seems little prospect of science ever being able to define a continuum of impersonal and purely material processes that would link the living and the dead in a coherent way. Admitting to a somewhat different context, we might even express this problem through the words of Christ spoken nearly two thousand years ago: "Why do you look for the living among the dead?" (Luke 24:5 NIV). It is, I am convinced, impossible to avoid the impression of intentionality in the living organism, even in its lowest forms. The question therefore remains: Where does this purposive order come from? Is not intention a property of mind? If so, then whose mind?

4

Birth of Life

A Popular View

Ⅰf the very concept of life poses a major problem for a materialistic science, then an even more difficult question remains to be addressed: How did life actually begin on this planet? How, when and where was that mysterious threshold crossed from the nonliving to the living state? How did the first fragment of life arise and, in the fullness of time, produce the boundless variety and sophistication of living forms that populate the biosphere? This is a question that holds enormous fascination and is one that popular science has embraced repeatedly and treated as if scientists have, at least in principle, solved.

Generally the issue is dealt with by appealing to one of several naturalistic scenarios, the most popular of which we will examine in this chapter.

The Magic of Megatime
Underpinning these so-called scientific explanations for life's origin is a single unifying principle: megatime. Almost all the origin-of-life hypotheses exploit the notion that, because vast periods of time were available for the evolution of life to occur, any apparent weakness or inadequacy in a particular naturalistic scenario is more than compensated for by the potential for creative innovation provided by the enormous scale of time—millions, even billions of years.

This kind of thinking, still common among scientists today, is no more clearly articulated than in the words of Harvard biochemist and Nobel laureate George Wald, one of the earlier origin-of-life researchers:

> Time is in fact the hero of the plot. The time with which we have to deal with is of the order of two billion years. What we regard as impossible on the basis of human experience is meaningless here. Given so much time, the 'impossible' becomes possible, the possible probable, and the probable virtually certain. One has only to wait: time itself performs the miracles.[1]

Wald's comment illustrates nicely how well the concept of megatime has served the materialist's cause. It appears to have relieved many of the obligation to provide rigorously argued scientific explanations, and it has done so without weakening the materialist's fundamental belief in a universe that is essentially self-evolving.

One of the intriguing aspects of the materialist's approach to the origin-of-life problem is that at the most critical points in the development of a particular reductionist theory a characteristic explanatory sloppiness often surfaces in which megatime becomes the instrument of creative change. It is used as a kind of magic wand, waved at appropriate points in the argument in order to accomplish quite remarkable feats of materialistic magic. I will revisit this issue of megatime toward the end of chapter six. For now, let us look at some of the ideas that have dominated popular treatments of the origin-of-life problem. We will briefly examine the way some influential writers of popular science have woven these ideas into their works so as to convey to the nonexpert a kind of "mystery solved" mentality.

Such Exciting Primordial Broths!

Popular naturalistic scenarios attempting to explain the origin of life typically describe a cocktail of simple chemicals, concentrated perhaps by tidal or thermal action on the ancient, lifeless earth and repeatedly struck by lightning. This process, replayed over and over again for many millions of years, sees the emergence of a primitive life form and the eventual evolution of the entire living world in all its amazing complexity (figure 4.1).

This popular naturalistic scenario draws its alleged scientific credibility from a series of supposedly historic experiments carried out at Chicago University by a young Ph.D. student, Stanley Miller, working in collabora-

---

[1]George Wald, "The Origin of Life," *Scientific American,* August 1954, p. 44.

tion with his research supervisor, Harold Urey, in 1953.[2] These experiments
were based on earlier hypotheses. The Russian chemist Alexander Oparin
had postulated that the complex molecular arrangements and functions of
living systems evolved from simple molecules preexisting on the lifeless,
primordial earth.[3] The English geneticist John Haldane had also speculated

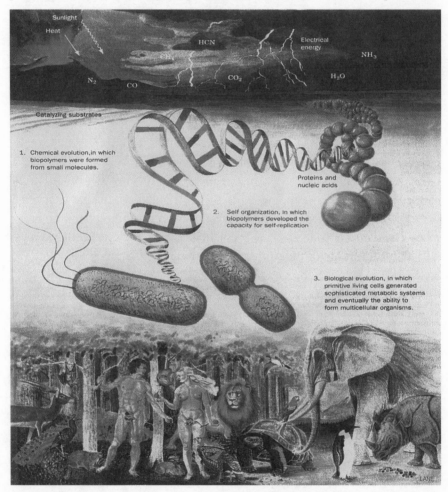

**Figure 4.1. The "grand naturalistic dream"—from molecule to man via a purely mate-
rial set of processes. (Reproduced with permission from D. Voet and J. G. Voet, *Biochemistry*, 2nd ed. [New York: Wiley, 1995].)**

[2]Stanley L. Miller, "A Production of Amino Acids Under Possible Primitive Earth Conditions,"
   Science 117 (1953): 528.
[3]Alexander I. Oparin, *Origin of Life*, trans. S. Morgulis (New York: Macmillan, 1938). Originally
   published in Russian in 1924.

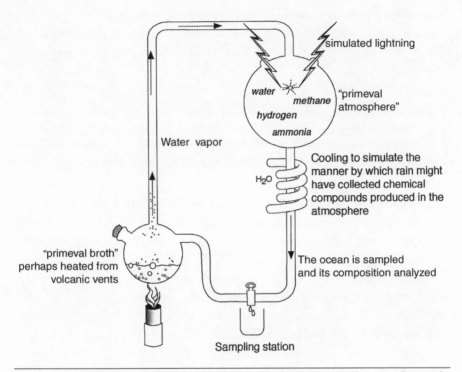

Figure 4.2. An arrangement similar to the one Stanley Miller used to simulate early earth conditions in which a soup of amino acids (building blocks of proteins) was produced. (Image by Vivian Ward, University of Auckland.)

that an energy source such as ultraviolet light might have acted on the earth's primitive atmosphere to produce increasing concentrations of organic molecules such as sugars and amino acids, and that life eventually evolved from these.[4] Miller's experiment was simple. It consisted of heating a mixture of the common gases methane, hydrogen and ammonia together with water in a laboratory flask. This flask contained a pair of tungsten electrodes providing a spark discharge to simulate the probable action of lightning (figure 4.2). After several days Miller observed the formation of a discolored residue, which on analysis was found to contain several types of amino acids—fundamental building blocks of proteins, the primary substance of living systems. Miller's prebiotic simulation experiments were heralded by many as vindication of the Oparin-Haldane hypothesis that life

[4]John B. S. Haldane, "The Origin of Life," *Rationalist Annual* 148 (1929): 3-10.

evolved by purely naturalistic processes on the ancient earth.

Great excitement, both in the popular press and in sections of the scientific community, followed the publishing of the Miller-Urey experiments. *Time* magazine reported the following in a feature titled "Semi-Creation":

> What they have done is to prove that complex organic compounds found in living matter can be formed, by chemical reactions, out of the gases that were probably common in the earth's first atmosphere. If their apparatus had been as big as the ocean, and if it had worked for a million years instead of one week, it might have created something like the first living molecule.[5]

Quite apart from the view now widely held by scientists that Miller's experiments actually have little relevance to the origin-of-life problem, to talk as the above quote does about "the first living molecule" is hardly meaningful. No living organism can be represented by a single molecule any more than a clay particle can represent a house. This loose and quite misleading kind of comment is unfortunately typical of the manner in which many of the complexities of science are popularized.

Pop Science on the Coffee Table

Old habits die hard, and scientific materialism has a disturbing tendency to appeal to Miller's now largely irrelevant experiment whenever the origin-of-life question needs a quick fix solution.

Cultural historian Jacob Bronowski views the evolutionary progression of life as a buildup of chemical molecules beginning from the materials that boiled on the earth at its birth. He then states that Stanley Miller's "beautiful experiment" answered the crucial question of how the first building blocks of life might have been formed.[6]

David Attenborough is equally embracing of Miller's experiment. He offers the same kind of reductionist scenario of a distant time in the past when the earth was completely lifeless and still cooling after its birth. He creates for his readers the following colorful primordial drama:

> The planet then was radically different in almost every way from the one we live on today. The clouds of water vapour that had surrounded it had condensed to form seas, but they were still hot. We are not sure how the land masses lay but they certainly bore no resemblance in either form or distribution to modern continents. Volcanoes were abundant, spewing ash and lava.

---

[5]"Semi-Creation," *Time*, May 25, 1953, p. 82.
[6]Jacob Bronowski, *The Ascent of Man* (London: BBC, 1973), p. 314.

The atmosphere was very thin and consisted of swirling clouds of hydrogen, carbon monoxide, ammonia and methane. There was little or no oxygen. This mixture allowed ultraviolet rays from the sun to bathe the earth's surface with an intensity that would be lethal to modern animal life. Electrical storms raged in the clouds, bombarding the land and the sea with lightning.[7]

Attenborough then points the reader to the Miller-Urey experiment, claiming that there can be little doubt that such a primitive-earth drama could have led to the formation of the essential protein building blocks. Given the passage of millions of years, with additional ingredients possibly added from outer space, Attenborough vaguely envisages the eventual development of the first replicating DNA molecules and of life itself.

The American astronomer Carl Sagan attempts to address the question of how the first molecules essential to the commencement of life might have been produced. Again the Miller-Urey work is used in order to convey to the reader that "the stuff of life, it turns out, can be very easily made." Sagan concludes his brief treatment of the origin-of-life issue with the following: "There is still much to be understood about the origin of life, including the origin of the genetic code. But we have been performing such experiments for only some thirty years. Nature has had a four billion year head start. All in all, we have not done badly."[8]

One other popular science writer should be mentioned here: Isaac Asimov. He comments on both Miller's experiments and a number of subsequent studies that built on those earlier successes in producing organic molecules of biological significance. He writes: "There is no question, then, but that normal chemical and physical changes in the primordial ocean and atmosphere could have acted in such a way as to build up proteins and nucleic acids." On the assumption that 1 percent of the primordial ocean may have been made up of these built-up organic compounds, Asimov then reasons:

> This would represent a mass of over a million billion tons. This is certainly an ample quantity for natural forces to play with; and in such a huge mass, even substances of most unlikely complexity are bound to be built up in not too long a period (particularly considering a billion years are available for the purpose).[9]

---

[7]David Attenborough, *Life on Earth: A Natural History* (London: Collins, 1979), p. 19.
[8]Carl Sagan, *Cosmos* (New York: Random House, 1980), pp. 23-43.
[9]Isaac Asimov, *Asimov's New Guide to Science* (New York: Viking, 1985), pp. 636-42.

I have quoted from the above four writers for two important reasons. First, in each we see the same spirit of blatant reductionist ideology. Straightforward physical and chemical processes, coupled with vast quantities of simple ingredients and megatime, are deemed to be all that are necessary to produce life. And as with George Wald (see his quote earlier in this chapter), it's taken for granted that qualitative development derives from the merely quantitative; that is, lots of matter plus lots of energy plus lots of time will produce lots of complexity. Second, each of the four writers' books referred to above is standard "coffee table" material—one may find any one of these books in the living room of an ordinarily educated family. The books are highly readable and well illustrated. Each is the kind of book that gives accessible, nicely packaged answers to even the most complex questions of science. And so for the crucial issue under discussion they represent a brand of popular science that is blatantly misleading and intellectually irresponsible.

The writers present a persuasive ideology—that life arose on this planet in the fullness of megatime, simply through the workings of natural processes alone. No other nonphysical force or influence was required. In principle, if not in exact detail, the riddle of life's origin is supposedly solved. In two main senses, though, no solution has actually been put forward in these typical stories of how life might have begun. First, not even a coherent sketch has been made of how life was actually arrived at from nonlife. A "soup" with some biggish molecules falls vastly, qualitatively short of life. Second, no such scenario, even if much more complete and supported by fact, can touch on the question of cause.

Reductionist Ideology Gone Mad

If Bronowski, Attenborough, Sagan and Asimov offer their readers a persuasive reductionist ideology, it is Richard Dawkins who must surely rank as chief spokesman for origin-of-life reductionists. Dawkins, a zoologist at Oxford University, is admired by many for his ability to retell his version of the drama of life in a popular, readable style. He is adamant that all can be explained entirely by the ordinary processes of physics and chemistry.

In confronting the issue of how life might have arisen in the supposed primeval soup, Dawkins is adamant: "There is no need to think of design, purpose or directedness. . . . There is no mystery. . . . It had to happen by definition."[10] But it is interesting to observe that Dawkins, while committed to showing that there is no purpose in nature, that there is no need to consider a nonmaterial force or influence, still resorts to the language of consciousness, intelligence and purpose to argue his case. Dawkins, in the same chapter, speaks of his so-called replicator molecules that "perhaps discovered how to protect themselves" or which "built survival machines for themselves to live in."[11] His replicators "have achieved notable triumphs"; they are "highly gregarious"; some "act as master genes controlling the operation of a cluster of other genes."[12] His fundamental unit of supposed organic creativity is the "selfish gene." Such language seems to betray the reductionist cause Dawkins so powerfully advocates. For, as philosopher Mary Midgley quips, "Genes cannot be selfish or unselfish, any more than atoms can be jealous, elephants abstract or biscuits teleological."[13]

There are of course many who would want to make excuses for Dawkins's extravagant use of this personified language by insisting that it is purely metaphorical and that behind his imagery lie the genuine, hard facts of science. He does in fact admit to metaphor. However, a closer scrutiny of his case reveals that without this personification in its literal sense Dawkins's entire case is, in Midgley's words, "bankrupt."[14]

The reasons for Dawkins's predicament are not difficult to find. Returning to Miller's experiment in which he obtained his broth of amino acids, it tells us virtually nothing about how the first proteins essential to a living organism might have been produced. This is because actual proteins require scores or hundreds of these amino acids to be arranged in a unique, non-random, meaningful sequence. In other words, the structure of the protein is immensely rich in coded information, and this simply cannot be achieved in the sort of experiment carried out in a laboratory flask like Miller's.

The formation of amino acids from simple reducing gases such as methane, ammonia and hydrogen involves chemical reactions in which more energy is released than is consumed. Technically this is called a negative enthalpy change, and it largely explains why they were produced with relative ease in Miller's prebiotic simulation experiment. However, protein for-

---

[10]Richard Dawkins, *The Selfish Gene* (Oxford: Oxford University Press, 1989), p. 13.
[11]Ibid., p. 19
[12]Ibid., p. 24
[13]Mary Midgley; "Gene-Juggling," *Philosophy* 54 (1979): 439-58.
[14]Ibid.

mation from these amino acids is a very different story. Not only is energy required to form a chain of amino acids, but also work must be done to "code" them, or arrange them in a meaningful sequence.[15]

A fundamental problem that science has never been able to solve is how to couple energy flow through the system to do this work of coding in order to produce, for example, a functioning protein.[16] Living systems do, of course, harness energy for this purpose, but only because the required, purposefully assembled metabolic machinery is already in place and functioning.

The fascinating process of photosynthesis has already been described briefly in chapter two. Plants capture solar radiation using the complex photosynthetic apparatus as a means of converting simple molecules—carbon dioxide and water—into complex organic molecules that can be used by the plant as sources of energy and molecular building blocks. However, this tells us little about how the sophisticated photosynthetic machinery could have arisen in the first place.

Dawkins uses a linguistic sleight-of-hand to attempt to get around the fundamental problem of explaining how his information-rich selfish genes might have arisen on the prebiotic earth. His molecules supposedly obey only the impersonal laws of physics and chemistry, but he then endows them with patently anthropomorphic qualities. In fact Dawkins insists that "genes have no foresight. They do not plan ahead. Genes just *are,* some genes more so than others, and that is all there is to it."[17]

If Dawkins is to insist that his genes just *are* (precisely how some genes can be more "are" than others is unfortunately not explained), then to prevent any possible confusion creeping into his intended meaning he should scrupulously avoid language that might possibly convey the suggestion that his selfish gene's behavior is anything other than purely material and impersonal. This he seems unwilling or unable to do. Holbrook similarly notes that Dawkins is forced into admitting to a nonmaterial guiding force while denying it, and attributing its operation to something else—mere matter in motion.[18]

One might counter that Dawkins is hardly taken seriously by scientists

---

[15]A helpful discussion of this issue can be found in C. B. Thaxton, W. L. Bradley and R. L. Olsen, *The Mystery of Life's Origin* (New York: Philosophical Library, 1984), chaps. 7-9.

[16]W. L. Bradley, "Thermodynamics and the Origin of Life," *Journal of the American Scientific Affiliation* 40, no. 2 (1988): 72-83.

[17]Dawkins, *Selfish Gene,* p. 24.

[18]David Holbrook, *Evolution and the Humanities* (New York: St Martin's, 1987), chap. 9.

who are genuine in their search for answers to the problem of biogenesis. However, the fact remains that his dogmatic materialist views on the origin of life do make, for many, exciting science reading and have been enthusiastically embraced by the media generally as well as by large numbers of the scientific community.

Pop Science, Prestigious Museums and the TV "Docutainment" Industry

Before I finish this chapter, let me revisit Miller's 1953 experiment. Despite his own relatively recent admission that "the problem of the origin of life has turned out to be much more difficult than I, and most other people, envisioned,"[19] the thoroughly misleading philosophical odors generated by his chemical broth continue to waft through the halls of popular science to this day.

During a recent stay in Chicago, I made a brief visit to the Field Museum of Natural History and viewed the "Life over Time" display on the upper floor. It might just as well have been called "From Molecule to Man," for it sought to portray in a most visual and interactive way the evolutionary development of life, beginning with simple molecules and ending with us humans.

I had no quarrel with the overall thrust and content of the display, but my faith in the sheer stupidity of origin-of-life pop science was sadly confirmed on entering the time tunnel. What immediately caught my eye (and stuck in it like a piece of grit) was a glass-case exhibit boldly headed "How Could Life Begin?" Two Pyrex glass flasks mounted on separate laboratory stands, connected in a simple circuit with glass tubing and incorporating a pair of sparking electrodes, were displayed in what looked to be a sanitized mockup of the apparatus used by Miller in 1953. The write-up stated that "a breakthrough in 1953 let us imagine life's beginning as a natural event" and identified the apparatus on view as the "terranium" built by Stanley Miller. Then followed the most outrageously irresponsible statement: "Miller's experiment broke our imagination barrier. Its message? Life could begin from chemical reactions between common materials found anywhere on earth."

As I explained earlier in this section Miller's work demonstrated nothing

---

[19]Quoted in J. Horgan, "In the Beginning," *Scientific American,* February 1991, pp. 101-9.

of the sort. But sadly, the impact of this exhibit's phony declaration, thrust on a largely unsuspecting public, is bound to be enormous. Huge numbers of people pass through the Field Museum's "Life over Time" display and are being subjected to what can only be described as the worst form of materialistic origin-of-life propaganda. In the interests of scientific integrity the Field Museum would do well to either pull down the shutters on this particularly bad piece of pop science or, better still, use it to explain to viewers that such a purely material approach to the origin-of-life question has nothing whatsoever to contribute.

The ghost of Stanley Miller's magical broth also reappeared in a recent BBC1 television spectacular *The Human Body*. The presenter of this internationally acclaimed series was Robert Winston, a British professor of obstetrics and gynecology and recently the recipient of the Michael Faraday medal in recognition of his contribution to the public understanding of science. Early in the first program of the series *The Human Body* Winston takes his viewing audience to the thermal vents in Yellowstone National Park, where, they are told, the story of life unfolded. Thousands of tiny heat-loving bacteria can be found in the hot pools around these vents billowing clouds of steam and sulphurous water. Winston's choice of such an environment is clearly suggestive of the primordial conditions that Stanley Miller's experiment sought to mimic. He stresses that these primitive organisms have survived practically unchanged for 3.5 billion years. And why? Because, according to Winston, the environment is so stable and unchanging. He then takes his viewers a short distance from the hot pools where there is an ebb and flow of the water and the temperature is constantly changing. Winston's story then continues something along the following lines: As living conditions changed, so the simple bacteria changed also. Through the generations there were minute, almost insignificant alterations, and enough of these added up through millions of generations to produce revolutionary transformations. Simple bacteria gave rise to single cells, the single cells to groups of cells, and these led to early plants and animals. Parts of bodies were adapted to meet new challenges and so on. All of this is summarized by Winston as the "miracle of evolution."

Now as a purely descriptive account of the possible (but by no means proven) pattern of the unfolding of life's marvelous complexity, Winston's story may well have some minor merit. But for him to convey to his vast viewing audience the idea that merely by moving from one kind of wholly material environment to another, coupled with "almost insignificant" changes occurring in the primitive organism, is sufficient to explain the evolutionary development of the entire living world is just hard-core, naturalistic propaganda. Winston omits any mention of those strikingly purposeful qualities that make an organism "alive" in the most fundamental sense of the word—recall, for example, Leon Brillouin's analogy of the self-repairing tire puncture described in the previous chapter. In Winston's primordial scenario there is no sense of mystery expressed over even the simplest organism's remarkable ability to adapt creatively to new and challenging environments. As always the reigning paradigm is constructed from a crude, physico-material essentialism. Searingly hot volcanic vents, billowing clouds of sulphurous steam and haphazardly changing watery conditions insert so much more conveniently in the materialists' truncated equation of life than does any hint of the transcendent.

Let me summarize what has been covered in this chapter. In all of the origin-of-life scenarios I have mentioned there is little offered but the parroting of a fairy-tale materialism constructed philosophically from atoms, molecules, heat, lightning, vast dollops of time and monumental leaps of fantasy. The inherent goal-centeredness of even the most primitive organism is completely ignored. The powerful sense of striving, of wanting to become, of wanting to survive are "colors" of biological reality clearly displayed by any living organism; however, these are conveniently ignored by the materialist. There is a serious problem of philosophical colorblindness endemic within the naturalistic community.

5

Serious Science & Life's Origin

In the previous chapter we surveyed the superficial and grossly misleading naturalistic answers that popular science has given to the origin-of-life question. But what more serious attempts have been made by the scientific community to deal with this important issue? The fundamental question to be addressed in this chapter is this: Could the highly complex molecular structures necessary for the construction of some kind of rudimentary living system have arisen by purely natural means? Is it possible to reconstruct, at least in principle, a reasonably plausible chain of purely material processes that might have given birth to some incipient form of life?

To Be or Not to Be in Equilibrium

I have a friend who spent several years with his wife and family living in China. He once shared with me his experience of approaching the turnstiles at Beijing Railway Station. He described how he became almost airborne, carried along by the sea of pressing humanity, prior to experiencing the rib-crushing saga of passing through the gate—here, temporarily, my friend was at the mercy of forces entirely beyond his control. Momentarily, he was far from equilibrium.

Science, by and large, is better equipped to study the state known as equilibrium, or near-equilibrium, than it is to handle phenomena far from equilibrium. It is much easier to observe the end result of a complex chemical process than to study the individual pathways the molecules them-selves might take on the way. Equilibrium has been described as the "full stop at the end of a chemical reaction."[1] The problem is that the living or-ganism is not at equilibrium. If it were, it would be dead! And this is where we need to consider a related concept—that describing the most probable state of matter.

Things tend inevitably toward a more disordered arrangement.[2] That carefully sorted pile of papers on my writing desk tends naturally toward a more chaotic state with the normal day's activity. The hot bowl of breakfast oatmeal soon cools to the temperature of its surroundings. The alluring fra-grance of a French perfume gradually abandons its fortunate wearer to per-vade the entire room.

The tendency for things to become more spread out from an initial, highly localized state is one of the realities of nature. This more uniformly spread-out arrangement of matter or energy is one way of describing a state of true equilibrium and, incidently, is precisely what helps to make the perfume business so lucrative. All those fragrant little molecules are driven by a tendency to become more uniformly distributed. Like the phys-ical universe itself, destined to an eventual "heat death" when all tempera-ture differences will vanish, so the wearer of perfume is a daily witness to a mini heat death—the inevitable tendency for those aromatic molecules to disperse until little of their sensual delight remains. All this can be summed up in the word *equilibrium,* referring to the state of bland uniformity.

It should, however, be stressed that much of our understanding of the material world given to us through the disciplines of physics and chemistry has been achieved by exploiting the powerful conceptual tool of equilib-rium thermodynamics—the science dealing with the relationship between heat energy and mechanical forces. The problem we are confronted with when studying the living world is that biological organisms are critically de-pendent on a complex array of mechanisms that operate under conditions far from equilibrium.

Consider, for example, how bacteria are able to meet their energy needs

---

[1]Peter Coveney and Roger Highfield, *Frontiers of Complexity: The Search for Order in a Chaotic World* (New York: Fawcett Columbine, 1995), p. 152.

[2]Technically the term *entropy* describes the degree to which any system has moved toward its least or most probable state, the lowest entropy state being the least probable (furthest from equilibrium) and vice versa.

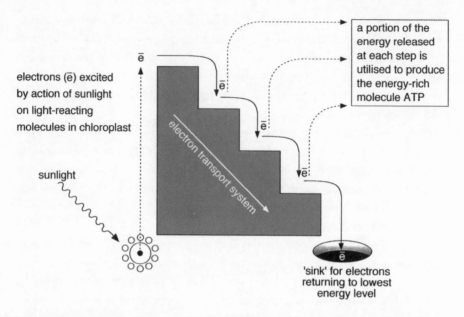

Figure 5.1. Electron flow (denoted by the symbol ē) is organized to make a controlled descent down the energy "staircase" of the electron transport system located within certain cellular membranes. The energy "currency" ATP is produced at three locations. (Image by Vivian Ward, University of Auckland.)

by feeding on almost any kind of organic material available to them. One of the essential pieces of cellular machinery used by the bacterium for this energy production is a quite remarkable molecular mechanism known as the electron transport chain. Many such chains are located in the stacked layers of membranes in the chloroplast bodies of the plant cell (see figures 2.4 to 2.7). Electrons cascade down a precisely configured voltage "staircase," or gradient, in a series of molecular steps, releasing at each step in this gradient the energy-transacting molecule ATP that is used to drive the entire cellular "factory." (See chapter two for a detailed discussion of this system.) If released all at once, most of the energy contained in the electrons at the top of the staircase would be dissipated simply as heat. However, with their controlled descent ending at the oxygen "sink," they are able to generate a supply of ATP at three consecutive steps in the chain (figure 5.1).

The electron transport chain is just one striking example of the way every living organism depends on exquisitely maintained "gradients," that is, far-from-equilibrium systems whose demise toward equilibrium would spell that organism's metabolic doom.

Tornadoes and Breeding Doughnuts

An obvious question must now be addressed. Could far-from-equilibrium processes possibly shed some light on the problem of life's origin? Many scientists today think so.

The concept of emergent complexity, or self-organization, is an area of physics that has found wide application in explaining many commonly observed physical and chemical processes, and it is considered by a growing number of scientists to be highly relevant to the problem of life's origin. It is a discipline that has grown rapidly since the 1960s, largely as a result of the earlier pioneering work of the Belgian scientist Ilya Prigogine.[3]

The essence of Prigogine's theory is that the gap between simple and complex, between disorder and order, is much smaller than was previously thought. Complex structures or behaviors may emerge spontaneously from chaotic or disordered systems in which intense gradients of, for example, temperature, pressure or concentration exist, that is, in systems that are far removed from thermodynamic equilibrium.

Figure 5.2. Tornado driven by the enormous concentration of energy contained in the vast supercell cloud structure above it. This is an example of one of nature's more frightening dissipative structures. (Photograph copyright © Howard B. Bluestein, University of Oklahoma.)

One of the most terrifying and destructive examples of a far-from-equilibrium phenomenon seen in nature, and one that displays emergent properties (albeit exceedingly transient), is the tornado (figure 5.2). Its simple external appearance disguises a complex internal system of double vortices of enormous energy driven by powerful pressure and thermal gradients contained in the huge supercell cloud structure above it.

One theory of a tornado's formation is that, under certain conditions where cold and warm air flows meet, a large horizontal cylinder of spinning

---

[3]Ilya Prigogine, *From Being to Becoming* (New York: W. H. Freeman, 1980). A more popular and less mathematical account of complexity theory is provided in Ian Stewart, *Does God Play Dice?* (New York: Penguin, 1990).

air, known as a vortex tube, is tilted on its end by the strong updraft of warm air. It may continue to feed on this warm rising air, shrinking in diameter and spinning with ever-increasing velocity, thereby giving birth to a twister that

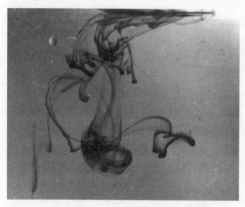

sucks into its interior much of what it encounters in its path of destruction. What we therefore observe on a vast and dramatic scale in the tornado is a highly ordered natural structure that exists as long as there is a sufficient and appropriate supply of energy in the form of intense, far-from-equilibrium pressure gradients. Exhaust these gradients and the dynamic structure of the tornado is destroyed—robbed of its frightening power.

Figure 5.3. A drop of dye falling into a vase of water generally produces a rather chaotic and unstructured swirling pattern. (Photograph by the author.)

On a completely different scale of magnitude this same kind of emergent complexity, produced as a result of conditions that are again far from equilibrium, can be demonstrated with an experiment easily performed in the kitchen. If a small amount of dark food coloring is dropped carelessly into a vase of clear water, a rather messy swirl generally appears but soon disappears with complete mixing of the dye and water (figure 5.3). However, if steps are taken to ensure that the water in the vase is completely still and the dye is then dropped carefully from a height of two or three centimeters above the surface, a fascinating pattern of behavior can be observed (figure 5.4). The dark-colored droplet, on entering the water, rapidly forms a doughnut-shaped ring that continues to expand in diameter as it descends through the still water.[4] A secondary set of structures then begins to appear within the simple symmetry of the downward-moving ring. In effect the original "doughnut" breeds a new generation of baby doughnuts, these new "offspring" sprouting at approximately regular intervals around the parent ring. With further down-

---

[4]The physical mechanism producing this ring structure is well known in fluid dynamics. A spherical droplet moving through a fluid medium will quickly become a ring because the pressure difference between its upper and lower surfaces effectively punches a hole in its center to form the doughnut shape.

ward movement, the offspring themselves begin to breed yet another generation. But "stillbirth" usually occurs because by this time the downward motion of the structure has virtually ceased. The emergent structure represented by the growing population of doughnuts, although a consequence of a complex set of interactions between the stationary mass of water and the moving droplet, actually feeds on this velocity difference, or gradient, and persists only as long as it is maintained; hence the term "dissipative structure" coined by Prigogine. The point in the doughnut experiment where a baby doughnut appears is called the *bifurcation point* by complexity theorists (the name given to scientists who study these far-from-equilibrium systems). Here the system reaches a crisis point, leaving the "steady state" of the single doughnut to form another.

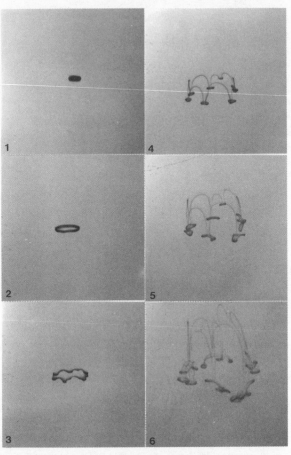

Figure 5.4. The "breeding doughnut" experiment: a drop of colored dye is allowed to fall into a vase of still water. If conditions are carefully controlled, a fascinating structure emerges as the drop descends through the still water as shown in the sequence of pictures 1 through 6. (Photographs by the author.)

Prigogine and others have suggested that a similar principle of self-organization may be inherent in organic systems and that it could account for the origin of the highly complex biological molecules found in living systems. Patterson somewhat optimistically comments: "The overwhelming majority of biochemists and molecular evolutionists who have looked into this matter realize that Prigogine's dissipative structures provide a very viable, perfectly natural mechanism for self-organization, perhaps even for the genesis of life from non-living matter.[5] But others have seriously challenged this claim, arguing that the complex behavior and order observed in these dissipative structures and predicted mathematically may be a direct consequence of their being highly constrained in an artificial manner.[6]

Some origin-of-life investigators have also pointed out that the complexity produced within the system will not exceed that of what is imposed on the system from the outside, commonly referred to as the boundary conditions.[7] In other words, it is only by setting up an external set of carefully controlled conditions that we can obtain the ordered dissipative structure. As shown in the doughnut experiment (figure 5.4) it is the careful release of the drop of colored water from a predetermined height above the surface of the still water that constitutes these boundary conditions. Unless these conditions are properly established and maintained, no such ordered doughnut structure will result; instead we get a chaotic mess.

Yet others have argued that dissipative structures in real, open systems lacking the constraints imposed by artificial boundaries will inevitably be chaotic and unstable and therefore have little relevance to living systems that show extraordinary stability.[8] Recall, for example, the dynamic symmetry and order of the tornado. Certainly this naturally occurring system is real, but it is hardly one that displays the persistence of complex order that is so powerfully demonstrated in the living world.

So while the observer's attention is easily drawn to the obvious symmetry or order of the emergent dissipative structure (almost three generations of "doughnuts" in figure 5.4), it is the properly maintained difference in relative velocity between the water and dye that provides the true ordering force. The slightest amount of stirring or convective motion of the clear water, or a careless release of the dye from the dropper, will prevent the

[5] J. W. Patterson, "Thermodynamics of Life," in *Scientists Confront Creationists,* ed. L. R. Godfrey (New York: W. W. Norton, 1983), pp. 99-116.

[6] G. Ahlers and R. P. Behringer, "Evolution of Turbulence from the Raleigh-Benard Instability," *Physical Review Letters* 40 (1978): 712-16.

[7] C. B. Thaxton, W. L. Bradley and R. L. Olsen, *The Mystery of Life's Origin* (New York: Philosophical Library, 1984), pp. 151-54.

[8] P. W. Anderson and D. L. Stein, "Broken Symmetry, Emergent Properties, Dissipative Structures: Are They Related?" in *Self-Organizing Systems: The Emergence of Order,* ed. F. E. Yates (New York: Plenum, 1987), pp. 445-57.

doughnut structures from forming (figure 5.3). This aspect is all too easily overlooked by those who have enthusiastically embraced dissipative structures as a potential solution to the problem of life's origin.

Canny Molecules

Most serious discussions about how life might have arisen on earth begin at the molecular level with an attempt to define what is generally considered to be the minimum set of properties a system of molecules would need to possess in order to represent a crudely living state. It is widely held among origin-of-life investigators that such a system would require, first, a mechanism for information storage that is chemically based, and second, a means of copying or replicating this information so as to produce repeated generations of new molecules in which "heritable" mistakes or changes could occur. It is then postulated that chance improvements in the efficiency of replication in the molecular "offspring" would produce an evolving complexity and eventually life itself.

In contemporary science there are several rival approaches that have largely dominated the debate surrounding the origin-of-life mystery. One popular view holds that the primordial "embryo" of life was based on a DNA-like or RNA-like molecule.[9] Another approach proposes a primitive proteinlike molecule as the first living entity. This view gathers its support from the Stanley Miller type of experiment demonstrating that the building blocks of proteins, the amino acids, can be generated easily under primitive chemical conditions (see chapter four for a critique of Miller's work). A different hypothesis argues that certain types of active minerals—for example, clays—may have played a key role in shaping the first molecular system that might be considered alive in some primitive sense. We will examine briefly each of these ideas in this chapter and then look at some recent conceptual developments that have become increasingly influential. Finally we will attempt an overall critique of the status of the origin-of-life question as it stands with its roots firmly planted within the framework of modern, materialistic science.

A Language in Molecular Form

The appeal of the DNA or RNA hypothesis is that all of life as we know it

---

[9]RNA (ribonucleic acid) is the nearest type of chemical to DNA, with similar properties but a wider range of molecular sizes and shapes. It is not usually two-stranded.

today uses an information storage and transmission system based on the giant molecules deoxyribonucleic acid (DNA) and ribonucleic acid (RNA). These giant molecular chains are made up from a huge number of individual linking units called nucleotides that are arranged in sequence along

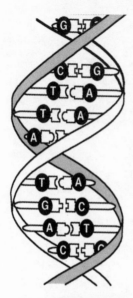

their length (in a typical human cell the length of DNA totals nearly two meters). Each nucleotide is identified by a kind of molecular tag or label termed a base, and it is these bases that provide the means of information storage by virtue of their particular sequencing along the long DNA chains. This molecular system employs the same principles of information storage that we find, for example, in the arrangement of letters in a sentence (twenty-six bases corresponding to the number of letters in the alphabet, plus commas and periods and so on). DNA can also be compared to the operation of the Morse code[10] in which there are just two bases, a dot and a dash, that are used in various combinations to represent the individual letters of the alphabet. These are then strung together in an appropriate linear sequence to convey a meaningful message.

Figure 5.5. The DNA double strand showing the coding sequence of the bases A, T, C and G. Note the "lock and key" form of complementary matching between the bases on opposite DNA strands. (Image by Vivian Ward, University of Auckland.)

In the DNA coding system there are four main molecular bases,[11] commonly abbreviated as A, T, C and G. In most living organisms DNA exists as two intimately related parallel strands. Within this form each A base on one strand bonds preferentially with a T base on the other strand. The same complementary bonding occurs between the C and G bases (figure 5.5). As a consequence the order of bases along one strand always determines the exact order along the other; that is, the same information is carried in a complementary form along each strand, but in opposite directions.

In contrast to DNA, RNA is a single-stranded sequence of nucleotides with a slightly modified language form, or "dialect." Three of its four main

---

[10]See chapter three for a more detailed discussion on how codes function.

[11]Much rarer, or "odd," bases also occur in DNA, but we have ignored these for the purposes of the present discussion.

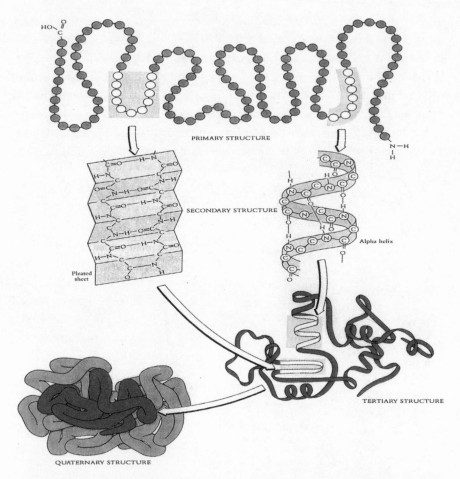

PRIMARY STRUCTURE

SECONDARY STRUCTURE

Pleated sheet

Alpha helix

TERTIARY STRUCTURE

QUATERNARY STRUCTURE

Figure 5.6. The various stages of protein assembly, beginning with a linear sequence of amino acids (analogous to a string of carefully sequenced beads), which is then folded into a complex three-dimensional shape to produce a functional protein. (Reproduced with permission from P. H. Raven and G. B. Johnson, *Biology*, 6th ed. [New York: McGraw-Hill, 1996].)

bases[12] are the same as DNA, but the fourth one, U, is slightly different from the DNA base T, which it replaces. This close similarity between the molecular "languages" of DNA and RNA is crucial to the transfer of the encoded information from DNA to RNA and thence to the success of the protein-manufacturing operations undertaken by the cell.

---

[12]"Odd" bases are relatively more common in RNA than in DNA but are still a small minority.

The proteins are crucial ingredients of all living organisms. They are made up of linear sequences of amino acids that are then folded into highly complex three-dimensional shapes. For example, figure 5.6 shows how the rather shapeless string of amino acid "beads" (referred to as the primary structure) can fold into a pleated sheetlike structure or a helical coil, depending on the exact sequence of individual amino acids involved. These highly ordered configurations are known as secondary structures and are further integrated into an even more complex tertiary arrangement, but they are all derived from a basic string of amino acid "beads." Finally, several of these tertiary structures derived from separate strings may be combined in order to produce a highly folded quaternary structure to give us the functioning protein.

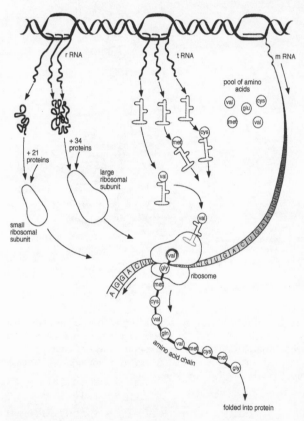

Some proteins provide the "bricks and mortar" for the construction of the organism's skin, bone, muscle, joint tissues, arteries and so on. Others, called enzymes, are organic catalysts, rather like highly sophisticated assembly or dismantling tools within the cell. Still other proteins perform molecular transportation duties and complex logistical tasks related to cellular function.

Figure 5.7. The orchestration of protein production within the bacterial cell. Note the remarkable coordination of logistical operations beginning inside the nucleus with the accessing of the genetic instructions and ending with a string of correctly sequenced amino acid units coming off the ribosomal machinery and ready for folding into the required protein structure. (Image by Vivian Ward, University of Auckland.)

In order for the cell to construct a specific protein it must obtain the cor-rect instructions from the DNA library within the cell nucleus. This occurs by the unzipping of the appropriate section of the DNA containing the en-coding instructions for that protein (see figure 5.7). This section of the complete DNA strand is known as a *gene* and is used by the cell as a kind of working copy to direct the synthesis of an RNA strand (referred to as messenger or mRNA) whose bases match in a complementary sense those of this DNA strand.

Each amino acid required for the construction of the protein is coded for by a specific set of three adjacent bases in the RNA strand. This group of three bases is termed a *codon*. There are a total of sixty-four possible triplet combina-tions that can be obtained from the four RNA bases A, U, G and C, but there are only twenty-two different amino acids actually used in pro-tein construction. Thus, several different codons generally code for each of the individual amino acids, and other triplets act in instructional ways that need not concern us here.

The messenger RNA, with its sequence of nucleotides transcribed from the DNA, then moves away from the DNA on to the "factory floor" of the cell—the cytoplasm. Here an incredibly sophisticated molecular machine called a ribosome comes into play. The ribosome is made of two distinctive parts—the large ribosomal subunit and the small ribosomal subunit. Each subunit is constructed from special proteins combined with sequences of RNA (called ribosomal RNA or rRNA) that are in turn derived from quite distinct regions of the DNA. For example, the bacterial ribosome is known to consist of fifty-five distinct proteins and three different RNA molecules (see figure 5.7). It is thought that these RNA molecules in the ribosome provide a three-dimensional framework on which the fifty-five different protein tools are correctly positioned. However, the detailed workings of the ribosomal machinery are still only poorly understood.

The ribosome attaches itself to a specific site on the mRNA and then a beautifully synchronized set of molecular processes takes place, leading to the creation of the exact sequence of amino acids that will eventually form the required protein.

The ribosome actually contains a "decoding" facility that reads the se-quencing on the mRNA, this recognition process being synchronized with the activity of another class of small courierlike RNA molecules called trans-fer-RNA (or tRNA), whose coding is read off yet another gene region of the

DNA. Each tRNA molecule is able to recognize a particular codon of bases in the mRNA but also associates with the particular amino acid specified by the codon. Thus each codon, as it passes through the decoding head of the ribosome, is read and then made to associate with its appropriate tRNA courier, which also carries the amino acid specified by that codon. A special protein in the ribosome then disconnects the amino acid from the tRNA so that it can be joined onto an adjacent amino acid previously translated in the same way. This process continues until the complete amino acid sequence required for the intended protein is produced. It is detached from the ribosome and then folds either automatically or by further molecular interactions into its unique three-dimensional shape to become a functioning protein. Figure 5.7 summarizes the technological sophistication and economy of the protein-making operation within the living cell.

Shape Really Is Important

The above is a greatly simplified description of the main steps in protein formation, and the reader should not be left with the impression that the process is completely understood. In fact our current knowledge of protein manufacture reveals layer upon layer of ever-increasing complexity and mystery at the cellular level. For example, we really do not know in detail how the ribosome actually functions, nor how it could have arisen in the first place, bearing in mind that it is itself constructed from specific RNA and protein molecules. Then there is the question of protein shape, which can be exceedingly complex (see figure 5.6). The ability of proteins to function as enzymes (think of an enzyme as a molecular version of a mechanical assembling or dismantling tool) is critically dependent on their being able to fold successfully into a precise 3-D configuration as the raw amino acid chain emerges from the ribosome. However, the problem of protein folding remains one of the unsolved mysteries in modern molecular biology.[13] There is a tendency for the as-yet-unfolded amino acid chain forming the incipient protein to coalesce into a completely meaningless blob, and this has to be prevented. Evidence has now come to light that special proteins called chaperonins (figure 5.8) are activated in the cell and that these guide the amino acid chain into the correctly folded shape.[14] One

---

[13]For a review of the problem of protein folding, see J. Maddox, "Does Folding Determine Protein Configuration?" *Nature* 370 (1994): 13.

[14]R. J. Ellis, "Proteins as Molecular Chaperones," *Nature* 328 (1987): 378-79.

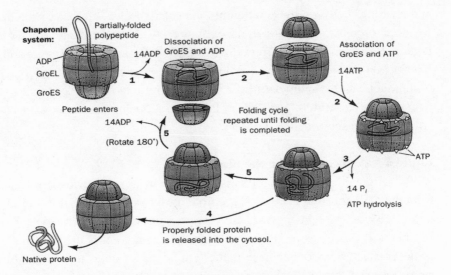

Figure 5.8. The chaperone machine guides the unfolded or partially folded amino acid chain through a repeating cycle of shape changes until its correct form as a functioning protein is achieved. In this now inaccurate representation the two "chaperone" proteins that perform the folding operation are labeled "GroEL" and "GroES" in the top left-hand side. (Reproduced with permission from D. Voet and J. G. Voet, *Biochemistry*, 2nd ed. [New York: Wiley, 1995].)

such mechanism involves the "chaperone" molecule capturing the as-yet-unfolded chain within its central, specially shaped cavity.[15] This encases the chain within a protective molecular environment shielded from other, still-unfolded chains with which it would tend to associate indiscriminately. The chaperonin somehow "persuades" the chain to fold into its correct configuration via a series of cyclic nudges, releasing it only when the correct shape is achieved.

All of the above serves to illustrate how one of the most fundamental activities carried out by the living cell is the result of a highly complex, marvelously orchestrated and purposeful set of processes involving two quite distinct classes of information-bearing molecules—the proteins and the nucleic acids. It is easy to see why many origin-of-life scientists believe that these or similar molecules were the most likely candidates giving rise to the first rudimentary living system.

We are also confronted with a cunning molecular conspiracy of "aiding

---

[15]F. Hartl, R. Hlodan and T. Langer, "Molecular Chaperones in Protein Folding: The Art of Avoiding Sticky Situations," *Trends in Biochemical Sciences* 19 (1994): 20-25.

and abetting" between these different molecular species—to make proteins we need proteins to be already in existence. To make DNA and RNA we need proteins, and to make proteins we need DNA and RNA. It is a genuine chicken-and-egg problem, a point that was made much earlier by Barry Commoner[16] and continues to pose major conceptual difficulties for those committed to a hard-line naturalism intent on reducing the living world to an impersonal set of material processes.

Could a Naked Gene Make the First Move?

While the genetic information that is processed within the living cell flows from the DNA through RNA to make proteins, information also flows in the other direction: protein enzymes are used to orchestrate the rich tapestry of biochemical processes in DNA and RNA. For example, it is the enzyme (a protein) called RNA polymerase that is employed to open up the double strand of DNA, "read" the information on a specific region of one strand, and then assemble a complementary molecular sequence in RNA language. In other words, it is the protein that is engaged in highly complex and creative biochemical activities within the cell; DNA and RNA, by contrast, possess encyclopedic amounts of "information" but lack the quite remarkable chemical versatility displayed by the protein.

So what might have come first in the origin-of-life conundrum? Two rather different possibilities have been advanced, and I will summarize these briefly.

Many investigators hold that DNA or a DNA-like molecule, functioning as a kind of "nude gene" unaided by any supporting proteins, might have been the first replicating molecule, which led to the commencement of life. However, compared to the relative ease with which amino acids—the building blocks for proteins—can be produced under artificial conditions that might conceivably simulate primitive earth conditions (these experiments have been described briefly in chapter four), production of the building blocks of DNA using comparably primitive conditions has proved extremely difficult. Another major problem is that to date it has not been possible to achieve replication of arbitrary sequences of either DNA or single-stranded RNA without specific protein enzymes being employed as essential molecular tools in the process.

---

[16]Barry Commoner, "Failure of the Watson-Crick Theory as a Chemical Explanation of Inheritance," *Nature* 220 (1968): 334-40.

An alternative idea that has received growing support in recent years is the possibility of a primordial "RNA-only" world.[17] Up until the early 1980s it was believed that only protein enzymes could perform the important task of aiding and stimulating the many biochemical reactions in living organisms by acting as catalysts. However, this picture changed when it was discovered that some RNA molecules could in fact perform such enzymic tasks. They were termed "ribozymes" for obvious reasons. Very quickly RNA was viewed in a new and creative light in terms of the origin-of-life problem. More recent experiments have lent further support to the idea that an RNA-like molecule may have appeared first on the ancient earth and that this could have made possible the evolution of the related structure of DNA, leading eventually to life itself.

To date no RNA molecules have been discovered in living organisms that can direct the replication of other molecules, this of course being a crucial element in the "RNA-only" hypothesis. However, some rather ingenious experiments have been carried out demonstrating that RNA can perform a number of the important chemical steps required for RNA replication. For example, naturally occurring ribozymes have been artificially modified so that they will join up individual or short lengths of nucleic acid sequences.[18] In another study a random pool of nucleic acid sequences was artificially created to approximate the random production that some scientists speculate might have occurred on the ancient, prebiotic earth. From this pool a ribozyme was isolated that could catalyze the linking together of individual nucleotide sequences. So in this rather contrived experiment was seen the possibility of a potential information-bearing molecule that bore some resemblance to actual RNA and that was also able to perform a crucial role previously considered to be the exclusive domain of protein enzymes. It has led some scientists to propose that the early earth may have been an "RNA world" in which the RNA acted as both the genetic code and the "convenor," or catalyst, of important reaction steps leading eventually to the commencement of life. But at the more practical level of functioning biological cells the many problems underlying the so-called evolution of a "nude" gene such as an already replicated

---

[17]For a review of this idea, see L. Orgel, "The Origin of Life on the Earth," *Scientific American*, October 1994, pp. 53-61.

[18]D. P. Bartel and J. W. Szostak, "Isolation of New Ribozymes from a Large Pool of Random Sequences," *Science* 261 (1993): 1411-18.

RNA-like molecule are considered by other origin-of-life investigators to be almost insurmountable.

Modern molecular biology has given us a truly remarkable depth of insight into the level of sophistication of the molecular machinery operating within the living cell. Consider again the making of a protein. This is accomplished through the supportive action of specific proteins that are already in existence and that can function as enzymic tools only within the highly complex biochemical and structural context of the cell. The persuasive simplicity of a nude RNA or DNA gene that somehow self-replicates and eventually gives us "life" really ignores the enormous problem of how this supporting cell biochemistry and structure might have been gathered up by the naked gene so as to achieve replication. One is reminded of the oft-quoted paradox: the nucleic acids that we know today are synthesized only with the help of proteins, but proteins themselves are synthesized only if their corresponding nucleic acid sequences are available. That is, DNA needs protein and protein needs DNA. And both, of course, depend critically on the "services" provided by the sophisticated cellular machinery itself.

Was Protein the Prime Mover of Life?

Another hypothesis is that proteins were the first molecules of life. The early Miller experiments discussed in chapter four, and the many related ones that have followed since, provided at least some justification for arguing that the early lifeless earth might conceivably have produced the necessary amino acid building blocks for protein construction by purely naturalistic processes. Although the protein enzymes found in living organisms today consist of scores or hundreds of amino acid building blocks in quite specific (that is, nonregular and nonrandom) sequences, it has been shown that even very short sequences can exhibit some tendency to act as reaction convenors.

More than two decades ago origin-of-life workers Sidney Fox and Klause Dose developed a remarkably simple method of producing large yields of amino acid chains (also known as polypeptides) by heating solutions containing many individual amino acids. They named their molecules "proteinoids," claiming they resembled actual proteins.[19] However, al-

---

[19]Sidney W. Fox and Klause Dose, *Molecular Evolution and the Origin of Life* (San Francisco: W. H. Freeman, 1972), chap. 6.

though large yields of amino acid chains can be produced with this method, there is little evidence to suggest that they represent anything more than random, meaningless sequences.[20] Certainly they are far removed from the highly specific sequences found in real, functioning proteins.

Another fundamental objection to the protein-first hypothesis is that it is difficult to see how a protein might actually replicate itself. Recall that DNA consists of two intimately related strands of nucleic acid chains in which there is a complementary matching between the bases on these two strands (figure 5.5). It is this unique base-pairing feature that permits DNA to be unzipped and then replicated. By contrast, in the complex three-dimensional shape of most protein enzymes there is no local amino acid to amino acid pairing or complementarity. There is therefore no obvious way by which the crucial amino acid sequence defining a given protein can be communicated to a new set of amino acids so as to provide a mechanism for faithful copying.

The Birth of Life in a Nursery of Clay?

The third rival hypothesis envisages the "cradle" of primordial life embedded in clay or some other chemically active but otherwise inert mineral. Graeme Cairns-Smith, a chemist at the University of Glasgow, contends that the first living system was not nucleic acid directed. In-stead he proposes that a crystalline mineral provided the first inorganic "crystal genes" and that the first life form was a self-replicating crystal of claylike material.[21]

Figure 5.9. Clay particles viewed under the scanning electron microscope at high magnification. Note the way in which the individual clay particles cling together like bees in a swarm. This property is a consequence of attractive forces arising from the clay's surface chemistry and is exploited by the potter in shaping wet clay. Some scientists have postulated that the first "living" organisms were clay-based. (Photograph by the author.)

---

[20]Stanley L. Miller and Leslie E. Orgel, *The Origins of Life on the Earth* (Englewood Cliffs, N.J.: Prentice-Hall, 1974), p. 144.

[21]A. Graeme Cairns-Smith, *Seven Clues to the Origin of Life* (Cambridge: Cambridge University Press, 1987).

Cairns-Smith argues that clays (figure 5.9) have several characteristics that might enable them to form the basis of a primitive genetic system. First, clays can form continuously in an aqueous environment and might conceivably provide a kind of "breeding" mechanism necessary for replication. Second, the crystalline structure of clay is based on oxygen and silicon atoms (the two most abundant elements in the earth's crust), and the crystals can accommodate numerous arrangements of substitute aluminum atoms, which in turn induce negative charges on their surfaces.

These clay minerals are chemically very active. (Incidentally, this is the reason why they may be shaped and "thrown" on the potter's wheel.) This surface charge, Cairns-Smith argues, could provide the basis of a mechanism for encoding information and would also enable the particles to attract a variety of organic molecules. They might therefore act as catalysts or facilitators of various organic reactions in much the same way that tiny particles of platinum are used in catalytic converters in automobile exhaust systems.

The local negative charges influence both the way the clay surface interacts with organic molecules and the manner in which the parallel stacks of clay particles interact with each other (figure 5.9). These stacks can be readily separated to expose the pattern of charges resulting from the substituted aluminum atoms. This pattern is then able to imprint the same pattern into a new clay platelet forming on top of it, thus, in theory, yielding a kind of crystal-based replication mechanism.

Cairns-Smith then hypothesizes that selection, and therefore evolution, could be achieved if the distribution of charges in a layer determined how efficiently that particular layer would be copied. He proposes that the clay crystals used organic molecules to help them survive and replicate and that these eventually replaced the crystals.

There is, however, little experimental evidence available to support Cairns-Smith's hypothesis, and conceptually there are many weaknesses in his system. For example, he fails to explain how the genetic takeover of the crystals by the organic chemicals might be achieved. Also, what does he really mean by a "clay organism"? It would surely need some kind of internal biochemical machinery, approximately as complex as bacteria, and this is left unexplained. Cairns-Smith suggests that his clay organisms might have "invented" a form of photosynthesis because they could then have used the sugars produced by the process to aid their sticking together. This language hints rather strongly of purpose and intentionality and is hardly consistent with a purely material mechanism for explaining the origin of life.

In concluding this brief summary of Cairns-Smith's ideas it is probably sufficient to note that they have received little enthusiastic support from the wider community of origin-of-life investigators.

Exercises in Molecular Self-Improvement

A different approach to the origin-of-life issue has been taken by the theoretical biochemist Stuart Kauffman. Apparently committed to a thoroughgoing naturalism (in his scheme there is no "master choreographer") but unhappy with conventional naturalistic explanations for the origin of life, Kauffman seeks to add another fundamental ingredient—the laws of self-organization. He has developed sophisticated computer models in order to demonstrate, at least theoretically, that when a system of long-chain molecules made up of simple repeating units (termed *polymers*) react together with the help of reaction catalysts (this constitutes Kauffman's "chemical minestrone"), they can generate further molecular products that may in turn provide new raw materials and catalysts for further reactions to occur. This idealized theoretical system will therefore undergo dramatic change and thus have the potential to "evolve."

Rather than attempting to address the question of whether the primordial molecules of life were RNA, DNA or protein, Kauffman asks, "How hard is it to obtain a self-reproducing system of complex organic molecules capable of a metabolism coordinating the flow of small molecules and energy needed for reproduction, and also be capable of further evolution?"[22] Kauffman proposes an entirely general scheme for the emergence of self-reproducing systems of repeating sequences of molecules that are joined to other repeating sequences to form large molecules having the ability to act as self-catalysts. They can then bring about the splitting and joining of more repeating units, or polymers, thus further enhancing the complexity of the system itself. These large systems may be either strings of amino acids or polypeptides (the stage before proteins), RNA or other polymer systems.

Kauffman argues that such a mechanism could, at least in principle, provide the needed mechanism for self-reproduction of peptides, and there-

---

[22]Stuart A. Kauffman, *The Origins of Order: Self-Organization and Selection in Evolution* (Oxford: Oxford University Press, 1993), chap. 7.

fore for the eventual evolution of proteins. This is despite the fact that they do not have the property of complementary base pairing as is found in the double strand of DNA and between a single strand of DNA and RNA. We might call this scheme a kind of molecular "self-improvement program."

Kauffman also argues that because of the known existence of ribozymes (remember, these are RNA molecules functioning as enzymes) that can bring about both the breaking and joining of chains of nucleic acid sequences, the ribozyme may have been the more likely route to the formation of the first DNA (that is, the first meaningful sequence of nucleic acids), and thus ultimately to the origin of life. He favors this in preference to a mechanism that would have required the formation of a "nude" or stand-alone gene consisting of a replicating DNA or RNA-like molecule. Kauffman therefore postulates that life may in fact be a collective, emergent property of complex polymer systems and that, given a minimum level of complexity of such systems, life may even be expected.

Kauffman's concept of emergent complexity, or self-organization, is highly theoretical and a full treatment of it is far beyond the scope of this chapter. But he has his severe critics. For example, the well-known origin-of-life scientist Gerald Joyce argues that Kauffman's scheme rests on a "highly over-optimistic estimate of the probability that a random sequence of amino acid chains can bring about new amino acid chain formation with any significant degree of sequence specificity."[23] In other words, there remains a fundamental difficulty in seeing how the correct linear sequencing of the amino acids, so important to eventual protein formation, can be faithfully reproduced by such a mechanism. And of course this is absolutely essential to a living system that requires that information be transmitted through the generations with a high degree of fidelity.

LEGO Models on the Science Catwalk

It should be stressed that the kind of research conducted by complexity theorists like Stuart Kauffman involve simulation studies using sophisticated computer-based models. In some respects these idealized models are the mathematical equivalent of a child's LEGO construction, bearing a superficial resemblance to the real thing but lacking any vital substance.

A recent article in the popular science journal *Scientific American* sum-

---

[23]Gerald F. Joyce, "RNA Evolution and the Origins of Life," *Nature* 338 (1989): 217-24.

marizes many of the criticisms currently raised by sections of the scientific community in response to the often-extravagant claims of many complexity theorists.[24] One such criticism targets the seductive syllogism, or inference drawing, that tends to drive much of their thinking and the manner in which they use mathematical models and spectacular computer graphics to simulate real systems. Computer programs are devised that create a "world of molecules" that are instructed to follow certain rules of behavior akin to the rules of chemistry. These "molecules" then spontaneously organize themselves into more complex entities that "eat," "reproduce" and "evolve" and are thus deemed to be alive by analogy with actual biological organisms that really do eat, breed and evolve. It is then argued that because we can develop such highly complex systems from quite simple starting structures on the computer, and because the real world contains many complicated systems, it logically follows that real-world systems must also be governed by quite simple rules. And of course powerful computers will help us unravel these rules that have given us life!

The fundamental problem with this kind of approach is that real living systems (actual organisms) are enormously complex to begin with and our knowledge of them is vastly incomplete. Many mathematical models that purport to simulate living systems may be more accurately described as "a work of fiction."[25] Further, philosopher Naomi Oreskes and her colleagues have this to say about mathematical models:

> A model, like a novel, may resonate with nature, but it is not a 'real' thing. Like a novel, a model may be convincing—it may 'ring true' if it is consistent with our experience of the natural world. But just as we may wonder how much the characters in a novel are drawn from real life and how much is artifice, we might ask the same of a model: How much is based on observation and measurement of accessible phenomena, how much is convenience? Fundamentally, the reason for modelling is a lack of full access, either in time or space, to the phenomena of interest.[26]

In the same article these authors comment that a model may be used to "confirm our biases and support incorrect intuitions." In other words there is always the risk that a well-behaved theoretical model with all its simplify-

---

[24]John Horgan, "From Complexity to Perplexity," *Scientific American*, June 1995, pp. 74-79.
[25]An expression used by philosopher Nancy Cartwright in her book *How the Laws of Physics Lie* (Oxford: Clarendon, 1983), p. 153.
[26]N. Oreskes, K. Shrader-Frechette and K. Belitz, "Verification, Validation, and Confirmation of Numerical Models in the Earth Sciences," *Science* 263 (1994): 641-46.

ing approximations and assumptions, while presenting an apparent fit with reality, may actually prevent the scientist from grasping the full extent of nature's complexity.

In my own area of cartilage research our laboratory has developed simple physical models or analogues to illustrate the important relationship between this tissue's complex structure and its quite remarkable ability to carry the enormous range of forces the living joint must endure. The model

Figure 5.10. LEGO-like model of cartilage constructed by the author and former colleague Denis Marra from an interconnecting meshwork of string and inflated balloons. A load of 80 kilograms (176 lbs.) is easily carried without the balloons bursting. (Photograph by the author.)

shown in figure 5.10 was constructed by first assembling a three-dimensional cagework from lengths of string repeatedly interconnected at nodal points. Some three hundred inflated rubber balloons were then packed into the cell spaces to create a free-standing and highly effective load-bearing composite structure that in a grossly simplified way models the actual cartilage tissue. The string elements on their own would simply collapse under load. The balloons on their own, unconstrained by the network of strings, would burst under any substantial load. However, when integrated in the manner illustrated in figure 5.10, their mutual coupling produces an effective load-carrying system.

But I must emphasize here the strict limitations of such a LEGO-like string-and-balloon model for cartilage. It fails to acknowledge that this important tissue is 60 to 80 percent water and that this water actually weeps out of the microscopic pores within the tissue when it is loaded in the joint. In doing so this water plays a crucial role in both lubricating the joint and providing a means of optimizing contact between the opposing joint surfaces.

The point I merely want to stress is that such models can be helpful in a conceptual sense, but we must also acknowledge their limited ability to represent the true complexity of actual biological and physical systems in the natural world. The great danger of an eye-catching model, whether it be a chaos-driven fractal image on a computer, a computer-generated mathematical eye (see figure 1.2) or a string-and-balloon model of carti- lage, is that the quality of resolution often achieved with the model within the parameters chosen by the model maker can all too easily cre- ate a false sense of confidence that the real system has been represented. Models can be enormously helpful but they can also be exceedingly se- ductive, tempting us to draw conclusions that may not be fully war- ranted.

Let us return now to Kauffman's "chemical minestrone," his theoretical mix of interacting polymers. Even if he were to show that biologically meaningful or useful molecular sequences such as proteins and RNA could have emerged by some sort of interconnected chemistry occurring between relatively simple starting molecules, he is still faced with major conceptual difficulties.

First, who or what determines what is meaningful? His molecules have to "strike it right." This surely presupposes some sort of recognition of what is appropriate to achieve a certain goal—hardly consistent with a wholly material and impersonal system. I will discuss this aspect in more detail in chapter six.

Second, assuming for a moment that one could arrive at all these mean- ingful combinations of molecules, how are they then to be assembled into systems that will yield a living organism? Kauffman of course relies heavily on natural selection, as do most materialists, but this (as I will argue vigor- ously in chapter ten) is really a disguised form of vitalism. So again he has exceeded the bounds of his own naturalistic assumptions.

A more general criticism of Kauffman's attempts to simulate origin-of-life scenarios with his computer models is provided by Walter Bradley, who ar- gues that these models ignore important aspects of reality and that if in- cluded would simply "kill" his so-called "living system."[27] He notes, for example, the huge organizational problem of having a million different molecules in the right place at the right time, one which, Bradley argues,

---

[27]W. L. Bradley, "Nature: Designed or Designoid," in *Mere Creation*, ed. William A. Dembski (Downers Grove, Ill.: InterVarsity Press, 1998), pp. 33-50.

Kauffman's computer model ignores.

Finally, mathematician and philosopher William Dembski, in his critique of Stuart Kauffman's most recent book, *At Home in the Universe: The Search for the Laws of Self-Organization and Complexity,* has this to say of his computer-simulation studies. "Nowhere does Kauffman even attempt to establish a correspondence between the mathematical models he runs on his computer and the actual processes matter must undergo to form a biological system. I find this omission unconscionable, for it represents a descent into mysticism worse than any Kauffman claims to avoid."[28]

Molecular Breeding Programs

One of the fundamental characteristics of a living organism is its ability to make copies of itself, or reproduce. Thus origin-of-life researchers generally see the attainment of self-replication as the passing of a milestone on the road to the creation of life. This has led some researchers to propose that the incipient spark of something approaching life might be found in synthetic molecular systems created in the laboratory.

Chemist Julius Rebek describes several such systems that exhibit the important feature of molecular complementarity.[29] By virtue of the way a molecule is shaped, its "nook" might fit into the "cranny" of another somewhat in the manner of a key fitting into a lock. A brief but intimate association between the two molecules may allow for a reaction to occur, thus forming a stable complex. Rebek depicts a simple replication process based on the mechanism of molecular "recognition" in which a concave molecular surface, lined with appropriately "enticing" atoms, can recognize and surround its convex complement. The same molecular surface can act as a mold for assembling the convex molecule from its component parts. This now-assembled convex molecule then serves as a template for gathering and fusing the component parts of another concave molecule and so on. Each molecule then is able to form the other, establishing what Rebek calls a "bicycle." It is this kind of artificially created molecular mechanism that Rebek argues is a first step in "expressing life as a series of molecular reactions." However, Rebek's non-information-bearing molecular systems have little relevance to actual living systems known to us today.

Of much more significance are the attempts to obtain replication of in-

---

[28]William Dembski, *Origins and Design* 17, no. 2 (1996): 30-32.
[29]J. Rebek, "Synthetic Self-Replicating Molecules," *Scientific American,* July 1994, pp. 34-40.

formation-bearing molecules without the assistance of enzymes. Specifically, an important step would be to obtain replication of a specific sequence of nucleic acids or nucleic-acid-like units. There is, currently, a fervor of research activity focused on the behavior of these supposedly clever RNA and DNA molecules. For example, continuous production of copies (that is, replication) of a fourteen-unit DNA-like double helix with symmetrical sequencing has been achieved without assistance from enzymes. This molecule will act as a template for single strands of DNA fragments that bind in correct complementary order along the DNA-like helix to form a triple helix. This then splits to form a new strand, which in turn serves as a template for assembling further fragments to produce another double helix identical to the first. The whole process is then repeated to provide a continuous cycle of replication of the original sequence.[30]

Of course the molecular systems described in these types of experiments are far removed from the functioning DNA we see in living systems. But the assumption is that they can model, at least in principle, what might have taken place on the primitive Earth. It is then argued that simple systems established under such primordial conditions can be progressively upgraded by natural selection leading eventually to the living state. In the next chapter we will examine in more detail this highly questionable naturalistic assumption.

---

[30]T. Li and K. C. Nicolaou, "Chemical Self-Replication of Palindromic Duplex DNA," *Nature* 369 (1994): 218-21.

6

Trade Secrets of Origin-of-Life Science

In the previous chapter we examined the efforts of serious science to address the question of how life might have begun on the primitive earth by purely material means. We will now outline some of the important assumptions underpinning this science. These assumptions are rarely discussed or acknowledged by science, but they raise serious questions about the limits of a purely materialistic approach to understanding the problem of life's genesis.

Wanted: A Sound Mind and a Pair of Deft Hands

Whichever naturalistic scenario is proposed by origin-of-life researchers, seemingly intractable difficulties of a scientific kind persist at almost every level in this exceedingly complex issue. But so strong is the commitment to a materialistic view of life's origin that most investigators working under its spell appear to remain unperturbed by the immensity of their task. What is also disturbing is that the same investigators continue to creatively manipulate the material processes of nature while effectively ignoring the absolutely vital role of the person—that nonmaterial input of human cunning and inventiveness that guides and therefore transcends the material processes science so successfully describes. Each of the naturalistic approaches to the origin of life is characterized by a single ingredient that seriously weakens its ability to represent scientifically plausible primitive-

earth scenarios; they all rely on the creative and highly artificial intervention of the human experimenter (figure 6.1). The fundamental question
therefore is this: What would reasonably constitute an acceptable origin-of-
life simulation experiment given that no intelligent human being would
have been there to set things up in a nicely organized and creative manner?

This complex issue has
been discussed in considerable detail by Thaxton, Bradley and Olsen.[1] They weigh
the success of various origin-
of-life simulation experiments in terms of how much
human interference is in-
volved. For example, a large
number of laboratory experiments have been performed
in which amino acids and
other compounds have been
produced from simple ingredients using ultraviolet light
to simulate the irradiation of
the primitive earth with solar
energy. However, the experiment works only if short-
wavelength ultraviolet light
is used; the longer wave-
lengths have a destructive effect on the experiment. So

**Figure 6.1. The essential ingredient in science—
the human investigator. (Courtesy of the School of
Biological Sciences, University of Auckland.)**

here the investigator is required to impose a highly selective condition on
the experiment, one that would hardly have applied when the early earth
was exposed to the full solar spectrum.

Thaxton and coworkers then examine the legitimacy of using "traps," a
technique that is commonly employed in simulation studies in which energy sources such as heat and spark discharge are used to promote specific
chemical reactions. The trap is arranged so as to allow removal of small

[1]C. B. Thaxton, W. L. Bradley and R. L. Olsen, *The Mystery of Life's Origin* (New York:
Philosophical Library, 1984), pp. 99-112.

amounts of a reaction product as it forms. As the product is removed, this encourages more reaction to occur. But the trap also has the effect of shielding the product from subsequent destruction by the very energy source that produced it. It is questionable whether such selective trapping could have occurred under primitive earth conditions.

Simulation experiments also have an element of "hygienic unreality" about them. The reactions among the original ingredients are studied in relative isolation from the crude, primordial chemical broth (if there really was such a thing!). It is then commonly assumed that the ingredients will also exhibit similar behavior when they meet up in the broad chemical composition of the broth. No simulation experiment ever begins by studying what might conceivably have been the original chemical broth itself, and for obvious reasons—nothing much would happen because of the many destructive interactions occurring in this broad-spectrum pottage. Thaxton, Bradley and Olsen refer to this as the "concerto effect" and comment as follows:

> To state the case in general terms, substance A might react with substance B when isolated from substances C, D and E. When all these substances are mixed together, however, competing reactions can be envisaged which assure that virtually no product accumulates from the reaction between A and B. Also, the reaction between A and B may begin as it would in isolation, only to be interrupted at some later step. Simulation experiments have thus produced some products which conceivably *would never occur* in the primitive soup" (emphasis in original).[2]

In their discussion of the basic problem, Thaxton, Bradley and Olsen suggest that the various prebiotic simulation experiments be ranked on a scale of "geochemical plausibility" and arranged according to the degree of investigator interference. They suggest a threshold level of investigator participation beyond which the interference of the scientist becomes illegitimate, and then note the following:

> Usually in laboratory experiments, an experimenter employs a host of carefully worked-out procedures in an effort to guide natural processes down specific nonrandom chemical pathways. In other words it is the character of the constraint that determines the result. In some chemical reactions for example, it may be necessary to combine reactants in a particular order, or vary the rates of addition in order to control temperature, to adjust the pH at

---

[2]Ibid., p. 105.

a crucial color change, to remove products of reaction after ten minutes instead of twenty minutes, etc. Such manipulations are the hallmark of intelligent, exogenous interference and *should not be employed in any prebiotic experiment."* (emphasis in original)[3]

Their conclusion is that virtually all of the prebiotic simulation experiments that achieve even minimal synthesis of organic products lie above the threshold of legitimacy and that

> for each of the unacceptable experimental techniques, the investigator has established experimental constraints, imposing intelligent influence upon a supposedly 'prebiotic earth.' Where this informative intervention of the investigator is ignored, the illusion of prebiotic simulation is fostered. This unfortunate state of affairs will continue until the community of origin-of-life researchers agree on criteria for experimental acceptability.[4]

In a somewhat analogous context we might recall the "breeding doughnut" experiment described in chapter five in which the success of the experiment is critically dependent on the conditions under which the ink drop is arranged to fall into the water.

The Prolife Principle

Although Thaxton and colleagues were writing before much of the more recent work on RNA- and DNA-like systems was carried out, it is entirely appropriate to apply the same criticism to these so-called "clever" molecular systems. There is the same intelligent intervention by the experimenter who manipulates both the molecules themselves and the precise chemical environment in which the various processes of synthesis and replication occur.

That Darwinian-style natural selection could have operated in the prebiotic world is an assumption commonly made by many investigators working on the origin-of-life problem. In writing about his experiments with "evolving" RNA and DNA molecules Gerald Joyce says:

> Darwinian evolution fundamentally involves the repeated operation of three processes: selection, amplification and mutation. Selection, whether it occurs naturally or artificially, is a winnowing process that separates the "haves" from the "have-nots." In nature the haves among organisms are those that survive to reproductive age, find a suitable mate and produce viable off-

---

[3]Ibid., p. 109.
[4]Ibid., p. 110.

spring. In the laboratory the haves are molecules that meet whatever criterion is imposed by the experimenter.[5]

Now there is widespread agreement among scientists that, given that an organism is successfully reproducing, and given that there are heritable variations in the characteristics of the offspring, then under the influence of external environmental pressures, some of the offspring may, because they bear certain of these characteristics, achieve a competitive edge over the others. This might in turn lead to a favored flourishing and survival of some offspring. This process is termed *natural selection*.

Chapter ten describes in greater detail what I believe is a blatant distortion by the materialist of the proper meaning of natural selection. But for now we should simply note that there is a usually unstated but vital ingredient embodied in this idea. It is this: the organism has a will to live! It wants to survive. It is possessed of what we might call a "prolife drive." Any characteristic in the organism that supports and encourages the expression of this principle will surely be to its advantage.

But would this same principle have operated at the prebiotic, molecular level? I would argue emphatically, no. Rather, it is the human experimenter who provides the creative guidance and selection in all of the so-called molecular evolution experiments. Gerald Joyce, for example, describes how his own laboratory "has learnt to apply Darwinian evolution to virtually any population of RNA molecules. . . . Darwinian evolution in the laboratory, unlike Darwinian evolution in nature, is a process we can literally hold in our hands."[6] But this claim is surely false. For example, in the kinds of experiments described by Joyce the researcher uses a repertoire of techniques and procedures to selectively guide the RNA and DNA molecules to replicate and "evolve" in certain permitted directions. The success of the experiment depends critically on this carefully orchestrated human interference.

Joyce refers to a special molecular technique known as the "polymerase chain reaction," which he regularly uses in his own laboratory. This process, discovered by American biochemist Kary Mullis in the early 1980s,[7] enables chemists to make millions or even billions of copies of

---

[5]Gerald Joyce, "Directed Molecular Evolution," *Scientific American*, December 1992, p. 48.
[6]Ibid., p. 55.
[7]Kary B. Mullis, "The Unusual Origin of the Polymerase Chain Reaction," *Scientific American*, April 1990, pp. 36-43.

specific DNA sequences in the laboratory with remarkable speed. The technique begins with a DNA sequence that is to be copied. It might have been obtained from the contents of a single cell derived from a sample of body tissue, from a drop of dried blood or one human hair root from the scene of an unsolved crime, or from the mummified brain tissue of an Egyptian pharaoh. The experimenter then determines the sequence of nucleic acid units that flank the sequence of interest. Sequences complementary to these flanking regions are then prepared by a special technique and used as "primers" for the next stage as follows. The DNA containing the sequence to be copied is heated to "split" the two strands apart and "anneal" the primer molecules to the separated DNA strands. Using a special heat-stable DNA-copying enzyme (a polymerase), which is derived from bacteria that live at high temperatures, the separated strands are both copied and the process repeated many times. Over a period of several hours, billions of copies of the original DNA sample can be made (figure 6.2).

Clearly the success of such an experiment is critically dependent on the skill of the experimenter. In fact, reading Kary Mullis's own account of how he dreamed up this now widely used DNA-copying procedure will show how important the personal ingredients of intelligence and creativity really are. It also demonstrates just how far removed many of the so-called "molecular evolution" experiments in vogue today are from any

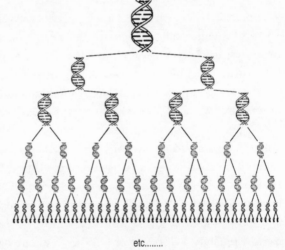

etc........

Figure 6.2. Using the polymerase chain reaction, billions of copies of the original DNA fragment can be made in a few hours since the copying rate increases exponentially. (Image by Vivian Ward, University of Auckland.)

realistic simulation of events that might conceivably have occurred on a lifeless planet devoid of any form of intelligence and, of course, of any enzymes, such as the protein polymerase, essential to the copying of DNA.

Vitalism—A Forbidden Eight-Letter Word

The creativity and ingenuity required of the experimenter to conduct the "directed molecular evolution" experiments described by Gerald Joyce in the previous section have their counterpart in the "prolife" drive expressed by the living organism. Put another way, just as the living organism always functions in a purposeful way, which at the most basic biological level we can recognize as a "striving to survive," so too are the evolving molecular systems described by Joyce. But in the latter, and this must be said emphatically, *it is the human scientist who provides this all-important element of intentionality.*

Try to imagine what those RNA-like and DNA-like molecules would achieve in an entirely unstructured chaotic environment in which there was no deliberate and thoughtful intervention by the human experimenter. Imagine that there was no deliberate separation of the different molecular species; no careful control of the purity, pH and temperature of the various solutions; and no human management of the precise timing and sequencing of each step in the experiment. These are all factors that are determined not by the impersonal laws of physics and chemistry but by the skill of the scientist.

This fundamental criticism applies to all naturalistic, origin-of-life models proposed to date (see previous chapter). It applies equally to Prigogine's dissipative structures as it does to Kauffman's theoretical argument that in a sufficiently complex mix of large, interreacting polymer molecules many potentially new and innovative structures may emerge.

We need to remember too that, whatever naturalistic mechanism is invoked in order to account for how increasing complexity might have arisen at the molecular level, it is usually argued that Darwinian-style natural selection would have then acted to achieve an ever-ascending progression leading finally to life itself. But this presupposes that a true gradient of intent exists such that those molecules most supportive of the as-yet-unrealized living state will be favored. The fundamental question is, Why should this profound element of intentionality be operating in a totally material universe? Why this strange premium on life?

So we can now expose one of the trade secrets of modern, naturalistic biology: Disguised beneath the rhetoric of a persuasive physicomaterial reductionism there is an implicit reliance on a transcendent quality—an essential striving toward the living state that must surely go under the dread name of *vitalism!* Of course no scientist worth his or her naturalistic salt would dare utter such a word. To use it would be tantamount to blaspheming the hallowed name of scientific orthodoxy. But in a strictly logical sense vitalism is precisely what is implied when the concept of natural selection is brought into the discussion.

In this context it is appropriate to recall a warning given by the distinguished evolutionary biologist Theodosius Dobzhansky. Speaking to an earlier generation of origin-of-life investigators, he had this to say: "I would like to plead with you, simply, please realize you cannot use the words 'natural selection' loosely. Prebiological natural selection is a contradiction in terms."[8] These are wise words that all materialists should heed.

In support of an entirely naturalistic explanation for the origin of life it is often argued that the scientist's intervention is legitimate because it is merely a way of speeding up a process that would, if left to its own devices, eventually succeed anyway. The investigator merely hastens the inevitable![9] Again this is a hollow argument. Time, indeed megatime, does not and cannot equate with intelligent intervention. Time can assist in the achieving of a goal that is aimed for by an intelligent being, but it cannot replace that being's role in achieving a creative end. It requires a substantial amount of intelligence to assemble, for example, an automobile engine from its component parts. More time might allow me, as a *person,* to discover the correct placement of parts that appear to have an uncertain location, but never will such a complex mechanical system be assembled with "unthinking" time alone—never in a billion years.

Despite the materialist's denial of purposeful intelligent design in the natural world, the reality is that this same materialist is forced to practice what he refuses to preach. Dembski sums up this grim fact of scientific life when he says:

> One can argue that many scientists are design theorists already, though in naturalistic clothing. . . . Most researchers studying biological complexity bring all their expertise and technical prowess to bear, especially when trying to reconstruct complex biological systems. . . . Intelligent design is one intelligence determining what another intelligence has done. There is nothing mysterious about this. The only reason it seems mysterious is because naturalism so dominates our intellectual life.[10]

---

[8]Theodosius Dobzhansky, quoted in *The Origins of Prebiological Systems and of Their Molecular Matrices,* ed. S. W. Fox (New York: Academic, 1965), p. 310.

[9]The persuasive but spurious notion of "megatime" being a creative force has been discussed already in chapter four.

[10]William A. Dembski, *Intelligent Design: The Bridge Between Science & Theology* (Downers Grove, Ill.: InterVarsity Press, 1999), chap. 4.

7

Games of Chance & the Evolution of Life

Naturalism or scientific materialism asserts that life in all its staggering complexity has emerged unaided from the "soil" of primeval simplicity. In this view, life has resulted from the accumulation of purely chance events occurring over vast periods of time and acted on by the sieve of natural selection, which is itself declared to be an entirely mindless or impersonal process.

In this chapter we will principally deal with the first two ingredients, namely, chance and time. We will endeavor to find out just how far these can take us down (or should I say up?) the path toward increasing complexity and sophistication. Ensuing chapters will look critically at naturalism's attempt to formulate a coherent theory of life by combining all three ingredients—chance, time and natural selection. This represents the grand materialistic synthesis that claims to have eliminated any need for God or the transcendent.

Literary Feats from Typing Monkeys

In the course of my research and academic life conversations have often drifted toward issues about the origin of life and the more profound question of cause. All too often one hears the uncritical parroting of a pseudoscientific story line that reveals the depth to which materialism has penetrated the mindset of the modern scientist and academic. I recall, during one such conversation with a fellow academic, airing my doubts about the importance of the role of chance in the development of the vast panorama of life. This particular person had been trained in the physical sciences but had spent much of his successful research career in biology. In response to my skepticism he retorted something to the effect, "Haven't you heard of Huxley's famous analogy? Six monkeys tapping away mindlessly on their typewriters for millions of years would eventually write all the books in the British Museum!" Another version has a team of chimps typing the complete works of Shakespeare, taking of course a comparably enormous length of time.[1]

My colleague's appeal to this oft-quoted analogy reflects an attitude expressed by many scientists when they are confronted with the considerable conceptual difficulties surrounding the origin and development of the living world. Given chance events and exceedingly large periods of time,[2] we are led to believe that we can explain the origin of almost everything. C. S. Lewis captures this popular notion rather nicely:

> To the modern man it seems simply natural that an ordered cosmos should emerge from chaos, that life should come out of the inanimate, reason out of instinct, civilization out of savagery, virtue out of animalism. This idea is supported in his mind by a number of false analogies: the oak coming from the acorn, the man from the spermatozoon, the modern steamship from the primitive coracle. The supplementary truth that every acorn was dropped by an oak, every spermatozoon derived from a man, and the first boat by something so much more complex than itself as a man of genius, is simply ignored. The modern mind accepts as a formula for the universe in general the principle "almost nothing may be expected to turn into almost everything" without noticing that the parts of the universe under our direct observation tell a quite different story.[3]

Returning then to our hypothetical team of typing monkeys, there are a number of serious conceptual flaws contained in this kind of analogy, which philosopher E. W. F. Tomlin has so masterfully pointed out.[4] First, we begin with monkeys who know how to type away at random on their

---

[1]James Jeans attributes this analogy to Thomas Huxley, Charles Darwin's friend and apologist. See James Jeans, *The Mysterious Universe* (New York: Macmillan, 1930), p. 4.

[2]Scientifically speaking, "megatime" is a perfectly valid concept to employ when we reflect on the enormous period of time spanned by the fossil record.

[3]C. S. Lewis, *Present Concerns* (London: Fount, 1986), p. 63.

[4]E. W. F. Tomlin, "The Dialogue of Evolution by Natural Selection," *Universities Quarterly* 38, no. 1 (1983-1984): 53-69.

machines in order to produce the required endless succession of scrambled letters; that is, the analogy assumes a highly structured system operating with appropriate nonrandom mechanical devices. The analogy certainly does not represent brute chance alone operating over megatime. The use of the typewriters introduces right from the beginning what Tomlin calls an "anti-hazard element." Thus even the chaotic fingerwork of the monkey is channeled and guided to a degree by the action of a sophisticated mechanical device.

Then we have the problem of recognition. The whole process assumes, again in Tomlin's words, a "phantom consciousness" or a "phantom Selector" stationed behind the monkeys, "choosing" or selecting specifically the works of Shakespeare. All this is a far cry from the intended point of the analogy, this being that pure chance operating over megatime represents the ultimate creative force behind the development of complexity in the biological world.

Finally, in keeping with the rather silly spirit of the analogy, if a group of monkeys typing at random could generate all of Shakespeare's works within the time available, the chances are that they would have, in the chaotic process, required so much paper, ink and typewriters (these would undoubtedly wear out) as to fill the earth with junk. Actual evolution has not been so wasteful.

Misleading Metaphors

In his highly popular book *The Blind Watchmaker* Richard Dawkins uses a compelling form of imagery in an attempt to convince his readers of the creative power of cumulative small changes. He describes his invention of a computer program that begins to draw from a simple predetermined form and that "evolves" an array of intriguing interrelated shapes as a direct result of small, random changes occurring in the instructional "genes" contained in his program (figure 7.1). Dawkins describes his own utter surprise and delight when he first ran his computer program:

> When I wrote the program, I never thought that it would evolve anything more than a variety of tree-like shapes. I had hoped for weeping willows, cedars of Lebanon, Lombardy poplars, seaweeds, perhaps deer antlers. Nothing in my biologist's intuition, nothing in my 20 years' experience of programming computers, and nothing in my wildest dreams, prepared me for what actually emerged on the screen. I can't remember exactly when in the

sequence it first began to dawn on me that an evolved resemblance to something like an insect was possible. With a wild surmise, I began to breed, generation after generation, from whichever child looked most like an insect. My incredulity grew in parallel with the evolving resemblance. . . . Admittedly they have eight legs like a spider, instead of six like an insect, but even so! I still cannot conceal from you my feeling of exultation as I first watched these exquisite creatures emerging before my eyes.[5]

Dawkins's main point is that, as the generations pass, the total amount of genetic difference between a particular "offspring" and its original "ancestor" can become extremely large. And while the offspring in any one generation are different from their parents in random directions, the choice of which progeny goes forward into the next generation is determined by a nonrandom selection process—the human eye. He does admit that the model is deficient in that it uses an artificial method to do the selecting, and he goes on to suggest that a really clever programmer might be able to devise a form of natural selection that in some way modeled a mechanism of survival or death based on his so-called "biomorphs" interacting with a simulated hostile environment.

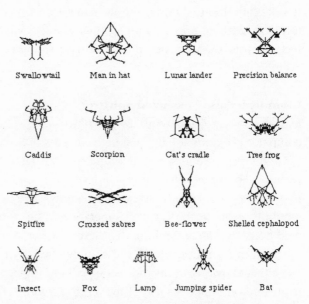

Figure 7.1. Richard Dawkins's biomorphs. Or are they just "anything-morphs" and "everything-morphs"? (Reproduced with permission from Richard Dawkins, *The Blind Watchmaker* [New York: Penguin, 1988].)

But there are glaring conceptual flaws in Dawkins's analogy. First, he has committed a fatal error by mixing his metaphors. In effect he has confused living systems with objects. What he produces are objects, a series of

_____

[5]Richard Dawkins, *The Blind Watchmaker* (New York: Penguin, 1988), pp. 59-60.

computer-generated doodles that certainly go through an intriguing sequence of transformations resulting from the accumulation of small, random alterations in the values of his shape-determining instructional
"genes." They are nothing more than this and can never be used to represent, in even the most childish way, any living system.

Dawkins is exploiting the fact that his computer model generates shapes
that crudely resemble all manner of objects, both living and nonliving. He
even calls them by a name designed, I suspect, to evoke in the reader's
mind a connotation of life—*biomorphs*. The unsuspecting reader might
then imagine a plausible connection between these computer-generated
doodles and the real thing. But in reality Dawkins's program produces pictures of anything and everything, living and nonliving—a huge variety of
recognizable shapes. They are crude and simplistic symbols of reality but
nothing more.

Biomorphs and Fossilized Spitfires

Dawkins's use of the word *biomorph* deserves closer scrutiny. For if his
computer program equally generates images of lunar landers, Spitfire fight-
ers and crossed sabers, as indeed he demonstrates, why doesn't he call his
pictures Spitfiremorphs, lunar-landermorphs, sabermorphs or whatever-
morphs? My hunch is that Dawkins knows that if he were to do this it
would destroy the power of his metaphor. The unsuspecting reader might
well be drawn in to thinking that here is a purely natural, wholly material
mechanism for producing all the complexities of the living world. It would
seem that Dawkins wants the reader to hold on to this powerful reductionist metaphor; hence his use of the term *biomorph*. This word may evoke in
the reader's mind an apparent causal connection between the real, living
thing and its computer-generated icon.

But this association is of symbolic value only. It offers nothing in the
way of explanation as to how living things might have come into existence. It provides no more satisfactory explanation than does a picture of
a Spitfire account for the existence of the real aircraft. For if it did, then
the obvious inference to be drawn is that it is equally possible to produce
a Spitfire fighter or a lunar lander by precisely the same set of purely
material processes. We might then quite legitimately expect to find the
fossilized remains of Spitfires (and lunar landers or whatever) embedded in the sedimentary strata along with trilobites or dinosaurs (figure

Figure 7.2. Why not fossilized Spitfires? The logical, though absurd, extension of Richard Dawkins's biomorph analogy is that the fossil hunter should not be surprised to find fossilized Spitfires along with trilobites and dinosaurs in the sedimentary rock record. Note: Reginald Mitchell was the aeronautical engineer who headed the design team that developed the Supermarine Spitfire aircraft. (Drawing by the author.)

7.2).[6] Given the generation of endless shapes of virtually anything by purely mindless material means, is there any fundamental reason why Spitfire fighter aircraft, complete with their high-performance Rolls-Royce Merlin engines and equipped with all the necessary flying controls, could not have emerged in the fullness of megatime without any human assistance? The obvious answer to this question is surely sufficient to expose the unsatisfactory nature of Dawkins's biomorph analogy.

A second conceptual flaw in Dawkins's analogy is that here is an intelligent human being programming a computer that itself has been built with an immense amount of creativity. This computer is then instructed to generate an intriguing array of pictures by sequential changes in the values of

---

[6]We will ignore for the sake of argument some rather obvious problems resulting from metallic corrosion.

the various shaping parameters (his "genes") made to occur at random (that is, "mutating"). In other words, Dawkins requires a carefully structured, nonrandom, highly sophisticated and intelligently constructed environment in which to produce his so-called biomorphs. This is no more a wholly material process than is implied in the use of monkeys to type out meaningless screeds on their typewriters.

For Dawkins's model to carry any real conviction, even as a mechanism for "evolving" an endless variety of geometric forms, he must be able to produce his biomorphs beginning only with completely material, impersonal mechanisms compounded with the chaotic action of brute chance. All ordering structures must be excluded absolutely. There must be no intelligence available to design, build and program the computer. He must be able to show that such utterly primitive conditions can produce a "system" whose interacting parts combine to *achieve* in a truly creative sense. Merely producing an object will not do. Frankly, I don't think Richard Dawkins would be nearly as enthusiastic about his "biomorphs" were he to remain faithful to the constraints actually entailed in the extreme materialist position he so vigorously expounds.

Dawkins could of course draw a much more modest conclusion from

his biomorph model. And it might go something like this: Given the necessary resources of human intelligence, computer hardware and software, the "random walk" biomorph analogy demonstrates how random instructions can be used to generate an endless variety of shapes that bear some purely superficial resemblance to the shape of both nonliving and living things.

Figure 7.3. Dendrite structures produced during the slow solidification of metals result from repeated branching of the newly formed metal grains along certain preferred growing directions. These dendrites are a metallurgical version of Dawkins's biomorphs. (Photograph by the author.)

His model tells us virtually nothing about how living systems might have evolved, nor what they are, but probably illustrates rather nicely the physical formation of dendritic structures found both in snowflakes and in solidifying metal alloys with their endless variety of form (figure 7.3). But Richard Dawkins, because he is committed to a thoroughgoing reductionist explanation for life, seems compelled to make much more of his computer doodles than is really justified.

The confusing of an object with a purposeful system is in many ways at the heart of the debate between the materialist and the transcendentalist. There is no doubt that quite complex objects can be produced by the action of the brute, unthinking forces of nature. I mentioned the tornado in chapter five as one such example (see figure 5.2).

One day during a leisurely stroll along one of Auckland's beaches I happened on a most interesting formation in the soft sandstone cliff face. There in all its sculptured magnificence was the unmistakably aquiline face of a Roman emperor (figure 7.4)—

Figure 7.4. Roman emperor Hadrian (perhaps!) sculptured in sandstone by the brute forces of nature. (Photograph by the author.)

perhaps, with a big stretch of the imagination, Publius Aelius Hadrianus. No intelligent mind had dreamed up and shaped this face. Over time the erosive forces of wind, sun and rain had done their unthinking bit on the variable strata of soft rock and produced by chance a recognizable object.

While sufficiently pleased with my find to record it on camera, I was unable to muster anything like the "feeling of exultation" that Dawkins admits to in seeing his biomorphs appear on his computer screen (figure 7.1). And yet my rocky Caesar is in many respects more of a material achievement than Richard Dawkins's computer-generated images. His biomorph objects depended on an intelligently operated and programmed computer. My sandstone caesar was produced entirely by the brute forces of nature. What we both have in our possession are crude, naive symbols of reality and nothing more.

Yes, I would certainly have experienced a great feeling of, not exultation, but complete and utter dismay had I stumbled across a fossilized lawn mower or a Spitfire aircraft, or any other purposeful machine, emerging from the cliff face and having been shaped by the brute forces of nature. Such a discovery would have destroyed the very soul of this book. It would have provided incontrovertible evidence that the raw forces and ingredients of an unthinking impersonal world are sufficient to produce purposeful systems. However, I have not a shred of doubt that the collective beachcombing of the entire human race over the eons of time will never lead to such a discovery.

Michael Polanyi summarizes in an economical way the main thrust of what I have labored to say in this chapter:

> If all men were exterminated, this would not affect the laws of inanimate nature. But the production of machines would stop, and not until men arose again would machines be formed once more.[7]

The activity of mind is fundamental to the existence of purposeful machines or systems.

Remember too that compared to any manmade machine the living systems and machinery of the biological world are, as I have already explained in chapters two and three, vastly more complex and sophisticated in their mode of integration and function. In many cases they are simply beyond the power of the human mind to fully understand. Should we then settle for the materialist's explanation that the brute forces of an impersonal law-bound universe have given birth to life? I believe not.

---

[7]Michael Polanyi, "Life's Irreducible Structure," *Science* 160 (1968): 1308.

8

Neo-Darwinism

*The Crown Jewel of
Materialistic Science*

If we are to take seriously the vast body of fossil evidence painstakingly won from the earth's geological strata, and if we accept that these fossils can be dated in many places with even a crude degree of accuracy, then it is reasonable to conclude that there has been an upward growth in complexity and sophistication in the living world over the vast period of time since life is thought to have begun some several billion years ago. This chapter provides a brief historical account of the development of the theory that purports to explain how this evolution in complexity has occurred within a wholly material or naturalistic framework.

Clarifying the Terminology

Technically the term *evolution* refers to this progressive elaboration of life from its earliest and simplest forms to the enormous variety of species seen both in those living today and in those now extinct. The materialistic explanation for how this evolutionary development has taken place is known today as neo-Darwinism, or the synthetic theory of evolution, and has gained widespread acceptance within the scientific community.

Many people, particularly those not trained in the biological sciences, may not appreciate the importance of correct terminology when discussing the subject of evolution. Any mechanism proposed to account for how evolutionary changes might have occurred must not be confused with the descriptive pattern of evolutionary development as read, for example, from the fossil record. Put simply, neo-Darwinism is not evolution but rather the widely accepted naturalistic explanation as to how the evolution of life has occurred.

So let's look now at the key players in the history of evolution and their ideas that have led to the formulation of a theory of life that has so profoundly influenced the modern mind.

Lamarck Versus Darwin—A Phony Duel

The concept of biological evolution is mainly associated with the name of the nineteenth-century English naturalist Charles Darwin (1809-1882).

However, the idea that life in all its diversity might have been the result of purely natural processes can be traced back to prescientific times and even to some classical thinkers of ancient Greece. But it is to the century immediately preceding Darwin that we will turn in order to understand the important influences that led to the development of modern evolutionary theory. In particular, we need to see the essential reliance of the theory on ideas that arise largely from a science that is committed to materialism.

Most controversial, and almost universally despised by neo-Darwinists even today, were the ideas on evolution proposed by the French zoologist Jean-Baptiste-Pierre-Antoine de Monet, Chevalier de Lamarck (see figure 8.1).[1] Although Lamarck spoke of a "sublime

Figure 8.1. A portrait of Jean-Baptiste-Pierre-Antoine de Monet, Chevalier de Lamarck (1744-1829) when old and blind. He was an important pioneer of evolutionary theory but is almost universally despised by neo-Darwinists. (Reproduced from *Lamarck: His Life and Work* by Alpheus S. Packard [New York: Longmans, Green, 1901].)

---

[1]Some commentators hold that it was Erasmus Darwin, the grandfather of Charles Darwin, who had stimulated much of Lamarck's thinking on evolution. Charles Darwin himself hinted in a letter to Thomas Huxley that the similarity between his grandfather's ideas and those of Lamarck might not have been entirely coincidental. However, a recent commentary, *The Spirit of System* by Richard W. Burkhardt ([Cambridge: Harvard University Press, 1995], p. 225), provides convincing evidence to the contrary.

Author," the "first cause of everything," he believed that it was possible to understand nature and its laws from a study of nature itself. Lamarck's most important contribution was the idea that evolution, from the first living organisms to the most complex (and this included man), occurred by nonvitalistic, natural laws. He argued that the enormous variability of organisms was proof that there was no such thing as a fixed, unchanging species but that each undergoes continuous change or transformation.

The mechanism Lamarck proposed to account for this process of evolution was *hereditary transmission of acquired characteristics*. He argued that in response to changing environmental conditions, an organism's needs will be altered, thus stimulating it to act in a different way. The acquired changes resulting from this modified behavior are then passed on to the organism's offspring.

How to Evolve a Very Long Neck

A popular example often quoted to illustrate Lamarck's concept of transformation is the giraffe, and it goes something like this: The original ancestor of the giraffe may have possessed a neck no longer than that of the modern cow. However, in attempting to reach the less accessible foliage higher up in the trees it would have stretched its neck slightly. This "acquired" lengthening would then have been passed on to its offspring. Over many generations this process would have continued until the giraffe neck evolved to a length appropriately adapted to feed from the tallest trees.

Lamarck's theory, however, required some sort of intelligent feedback or information-processing mechanism in which those changes acquired by the organism in response to its environment could then in turn influence the hereditary material being passed on to its offspring. No such mechanism was known.[2]

As noted earlier, Lamarck's mechanism for evolution was mostly rejected by the Darwinists. However, his contribution to modern evolutionary thinking was still an important one. Indeed the distinguished evolutionary biologist Ernst Mayr wrote: "It would seem to me that Lamarck has a much better claim to be designated the 'father of the theory of evolution.' No author before him had devoted an entire book exclusively to the presentation of a theory of organic evolution. No one before had presented the entire

---

[2]That lack of factual knowledge did not, of course, destroy Lamarck's main concept.

Figure 8.2. An engraving of Charles Darwin at about sixty-five years of age. (Reproduced from *The Life and Letters of Charles Darwin*, vol. 2 [London: Murray, 1887].)

system of animals as the product of evolution."[3] It is also interesting to note that Charles Darwin (see figure 8.2) himself was sympathetic to Lamarck's idea that changes occurring in an animal resulting from use or disuse of a certain organ could be transmitted to the animal's offspring. However, Darwin did not see this as the only factor in evolution.

Darwin was awakened to a further dimension of evolution through his reading of an essay on population by the English economist and clergyman Thomas Malthus (see figure 8.3). Malthus's work titled "An Essay on the Principle of Population" appeared first in 1798 and passed though six editions by 1826. He developed his ideas in the context of late eighteenth-century England amid dreams of social improvement taking place as the result of increased productivity, which would in turn provide plenty for all.[4] Malthus argued that it was impossible for all the seeds of life to survive when scattered so abundantly, and that they were kept in check by vice (which he defined only vaguely), famine, disease and war. If the living standards of the poor were raised, their numbers would increase until they were again reduced to poverty.

Prevailing economic theory held that the population will always increase more rapidly than the means of production. Malthus therefore saw people as doomed to a "struggle for existence" and trapped in an economy barely adequate to sustain life. He was an economic pessimist. In his essay's preface he said of himself: "The view which he has given of human life has a melancholy hue; but he feels conscious that he has drawn these dark tints, from a conviction that they are really in the picture; and not from a jaun-

---

[3]Ernst Mayr, quoted in Ernest Boesiger, "Evolutionary Theories After Lamarck and Darwin," in *Studies in the Philosophy of Biology,* eds. Francisco Jose Ayala and Theodosius Dobzhansky (London: Macmillan, 1974), p. 26.

[4]For more insight into the life and theories of Thomas Malthus, see Patricia James, *Population Malthus: His Life and Times* (London: Routledge & Kegan Paul, 1979).

diced eye, or an inherent spleen of disposition."[5]

Over a period of several years Malthus's ideas served to crystallize Darwin's thinking about the process of evolution in a new way. It occurred to him that under the pressure of competition favorable variations would tend to be preserved and unfavorable ones destroyed. Thus, combining the three ingredients—that all organisms varied, that these variations could be passed on to the organism's offspring, and that there was an intense competition for existence—Darwin conceived the idea of evolution by natural selection (see figure 8.4).

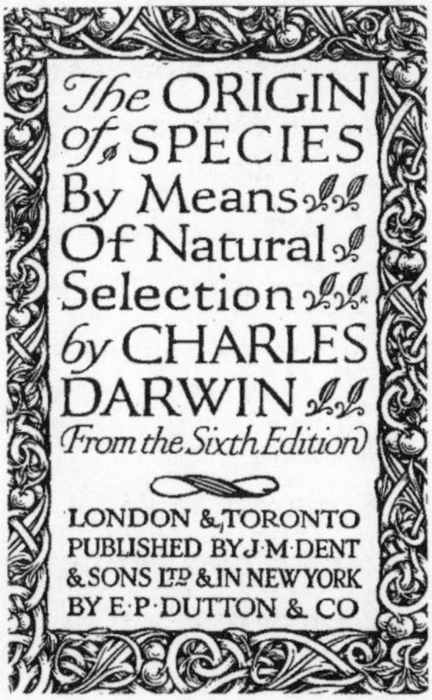

Figure 8.3. The only known portrait of Thomas Robert Malthus (1766-1834), the English economic theorist and clergyman whose essay on population greatly influenced both Darwin and Wallace. (Reproduced from James Bonar, *Malthus and His Work* [London: Allen & Unwin, 1885].)

I must hasten to add that the historical events that led to the idea of the origin of species through natural selection are considerably more complex than what I have just described. The Welsh-born naturalist Alfred Russel Wallace (see figure 8.5) had quite independently arrived at the same idea. Wallace's life, with his lack of formal education and his impoverished family background, provides a striking contrast with the privileged social and intellectual environment that Charles Darwin grew up in.

In 1858 Wallace was on an extended collect-

The ORIGIN of SPECIES By Means Of Natural Selection by CHARLES DARWIN (From the Sixth Edition)

LONDON &,TORONTO PUBLISHED BY J·M·DENT & SONS LTD & IN NEW YORK BY E·P·DUTTON & CO

Figure 8.4. Title page from Charles Darwin's *The Origin of Species*. Sixth edition of Everyman's Library. (Reproduced with permission from J. M. Dent, London.)

[5]T. R. Malthus, *First Essay on Population* (1798; reprint, London: Macmillan, 1926), p. iv.

ing expedition in the Malay Archipelago. In the grip of a tropical fever his mind recalled Malthus's essay on population and saw clearly its relevance to the way the natural world operates: "From the effects of disease the most healthy escaped, from the enemies the strongest, the swiftest, or the most cunning; from famine, the best hunters."[6] In the space of a few days Wal-

Figure 8.5. Alfred Russel Wallace (1823-1913). (Reproduced from A. R. Wallace, *The Wonderful Century* **[London: Swan Sonnenschein, 1901].)**

lace wrote an essay called "On the Tendency of Variations to Depart Indefinitely from the Original Type" and quite innocently sent it to Darwin in England. Darwin, who had been working for more than twenty years on his own origin of species, was stunned, for there in this essay from the young and virtually unknown naturalist on the opposite side of the world were the elements of his own theory.

Even in those days science was a rat race. The issue as to who should have prior claim to the theory was defused by a joint reading arranged before the Linnean Society of London of both Alfred Wallace's essay and a paper by Charles Darwin summarizing the elements of his own theory. Neither man was present at this scholarly meeting: Wallace was thousands of miles away adding tropical insects to his collection, and Darwin was keeping vigil over a sick child.

What Darwin (and of course Wallace) offered was an explanation for evolution that did not seem to require any inner drive or "destining force" to shape the course of transformation of an organism over time. Darwin knew nothing of the mechanism of heredity. The first clues to this were discovered quite separately by the Moravian monk Gregor Mendel (figure 8.6), who demonstrated in his breeding experiments with sweet peas that specific characteristics were passed on from one generation to the next by definite hereditary units (whose physical nature remained unknown).

Darwin was convinced that the mechanism responsible for the observed

---

[6]Quoted in Loren Eiseley, *Darwin and the Mysterious Mr. X* (New York: Dutton, 1979), p. 26.

variations between individual organisms of a kind could have been entirely blind to its requirements. If a variation occurred that gave an organism some slight advantage or improvement, this might be entirely accidental in the sense that all variations were undirected. They were just as likely to be harmful, helpful, or neutral in their consequences for the organism. It was this idea of undirected, heritable, chance variations that set Darwin's concept of evolution apart from all other theories of evolution that required some form of directed influence or control.

Darwin's ideas accordingly led to a radical redrafting of the neck-of-the-giraffe story. We begin with the same short-necked ancestor of the modern giraffe. But now chance variations lead to some offspring being born with either slightly shorter or longer necks than their parents. The longer-necked protogiraffe

Figure 8.6. A portrait of Gregor Mendel about the year 1862. (Reproduced from W. Bateson, *Mendel's Principles of Heredity* [Cambridge: Cambridge University Press, 1909].)

has a selective advantage in being able to feed from the higher branches. Therefore in times of drought or feed shortage it has a survival advantage over its shorter-necked brothers and sisters. This long-necked characteristic is then passed on to its own offspring and the same process, repeated over many generations, evolves eventually into the modern giraffe.

So at the very heart of the Darwinian explanation of evolutionary change was a set of purely material mechanisms that stood in compellingly clear, scientific rationality over and against the supernatural claims of both vitalism and religion.[7] Grand design by a Creator was no longer fashionable. Chance events, acted on by an impersonal principle of nonrandom death, was now the official doctrine of scientific orthodoxy. Although Darwin himself never rejected the need for an ultimate first cause, and although he even went so far as to express this need in vaguely religious

---

[7]Nancy Pearcey explores this aspect of Darwinism in more depth in her essay " 'You Guys Lost': Is Design a Closed Issue?" in *Mere Creation*, ed. William A. Dembski (Downers Grove, Ill.: InterVarsity Press, 1998), chap. 3.

language (he spoke for example "of the laws impressed on matter by the Creator"),[8] the essentially materialistic nature of his theory ensured that the philosophical framework of the rapidly developing biological sciences moved quickly toward a thoroughgoing naturalism that had no need of God.

In his later years Darwin became increasingly uncertain that natural selection alone could fully explain the process of evolution. His theory required that a beneficial new trait be inherited by the organism's offspring. But how this might have occurred seemed beyond his grasp. Darwin died in 1882 apparently unaware that this problem of inheritance had been solved by Mendel's discovery of the fundamental unit of heredity.

It should also be noted at this point that Darwin's main idea was not necessarily in conflict with Lamarck's. The phony argument between their respective adherents is as intellectually unsound as that much more important argument alleging that evolution and creation are mutually exclusive. The two sides of this historically divisive issue are these: (1) if evolution has occurred, then that fact obviates God; and (2) if God is accepted as Creator, then evolution cannot be the process whereby creation is performed. To the contrary, I believe it can be argued reasonably that a process of evolutionary development actually demands recognition of a transcendent, nonmaterial dimension. The Christian believer need never fear that his or her faith in a personal Creator is threatened by the recognition of a living world that progressively unfolds or evolves with increasing complexity and sophistication.[9]

I will attempt to show in the next chapter that such a process is, contrary

---

[8]Charles Darwin, *The Origin of Species by Means of Natural Selection,* Everyman's Library (London: J. M. Dent, 1928), p. 462.

[9]I am conscious that many Christians find any thought of an evolving creation totally at odds with their understanding of the creation texts in the Bible. The issue is both complex and much debated within Christian circles with sincere viewpoints held both for and against. For many, the issue of whether or not evolution has occurred focuses around a literal reading of the first two chapters of Genesis. One position argues, often quite strenuously, that Genesis outlines quite *literally* the actual history and scientific principles of creation, and any secular science that contradicts this "Bible science" must be rejected outright.

In this literal interpretation of a particular part of Scripture, creation is assumed to have taken place over six twenty-four-hour days and perhaps no more than ten thousand years ago. "Creation science" rejects any thought of an ancient earth spanning periods of geological time of many millions of years, and denies any gradual development or evolving of life forms. It is a philosophical position that necessarily rejects a huge amount of scientific evidence gathered to what the materialist would claim, crucially dependent on the activity of something akin to mind.

Gemmules, Genes and Heredity

Modern Darwinism, referred to as neo-Darwinism or the synthetic theory of evolution, brings together three important conceptual elements: Darwin's concept of natural selection, the mechanisms of inheritance, and the mathematics of population change.

---

by a vast number of scientists who may hold a wide spectrum of religious (Christian and otherwise) or atheistic convictions about the origin of life.

My personal conviction is that "creation science" is fighting the wrong battle, and I say this for two important reasons. First, it makes the dubious assumption that Genesis 1—2 must be read in a strictly literal sense if it is to be read in a God-honoring way. It is not at all clear to me that the language is literal and even remotely scientific in its intent. The passage contains a very simple story line that is timeless and relevant for all people for all time. But is it science? Science wasn't even invented when the Genesis narrative was written. Second, the burning issues of the time were probably theological, certainly not scientific. In the religious context of the day the big questions would have been: Who is in charge of the cosmos? Who is to be worshiped? Was it the many divinities of polytheism or the one true God of monotheism?

It seems to me that the main point of the creation narrative is to put nature (including humankind) fairly and squarely in its place as *created,* and thus as a consequence never to be accorded the status of divinity. No part of nature is to be the object of human worship. No part of nature, including the heavenly bodies, is to shape human destiny. God alone is the source and sustainer of all created things.

Clearly the reader needs to discern very carefully the type of literary narrative being using in each part of Scripture. It will be disastrous if we apply an interpretation not intended by the author. It seems to me that when we come to a central Christian truth such as the resurrection, the various accounts given in all four Gospels confront us with a flesh and blood, time and space narrative that demands to be read in a literal sense. Everything about the resurrection accounts seems to insist we take them literally.

By contrast the early chapters of Genesis do not read in this same flesh and blood, historic way. They have an entirely contrasting literary flavor. Their structure is much more poetic and stylized. The already established seven-day Hebrew week is, in all probability, used as a literary vehicle for systematically working through each realm of the created world with the very powerful pronouncement that all such realms and their inhabitants were the creation of God.

The creation texts read more like a series of epic declarations—that God is the supreme commander of the universe and that all things large and small owe their existence to him. They are, perhaps, words that attempt to describe the indescribable—events of such cosmic proportions as to be literally beyond our understanding as created beings. Most crucially, the creation narratives are resoundingly antimaterialistic, for they declare all of nature to have a personal rather than impersonal origin. (Those wanting to explore this whole issue in much greater depth may find aspects of Conrad Hyers's book *The Meaning of Creation: Genesis and Modern Science* [Atlanta: John Knox Press, 1984], helpful.) Thus, if divine intent is at the very heart of all creation, both in the sense of causation and its constant sustenance, then any science that ignores or denies this transcendent aspect of reality will be a hugely impoverished science.

Darwin had argued that the variations among individuals of a kind were in fact continuous and that these differences blended in heredity. However, Fleeming Jenkin, a prominent electrical engineer and a business partner and former student of the famous Irish-Scottish physicist and engineer William Thomson (later Lord Kelvin), drew attention to an apparent flaw in Darwin's scheme. Jenkin argued that if differences did blend continuously in heredity, then any beneficial variation would be blurred or diluted by breeding with another individual lacking this improvement. Therefore a given variation would be unable to persist long enough to provide a selective advantage except in the most unlikely situation where the same variation occurred repeatedly in subsequent generations. Jenkin's counterargument was that variations might instead be abrupt and discontinuous, and these could then be inherited by all offspring without blending. But this was not what Darwin had proposed. In Darwin's own words, "Species have been modified during a long course of descent. This has been effected chiefly through the natural selection of numerous successive, slight, favourable variations."[10]

Darwin, it seems, yielded to the pressure of Jenkin's criticisms and gradually retreated toward a Lamarckian position in which acquired characteristics were inherited. He particularly emphasized the important role that use and disuse of particular parts of an organism would play in providing a source of variability along with the contribution of chance variations. Darwin then set out to devise a mechanism for this Lamarckian inheritance that he termed *pangenesis.* He proposed that environmental pressures influenced certain parts of the body and that the products of these changes, which he called gemmules, were gathered up in the germ cells and then passed on as hereditary material to the offspring.

In the midst of Darwin's retreat toward some degree of accommodation with Lamarckism, Gregor Mendel had independently discovered in 1865 a fundamental pattern of inheritance. He demonstrated with his famous breeding experiments using sweet peas that specific plant characteristics were passed through the germ cells[11] as nonblending units (now known as genes) and that the characteristics of an individual are influenced by a statistical combination of these gene units, which remain discrete and unaltered except by relatively rare changes called *mutations.* The genes are

---

[10]Darwin, *Origin of Species,* p. 454.
[11]His experiments did not illuminate what was happening at the level of the cell.

more or less completely isolated from the environment of the organism and are therefore not diluted or averaged out by mating and reproduction. Darwin's retreat into Lamarckian inheritance, and his need to postulate the existence of gemmules, would have been entirely unnecessary had he known of the significance of Mendel's discoveries.

Mendel's work, which lay virtually unrecognized until 1900, was rediscovered by the Dutch botanist Hugo de Vries, who unearthed two monographs by Mendel setting forth with remarkable precision his laws of heredity. De Vries himself had conducted a painstaking investigation into the breeding of the evening primrose and was able to demonstrate for the first time the sudden appearance by mutation of a new species of this flower. These crucial discoveries were to provide the all-important foundation for the development of modern genetics and had a profound influence on the development of evolutionary theory in the first half of the twentieth century.

Mendel's laws of inheritance initially appeared to contradict Darwin's concept of continuous variation. However, by the 1930s Mendelian inheritance was integrated with both Darwinian selection and the mathematics of population change to produce the synthetic theory of evolution, or neo-Darwinism.[12]

Because genes are not averaged out with breeding but persist in different combinations in the offspring, a characteristic can be carried and spread throughout a wider breeding population even if it is recessive, that is, carried by the genes but not expressed as an observable characteristic or phenotype in the body. A beneficial characteristic may spread rapidly through the breeding community. But conversely, an undesirable or even lethal one will be suppressed and possibly eliminated.

In sexual reproduction variability arises from the essentially random nature of the two principal mechanisms involved. In the production of both the egg and the sperm there is a random segregation into two halves of the original complement of chromosomes that carry the genetic material. The fusion of the sperm and egg to reconstitute the full complement of chromosomes is largely a random process. Thus, in an ideal population (one of "infinite" size), providing there is no mutation, no migration in or out of the group and completely random breeding, there will be no change over time

---

[12]In her book *Man, Time and Fossils* (London: Cape, 1954), Ruth Moore provides a thoroughly readable account of the historical development of evolutionary theory.

in the frequencies of the genes comprising the population's gene pool. In reality, however, populations are often not large, and in small breeding groups that have become isolated from the parent population, the gene frequencies may be highly susceptible to sampling bias such that the gene frequencies of the isolated breeding group are no longer the same as those of the parent population. This is referred to as *genetic drift.*

Further, mutations (that is, changes—supposedly random—in the structure of the DNA itself) are always occurring, and these will tend to bring about a slow shift in gene frequencies. Migration into the parent pool of new genetic material from another breeding population, or loss of genetic material through emigration, will also contribute to changes in the gene frequencies. Finally, reproduction is hardly ever random. Mate selection, the physical efficiency and frequency of the mating process, fertility, the total number of fertilized eggs produced at each mating and the percentage of viable eggs leading to successful embryonic development and birth are all factors that make reproduction highly nonrandom.

For all of the above reasons complete stability of the gene pool in a population is not expected. Rather, there will be an ongoing shift in its gene frequencies. Thus in a reproducing community of individuals there will be available a large number of different combinations of the total pool of genetic material, giving rise to hereditary variations between individuals. Natural selection can then act on this variability and change the genetic balance within such a community. Agents such as predators, parasites and infectious diseases, competition for food and space, and climatic conditions can all bring selection pressures to bear on a population and thus substantially alter its genetic balance.

Taking Potshots at DNA

Without fundamental changes taking place in the actual structure of the genetic material (mutations), the degree of change possible in a population is limited by the amount of variety represented in the common pool of genes. Mutations are the result of structural alterations in the DNA molecules comprising the genetic material. They can arise through the action of radiation, because of certain chemicals, or when errors in copying the genetic material occur within the nucleus of the cell.

Mutant genes are continually being introduced into the population in an entirely unpredictable and essentially random manner. Most of these genetic errors are either insignificant or harmful in the way in which they are expressed in the body and behavior of the organism (known as the pheno-type) and would therefore tend to be either retained in the population's gene pool or eliminated under the action of natural selection.

A well-known example of a disease resulting directly from a harmful mutation is sickle cell anemia. The red blood cell contains the important protein hemoglobin, of which there are known to be at least three hundred naturally occurring genetic variations in the human population. One partic-ular mutation involves a single error in just one of the amino acid units making up the full protein. This causes the protein structure to fold incor-rectly and results in a highly dis-torted sickle-shape blood cell that is fragile and is rapidly destroyed by the body (figure 8.7). This inherited dis-order occurs pri-marily in people of African de-scent and may result in severe

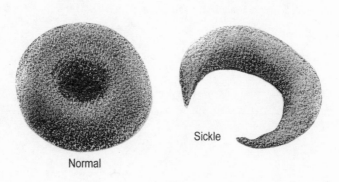

Figure 8.7. Sickle cell anemia results from just one amino acid error in the structure of the hemoglobin protein. (Drawing by the author.)

anemia and even death. Interestingly, in the malarial environment of West Africa, people with sickle cells actually have reduced mortality from ma-laria, and hence the mutation is beneficial within that environment.

It is assumed that very infrequently a beneficial mutation will occur, and in neo-Darwinian terms it is the gradual accumulation of such random changes under the action of selection pressure that eventually leads to the development of new biological structures and therefore to the origin of a new species. Thus a nonnegotiable claim of neo-Darwinism is that ulti-mately, in the words of Francis Crick, "chance is the only source of true novelty,"[13] and that the evolution of living organisms from one distinct spe-cies to another—that is, macroevolution—is in essence nothing but the ex-

---

[13]Francis Crick, *Life Itself: Its Origin and Nature* (New York: Simon & Schuster, 1981), p. 58.

trapolation of an entirely observable set of naturalistic processes occurring within any normal population of a given species.[14]

Such a claim, if true, will have far-reaching implications for how we deal with issues relating to the meaning of life and to the place of humanity within the cosmos. We must therefore look more closely at the underlying foundations of neo-Darwinism. Are these as solid and secure as a large section of the scientific community would have us believe? This question will be addressed in the next chapter.

---

[14]It should be noted here that many scientists would view the word *chance* as meaning that we do not know of any cause in detail.

9

Neo-Darwinism's Struggle to Survive

Within mainstream scientific culture, popular support for neo-Darwinism as the mechanism for evolution is not necessarily founded on solid scientific evidence. Other, more subjective influences have played a powerful role in shaping the neo-Darwinian belief system of our modern, materialistic culture.

Neo-Darwinism offers an explanation for the staggering diversity and complexity of the living world in terms of completely material or natural processes. Neo-Darwinian fundamentalism totally rejects any need for a nonmaterial dimension, a vital force or the transcendent. Richard Dawkins, in the spirit of his own materialist position, declares, "Darwin made it possible to be an intellectually fulfilled atheist."[1] Dawkins's words do in fact reflect the pivotal doctrine of scientific materialism, which is that Darwin and the resulting formulation of the synthetic theory of evolution, or neo-Darwinism, effectively eliminated God from the equation of life. This chapter examines the current "state of health" of this central dogma.

A Culture-Shaping, Materialistic Legacy

Darwin's idea of natural selection and the ensuing formulation of the synthetic theory—neo-Darwinism—has probably been the one idea aris-

---

[1]Richard Dawkins, *The Blind Watchmaker* (London: Penguin, 1988), p. 6. m

ing from modern science that has most profoundly shaped humanity's view of itself, particularly in the West. Although Darwin might well have felt some unease had he been alive to hear the belligerent, atheistic extrapolations of his theory by modern popularizers of neo-Darwinism such as Richard Dawkins, there has nonetheless been an enormous investment in these ideas by the contemporary secular mind. The idea that we have evolved by natural selection seems indelibly imprinted on the belief system of our culture. And even if we have not personally examined the underlying concepts and assumptions involved, we know it to be "truth"—the "truth" brought to us by the high priests of the neo-Darwinian creed.

But every creed has its apostates and renegades, and neo-Darwinism is no exception. While up until the 1980s the synthetic theory stood, for the greater part, unchallenged as the fundamental framework for understanding the origin and development of the living world, the last two decades have seen a growing number of scientists expressing serious reservations about its conceptual soundness. It should also be noted here that neo-Darwinism has always had its critics, but their voices have gone largely unheard amid the clamor of mainstream scientific opinion.

Sense, Nonsense and the Language of Life

The challenges to neo-Darwinism have come from a variety of directions that reflect a growing interest in the subject from outside the discipline of biology itself. In recent decades it has attracted the close attention of increasing numbers of scientists from backgrounds as diverse as mathematics, computer and information science, and physics and engineering as well as the critical scrutiny of lawyers and philosophers.

At the most superficial level the numbers game underlying evolutionary theory has been vigorously challenged. In 1966 a symposium was held at the Wistar Institute of Anatomy and Biology at the University of Pennsylvania. This conference brought together evolutionary biologists, geneticists, mathematicians, computer scientists, engineers and physicists to debate the mathematical plausibility of neo-Darwinism. Much of the often-heated discussion centered around the challenge from the nonbiologists concerning the sheer improbability of enrichment of the genetic code by random mutations. Murray Eden, an engineering academic at the Massachusetts Institute of Technology, observed at one point in the discussions:

Clearly, we have the evidence available to us, namely, that we are alive, and the evidence that life has developed to this state in a relatively small number of generations; so we have what a mathematician might call an existence theorem. There is some path by which we have arrived at this relatively small corner in this large space, on the basis of a relatively small number of generations. What I am claiming is simply that without some constraint on the notion of random variation, in either the properties of the organism or the sequence of the DNA, there is no particular reason to expect that we could have gotten any kind of viable form other than nonsense. It is the character of the constraint that makes things possible, not the variation.[2]

Thus whereas the neo-Darwinists have gone to great lengths to establish what they believe is a rational mathematical basis for organic variability based on the natural selection of changes in the organism resulting from random variations in its genetic material, Eden argues that the very "achievements" so strikingly observed in the living world point to a necessary constraint on this randomness.

Eden also sees the genetic structure of a living organism as a kind of generative algorithm, that is, a carefully spelled out, largely foolproof recipe for producing a living organism of the right kind within an appropriate developing environment. He argues that this algorithm or recipe must be written in some kind of abstract language. And while molecular biology has elucidated the alphabet of this language, there is an enormous leap from a knowledge of this alphabet to a rigorous understanding of the language itself. Eden comments:

> A language has to have rules, and these are the strongest constraints on the set of possible messages. No currently existing formal language can tolerate random changes in the symbol sequences which express its sentences. Meaning is almost invariably destroyed. Any changes must be syntactically lawful ones. I would conjecture that what one might call "genetic grammaticality" has a deterministic explanation and does not owe its stability to selection pressure acting on random variation.[3]

In other words, the very notion of changes being produced randomly in the genetic makeup of an organism, even when combined with the action of natural selection, is largely a sense-destroying process. We are therefore

---

[2]Murray Eden, "Inadequacies of Neo-Darwinian Evolution as a Scientific Theory," in *Mathematical Challenges to the Neo-Darwinian Interpretation of Evolution*, ed. P. S. Moorland and M. M. Kaplan (Philadelphia: Wistar Institute Press, 1967), p. 14.
[3]Ibid., p. 11.

left with what might loosely be termed the "natural selection of potential nonsense."

So, whereas neo-Darwinism sees randomness as the rich source of variability from which new and potentially creative biological novelties can emerge, Eden's basic thesis appears to be almost the reverse. It stresses rather the importance of constraining this potentially chaotic variability so that organic change can be channeled in certain meaningful directions. It would seem then that the central concept of neo-Darwinism, which requires that the highly sophisticated instructional language of biological systems be randomly altered in evolution, actually runs counter to what is absolutely fundamental to the operation of any formal language system. And remember, at the heart of the living world is a sophisticated information-communicating system based on the language of DNA.

Genetic Code—Algorithm or Blueprint?

Physicist Anthony Ruffa has examined the genetic code from the perspective of an information system. He draws attention to the important difference between the functioning of a blueprint and that of an algorithm.[4] The former works by providing a series of explicit instructions that detail every single step required for the process of construction. By contrast, an algorithm, rather than detailing every single step, provides what Ruffa calls a "minimal regenerative procedure" for constructing the device or end product. In essence it compresses much of the monotonous and repetitive detail contained in the blueprint. This algorithmic method is also used in computer programming.

Ruffa illustrates this important difference between the two types of information systems using the familiar example of a knitting pattern. The blueprint for knitting a particular garment would specify every single "knit," "pearl," "slip" and "cast" operation required to be followed. The size of this blueprint-type knitting pattern would be rather long and would increase in proportion to the size of the garment. By contrast, the algorithm for the same garment would be greatly abbreviated. Instead of specifying every single operation in each row, the algorithm might, for example, specify "knit, repeat one hundred times" or "knit one, pearl two, repeat thirty times." Further, if any of the rows are to be identical, as is often the case, a

---

[4]Anthony Ruffa, *Darwin and Determinism: The Role of Direction in Evolution* (Brookline Village, Mass.: Branden, 1983), pp. 67-97.

single instruction specifies the repetition of the row and therefore shortens the length of the pattern considerably. For example, the set of instructions required to complete the first full row of seventy-nine stitches marking the

commencement of the repeating cross-shaped pattern in figure 9.1 is given by the following brief code: "P8, KB3, *P9, KB3; rep from * to last 8 sts, P8."[5] By contrast, the instructions for a piece of embroidery (figure 9.2) are required to detail every single stitch and

Figure 9.1. The pattern in a knitted garment is generated from a highly "compressed" algorithmic-type code. (Photograph by the author.)

color of thread and therefore constitute a blueprint-type code.

Apart from the obvious advantage of greatly increased efficiency in storing the encoded information with the algorithmic method over that of a blueprint, there are several other important differences that Ruffa draws attention to.

First, to create an algorithm requires a considerable amount of ingenuity compared to that needed to make a blueprint. The algorithm can reduce a large number of individual instructions to relatively few commands. In the context of computer

Figure 9.2. An embroidery pattern specifies each individual stitch with no code compression. The instructions therefore constitute a type of blueprint. (Photograph by the author.)

programming, a blueprint-type program written without the generative "loops" that characterize the algorithmic-type code can operate very fast

---

[5]Knitters will appreciate the functional significance of this sequence of instructions.

but requires a large working store. Also, the blueprint requires much time to write and put into the computer.

Second, the length of the algorithm is largely insensitive to the size of the thing being constructed. Whereas the blueprint knitting pattern for two garments of similar design, one of which is twice the size of the other, would require double the number of instructions for the larger size, the algorithmic knitting pattern would be identical in length for each. Writing the necessary instructions for the larger garment merely requires an appropriate doubling factor to be incorporated into the algorithm.

The third characteristic of an algorithm is that it is more sensitive to minor errors. If the algorithmic knitting pattern specifies "knit, repeat one hundred times" but the knitter misreads this as "knit, repeat ten times," this single mistake would have disastrous consequences for the shape of the completed garment. Contrast this with a single misread of a blueprint knitting pattern for the same garment—the mistake would amount to a single discordant stitch and thus usually go unnoticed.

Now what has all this got to do with living things? Well, we know that in the living cell there is a highly sophisticated and extremely rapid transfer of an enormous amount of complex information from the genetic library contained within the DNA to the cellular metabolic machinery. The sheer complexity of this information-transfer process, together with the extremely efficient functioning of the cellular machinery, suggests an algorithmic-like, rather than a blueprint-like, method of communication within the cell. Further evidence for this is seen from the fact that just as minor errors in a knitting algorithm can result in massive distortions in the final form of the garment, so living organisms may similarly exhibit gross deformities when their genetic material is damaged by ionizing radiation or other mutagenic agents.

Molecular Orchestration

Modern molecular biology has been enormously successful in showing how at least part of the information carried in the genes is used by the cell to assemble a vast array of complex protein molecules. These proteins are highly diverse in both their structure and the roles they perform. They are required for the direct metabolic function of the cell, for its reproduction and for the manufacture of complex raw materials used for the construction of new biological structures.

The class of proteins called *enzymes* controls highly complex sequences of chemical reactions with exquisite timing and efficiency. They are extremely large and complicated molecules that can undergo subtle changes to their three-dimensional architecture in response to changing conditions within the cell. These shape changes, in turn, alter the enzyme's influence on the chemical reactions they control, thus orchestrating an intricate web of processes that enable the cell to respond and interact in a meaningful way with its environment.

Although there is still much that is unknown about the detailed structure of the genetic algorithm and the language in which it is specified, modern molecular biology has demonstrated that the processes of life are critically dependent on the precise operation of this immensely sophisticated and ingenious information-processing system. As we have noted in the previous section, its very sophistication makes the genetic algorithm vulnerable to random disturbances. Thus any mechanism for evolution that depends ultimately on random changes to the genetic code as a source of biological novelty would appear to be largely incompatible with what we know about complex information systems.

Neo-Darwinism also faces a fundamental problem in its attempt to address the question of how biological systems actually develop. The living world presents us with a truly staggering array of the most ingenious and creative structures and systems imaginable. Even the most intricate man-made devices cannot compare with the sophisticated biochemical systems that operate within the living cell. The central claim of neo-Darwinism is that the information contained within the genes is what determines all biological processes; that is, the organism is the byproduct of genes, and these genes can be explained by mutation and natural selection. The concept fits perfectly within the reductionist framework but actually explains little about the real nature of life itself and how it might have arisen in the first place. The very expression "natural selection" has become a mantra, a sacred utterance for the materialist, with the power to coax the mutation-battered gene into performing ever new and wondrous feats of biological innovation.

I will critique the neo-Darwinian idea of natural selection in much more depth in the next chapter. Right now our task is to examine just what a gene can and cannot do.

Molecules with Minds

To claim that the gene is the fundamental ordering substance in nature is to attribute to it quite remarkable powers of intelligence and creativity. However, such attributes claimed for the gene have never been demonstrated by science itself. Much of the persuasiveness behind the "gene is God" doctrine lies in the rhetoric and language used by its adherents.

Richard Dawkins, who as I noted in chapter four is an outspoken advocate of the neo-Darwinian cause, has the gene thoroughly anthropomorphized.[6] His genes compete with fellow genes; they break up rivals; they discover how to protect themselves; they construct containers for their own continued existence. Dawkins sees the entire drama of life arising from its supposed humble beginnings in the "primeval soup" as the inevitable consequence of his "selfish genes" forever asserting themselves in the face of natural selection. He leaves his readers in no doubt that the most fundamental problems and mysteries presented to us by the living world are solved, at least in principle, by his own version of gene-centered reductionism.

Having supposedly explained how these genes (or as he calls them, "replicators") rose to biological supremacy on our once-lifeless planet, Dawkins continues:

> Four thousand million years on, what was to be the fate of the ancient replicators? They did not die out, for they are past masters of the survival arts. But do not look for them floating loose in the sea; they gave up that cavalier freedom long ago. Now they swarm in huge colonies, safe inside gigantic lumbering robots, sealed off from the outside world, communicating with it by tortuous indirect routes, manipulating it by remote control. They are in you and in me; they created us, body and mind; and their preservation is the ultimate rationale for our existence. They have come a long way, those replicators. Now they go by the name of genes, and we are their survival machines.[7]

But this is surely a vulgar misrepresentation of biological realities. By what means can a gene, however rich in coded information it might be, achieve such evolutionary feats? Paul Weiss, writing several decades before Dawkins, points out the absurdity of the "gene is supreme" idea: "The claim of the gene for recognition as the sole ordering principle in organisms . . . rests on sheer assertion, based on blind faith and unqualified reductionistic preconceptions."[8]

Weiss further accuses the reductionists of

---

[6]Richard Dawkins, *The Selfish Gene* (Oxford: Oxford University Press, 1989), chap. 2.
[7]Ibid., p. 19.
[8]Paul Weiss, *Within the Gates of Science and Beyond* (New York: Hafner, 1971), p. 301.

glossing over the difficulty of explaining just how gene interaction could achieve any real creative synthesis of more complex biological systems by taking recourse to pretentious anthropomorphic terms, which evaded and obscured the issue. One simply bestowed upon the gene the faculty of spontaneity, the power of dictating, informing, regulating, controlling, etc.[9]

This painting over of the cracks in a deficient science with thoroughly misleading and inappropriate anthropomorphized imagery is precisely what Richard Dawkins resorts to in his *Selfish Gene* and later books.

If the practitioners of science are at times guilty of disguising their real ignorance of some of the most fundamental aspects of their discipline, popular science feeds voraciously on this ignorance, thriving on the simplistic and trivialized kind of science that is promoted by certain sections of the scientific community. A feature article in *Time* magazine titled "Genetic Revolution"[10] presents its readers with a powerful visual feast, literally a laboratory test tube containing DNA—the "essence of life," the "Master Molecule." It is described as a clear watery fluid which turns out to be as sticky as molasses, a giant spiral staircase-shaped molecule that acts like a "biological computer program" for making proteins, the basic building blocks of life. So a molecule that is admitted to be exceedingly complex (it is even likened to a computer program), but equally, whose chemical structure is thoroughly understood, is put on public show in a test tube and declared to be the ultimate inspiration of life. This glamorized "magazine science," so typical of the manner in which serious scientific issues are re-packaged for the popular media generally, is used more for its entertainment value than for conveying to the reader the real limits of human knowledge and a sense of the vast unknown.

The test-tube image of DNA in the above-mentioned *Time* article has all the ingredients of a no-nonsense reductionism, leaving the nonexpert reader in no doubt that scientists have, to all intents and purposes, solved the weighty problem of biological existence. The reader is served up a compellingly simple message—the mystery of life can be explained by a chemical substance in a test tube that we can hold in our hands. And the take-home message—it really is so very simple!

Now no right-minded scientist would question the central importance of DNA in its role as a highly sophisticated molecular source code that is cru-

---

[9]Ibid., p. 302.
[10]*Time,* January 17, 1994, pp. 26-42.

cial to the entire workings of the living cell. We now know in considerable detail how the DNA molecule is replicated and how it codes for a vast range of the important molecules assembled by the cell and used in the construction and function of a living organism. Richard Dawkins uses this knowledge to construct an entire philosophy of existence around the supposed preeminence of DNA (i.e., the gene). He would have us believe that "they are in you and in me; they created us, body and mind; and their preservation is the ultimate rationale for our existence."[11] But this is surely biological nonsense. Life cannot be defined so simplistically.[12] DNA is not the ultimate "explainer" of all living things. And the reason is quite simple: DNA does not produce life. Rather, it is the source code that the cell reads in order to manufacture proteins that are, in turn, used as the bricks and mortar and metabolic machinery of the living world. And this fact contributes virtually nothing to solving the central problem in developmental biology—how the living organism is actually assembled in all its structural and functional complexity from these basic molecular building blocks.

Recall that DNA functions rather like a set of blueprints, or rather a series of algorithms, providing the correct recipe for making each of the many different proteins required to be manufactured by the cell at each moment in time and space. The exact coordination of this process is absolutely crucial to the correct functioning of the cell but is left largely unexplained by the DNA itself. A higher level of control is required, and the process goes something like this: At a given moment a particular protein enzyme is required by the cell. The cell reaches into the appropriate DNA "pigeon hole" (that specific part of the DNA library containing the coding instructions for the required protein), takes it out, makes a "photocopy," returns the original to its correct place and delivers the copied instructions to the cellular machinery, thus enabling protein production to commence. It is not the DNA that orchestrates this exquisitely synchronized set of events. Rather, it is the whole cell within the living organism that is somehow orchestrated to bring about the retrieval of the required protein recipe from the vast library of coded information stored in the DNA. And don't forget: this entire process is resoundingly goal-centered. The cell is intent on pro-

---

[11]Dawkins, *Selfish Gene*, p. 20.
[12]Even the well-known American paleobiologist Stephen Gould, who appears to be no friend of theism, writes scornfully against this reductionist mentality. See Stephen J. Gould, "Message from a Mouse," *Time*, September 27, 1999, p. 56.

ducing a particular protein for a particular task.

Codes in Context

The British biologist Brian Goodwin has written extensively about the conceptual problems surrounding neo-Darwinism. In particular he challenges the widely held claim that the essence of life resides in the germ plasm, or the genes, which, it is argued, have the power to make specific organisms according to the genes' specific structure. Goodwin takes particular issue with Dawkins's reductionism, as articulated in his "grand strategy" of the genes (replicators). Goodwin comments as follows:

> What makes organisms is not replicators but organisms, via the process of reproduction. No autonomous (nonparasitic) organisms are made by replicators. Understanding the process of reproduction is the fascinating but unsolved problem of development. During this process the genetic material of the organism is replicated by the remarkable mechanism of "template copying," using one strand of DNA as a template to make another. This distinctive property of nucleic acids is the molecular basis of inheritance. But the process occurs within a highly organised context, the living cell. Without such a context there is no known mechanism whereby the DNA of a particular species can be completely and accurately copied. So the reproduction of the organism and the replication of its genome are mutually dependent processes.[13]

We need to remember that information, whether it be contained in DNA or any other medium, is not something that can be poured into an unstructured environment as one might pour water into an empty container. The gene is captive within its highly structured cellular environment—what Goodwin calls the "context." It expresses itself as a rich, information-bearing molecular code only by virtue of the profoundly complex and sophisticated system of which it is but a part. This system is specially designed to receive, make sense of and act on the instructions transmitted from the source code or DNA. It is the total, integrated system that "achieves," not DNA as a kind of molecular maestro.

To the illiterate mind a page of scribble and a portion of text ripped from the *Encyclopedia Britannica* will have little difference in value. But provide that same mind with an appropriate context of education and the portion of text takes on a rich depth of meaning. Thus, the central claim of

---

[13]Brian Goodwin, "Rumbling the Replicator," *New Scientist* 10 (March 1988): 56.

neo-Darwinism that genes acting autonomously (that is, without a meaningful context, as in Dawkins's "selfish gene"), under the action of natural
selection, are somehow sufficient to explain the origin and development of
life would seem to be a fatal flaw in its formulation.

Think of the modern hi-fi stereo system. The source code is contained in
either the physical undulations in the record grooves, the variations in
magnetic flux in the cassette tape, or the optical patterns on the compact
disc. This code is then made to interact with an appropriately designed,
richly structured electromechanical system so as to achieve a meaningful
detection, transmission, reception and processing of this source code, and
then it is finally translated into the meaningful "language" of music. The
source code, however complex it might be, is quite incapable of giving us
the music on its own. Every music lover knows only too well that there has
to be a considerable financial investment in the electromechanical system
(the stereo player itself) if the source code is to be converted into music.
And we must go even further. The source code itself is the product of a
musical mind, that of the composer. So again we are reminded of Aristotle's
efficient and final causes (see chapter three).

The same is true for the source code of the living organism. Without the
rich complexity of the cellular system, the genetic code is incapable of giving us the magnificently composed and orchestrated "symphony" of biological life. The sheer richness of the melody of life, its coherence and unity
and its innovating freedom must surely compel us to acknowledge the
hand of a great Composer.

In brief, the operation of even the simplest form of code is an expression of intelligent design rather than impersonal forces.[14]

The Wright Brothers Versus *The Blind Watchmaker*

A cornerstone of Richard Dawkins's all-encompassing materialistic vision is
the creative power of cumulative small changes. He describes in considerable
detail this concept in his popular book *The Blind Watchmaker*. These small
changes, wrought by random mutations and acted on by the sieving action of
natural selection, are deemed to provide a totally naturalistic mechanism for
achieving major innovation in the living world. However, many critics of neo-

---

[14]William Dembski in his book *Intelligent Design* (Downers Grove, Ill.: InterVarsity Press, 1999)
offers a compelling justification for enveloping the activity of science within a theistic
framework of intelligent design.

Darwinism have argued that complex organs such as the human eye could not have evolved by a process of gradual, step-by-step improvement. Rather, such evolution must have required the coordinated integration of all its parts, their evolving in synchrony, so as to produce a functioning organ of sight. No half measures would have been permitted since these, having no survival value, would be eliminated by natural selection.

In the face of this challenge Dawkins lashes back at his critics: "Vision that is 5 per cent as good as yours or mine is very much worth having in comparison with no vision at all. So is 1 per cent vision better than total blindness. And 6 per cent is better than 5, 7 per cent better than 6, and so on up the gradual, continuous series."[15] And again: "A simple, rudimentary, half-cocked eye . . . is better than none at all. Without an eye you are totally blind. With half an eye you may at least be able to detect the general direction of a predator's movement, even if you can't focus a clear image. And this may make all the difference between life and death."[16]

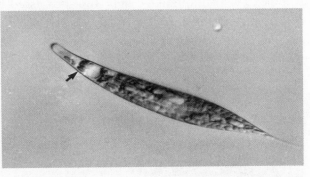

Figure 9.3. The tiny aquatic animal *Euglena* has a light-sensing spot, or primitive "eye," located near one end of its body (see darkish spot marked with arrow). The author collected this specimen from a sewage-treatment pond. It was photographed alive at approximately one hundred times magnification in a "slowing down medium" similar to clear wallpaper paste. (Photograph by the author.)

Superficially Dawkins seems to have a compelling argument. No one in their right mind would disagree that a poor sensory organ (if this is what he means by "half-cocked") is more useful to the animal than none at all. It is easy to see that any slight improvement in vision will constitute a functional advantage and might therefore be retained under the pressure of selection. Dawkins further buttresses his argument by rightly noting that in nature there exist many single-celled and multicelled organisms that possess very simple light-sensing systems (see figure 9.3), thus providing com-

[15]Richard Dawkins, *The Blind Watchmaker* (London: Penguin, 1988), p. 81.
[16]Ibid., p. 41.

pelling evidence in support of a continuum of evolutionary development from the most primitive light-sensing pigmented cell to the immensely sophisticated workings of the mammalian eye. However, there is a fundamental flaw in Dawkins's reasoning. When, for example, he talks about having "half an eye," I don't think he means an eye that is only halfway to achieving even a minimal level of rudimentary sight. This confusion makes his whole argument highly suspect, as I will attempt to demonstrate in the remainder of this chapter.

Richard Dawkins is, I believe, referring to an eye with a degree of seeing power that is some fraction of that possessed by the fully developed complex eye. The primitive light spot possessed by the little protozoan organism *Euglena* shown in figure 9.3 actually functions as a real light-sensing device, albeit at a low level of sophistication. The light spot is a crude eye, not half an eye. Our little *Euglena* doesn't almost see. Rather, it sees to a degree of sophistication that suits its needs as a simple aquatic creature.

Now it is important to emphasize that any system that achieves some degree of function, whether it be biological, electrical, mechanical, optical or whatever, is an *achieving* system, not a *nearly achieving* system. In evolutionary terms there is no selective advantage in having a system that claims to work but doesn't. Apply this principle to the first controlled, heavier-than-air flight of the American cycle engineers Orville and Wilbur Wright (see fig. 9.4). They could not have taken off in their gas-powered biplane "Flyer I" and remained airborne for those twelve momentous seconds had they not first created a *minimally flyable* system.[17]

Figure 9.4. The Wright brothers' first flight. They achieved twelve seconds of sustained, powered flight, not almost-sustained flight. (Courtesy of Special Collections and Archives, Wright State University.)

When it comes to achieving flight it is complete nonsense to call some-

---

[17]I cannot resist adding a decidedly patriotic footnote at this point. Although popular history has accorded the Wright brothers with having achieved the first sustained and controlled flight in December 1903, more recent historical research has uncovered convincing evidence that the

thing a flying machine when it cannot fly but has say 5 , 50 or even 90 percent of the requirements of a machine that will fly (see figure 9.5). It will
remain firmly stuck on the ground and cannot be considered in terms of
the evolution of the air-
plane as achieving even a
fraction of a percent of
flight. An improvement in
flying performance of say
just 1 percent cannot be
claimed unless there is
some actual flight in the
first place.

The Wright flyer was
not simply a lucky piece of
invention that happened to
fly. It deserved to fly because it met the minimum

Figure 9.5. Powered flight was achieved because a flying machine, not a "nearly flying machine," had been successfully built. (Cartoon by the author.)

requirements of aerodynamic stability, self-power and means of control. Of
course there are degrees of successful flight. The twelve-second flight of
the Wright flyer cannot compare with the superb aerodynamic performance
of modern aircraft. However, both have flown.

There is an enormous qualitative, technological leap from nonflight to
flight. And in an analogous sense there is an enormous qualitative leap
from no sight to sight. Yes, there are degrees of sophistication of vision organs ranging from the primitive light-sensitive spot possessed by the tiny
Euglena (figure 9.3) to the highly sophisticated optical system of the human eye. But all are, optically speaking, going concerns—they all "see."

Dawkins would have us believe that "part of an eye is better than no
eye at all."[18] This is nonsense. A "pre-eye" or a "pre-light spot" that cannot
see in even the most rudimentary sense cannot be called an organ of sight.

---

reclusive New Zealand farmer Richard Pearse achieved a successful powered, though largely
uncontrolled, take-off in his home-built monoplane, probably in March 1903. A recent issue
of *Time* magazine (October 25, 1999) makes brief mention of Pearse's pioneering
achievements, and the interested reader is referred to Gordon Ogilvie's painstakingly
researched book *The Riddle of Richard Pearse* (Wellington, N.Z.: A. H. & A. W. Reed, 1973)
for a deeply moving account of this enigmatic man's life and remarkable but largely
unrecognized aeronautical achievements.

[18]Ibid., p. 85.

We might well ask, "What happened to the burden of accumulated small mutations toward an eye but as yet conferring no degree of vision?" Neo-Darwinian theory would select against such meaningless burdens, thereby making the evolutionary passage from raw componentry to a connected assemblage of parts with the crudest degree of sight highly improbable.[19]

What I believe is important to appreciate is that Richard Dawkins has completely blurred the quite fundamental distinction between a lesser eye

---

[19]It should perhaps be noted here that although Richard Dawkins holds to a thoroughgoing gradualism to account for the evolution of biological complexity—that is, "part of an eye is better than no eye at all"—he does admit elsewhere that a different kind of explanation may be required to avoid any reliance on large, single-step mutations in order to achieve some functional advantage that may be open to selection. For example, in his book *Climbing Mount Improbable* (Harmondsworth, U.K.: Viking, 1996), chap. 4, he discusses the evolution of insect flight and animal flight generally. He argues that the first insect wings may have been stubs of insufficient length to achieve any significant degree of lift but that they were preadapted for a completely different purpose, that of equipping the animal with heat-gathering solar panels. Darwinian selection might then have acted to increase gradually the length of these "wing stubs," thus providing a smooth gradient of improvement in solar heating performance for the insect. This increased size would then have been exploited perhaps much later in evolutionary time for the very different purpose of flight.

Dawkins also discusses a number of other sideways diversions in evolutionary development. For example, he suggests that feathers in birds perhaps evolved not initially for flight but for thermal insulation, or possibly as a kind of net for catching insects. Flapping movements in the wings, he suggests, might have come originally from the need for a tree-leaping animal to develop some degree of control over pitching and rolling movements—it might do this best by some kind of arm flapping that eventually evolved into winged power.

However, all this does little to get around that fundamental issue the neo-Darwinist so desperately seeks to avoid—the all-important element of intentionality, or purpose, in the living world. Dawkins's sideways diversions merely shift this problem into a different biological realm. Even if it could be shown that wings did evolve originally as thermal panels, he is still required to express the gradual increase in wing length in intention-laden language—they "become better solar panels."

He similarly speaks of muscular movements that are used "to control glide direction, so average time to landing is postponed over evolutionary time." In discussing the flying squirrel, with its special membranes of skin stretching from wrists to ankles, he argues that its evolutionary ancestor possessing even a slight flap of skin would have been able to leap that little bit farther and in a critical situation "save its life." But such purposeful language is surely a blatant contradiction of the materialistic assumption that lies at the core of neo-Darwinism.

Sideways diversions that turn out to be advantageous are not of course uncommon. But they all require that *personal* element of being able to sense whether a particular innovation might be useful for something else. The space race is a good example in that a number of technologies developed originally for the exploration of space have been exploited to great advantage in many earth-bound situations, always because they have been *recognized* as being useful. Richard Dawkins, when he invokes sideways diversions to maintain his belief in a wholly material process of evolutionary gradualism, is in my view using neo-Darwinian *ad hoc*-ery to disguise his real reliance on this essential, nonmaterial element of purpose.

(one that works but with limited sophistication) and something that is part-way to becoming an organ capable of seeing to some degree. In neo-Darwinian terms a lesser eye, because it can see to a degree, may be open to functional improvement by selection. Minor structural variants of a primitive eye, perhaps the inclusion of a light-restricting aperture or iris, or a crudely shaped lens that confers on the organ a tiny increase in image sharpness, will be advantageous to the animal's survival and therefore be favored under selection pressure. But merely having some part or parts of an eye that on their own have absolutely no seeing function cannot be open to selective improvement, simply because there is no seeing function that can be selected in the first place.

One cannot select from what one doesn't have. I cannot pick an apple from a fruit tree unless there are apples on the tree to begin with. Nor can I pick a better apple unless there are a range of apples of varying quality to choose from. Finally, in order to pick a better apple I need to know what constitutes apple quality. I require that all-important element of discernment.

The only way Dawkins's scheme could make sense is if he admits to what he and his neo-Darwinian colleagues so resolutely deny—an essential purposeful dimension that inspires and directs innovative development in the biological world. Put another way, an assemblage of bits and pieces that represent just part of an eye and that in themselves cannot see may be exploited for the purpose of sight provided that sight is being sought in a purposeful and creative way.

The same is true of flight. A batch of components representing, say, 1 percent or 5 percent of an airplane (perhaps a box of rivets, a wheel assembly, a wing spar or a propeller), although essential to a flying machine, would not be better than no airplane at all when it comes to achieving flight (figure 9.6). A wheel assembly, a wing spar, a propeller or a gob of metal will not take off in any sense. A propeller or wing spar will contribute to the achievement of flight only if flight is being sought in a purposeful and creative way. What is required is a concept of flight that is being striven for. One cannot select for improved flight unless there is actual flight to begin with and, moreover, unless an improved performance can be recognized. The function of discernment attaches to persons. We must therefore acknowledge the crucial role of a personal dimension that transcends the concept of a purely material world the neo-Darwinist so aggressively promotes.

What Dawkins has failed to point out is that any improvement in a system—remember, this is what he is trying to explain in purely material terms—is possible only if two crucial, nonmaterial conditions are fulfilled. First, the idea of the system must exist. In this regard we might recall the concept of final cause as stated originally by Aristotle (see chapter three).

Second, there must also be the ability to recognize whether or not a given subset of components, arising either by chance or by design, will actually constitute a step toward the achievement of what was originally conceived. Without this essential element of intentionality, it is plain nonsense to talk of the power of small changes to produce any

Figure 9.6. A rivet, although an essential component of a modern aircraft, will not fly. (Cartoon by the author.)

achieving system in the biological world.

In a wholly material universe things just are. There is no logical reason why a purely material system should want to embark on a self-improvement program. Why should a functionally superior system be favored over a functionally inferior one? On what purely material grounds is "superior" or "inferior" function to be judged? Here we seem to have exhausted the answers that a purely naturalistic science can supply. Here, it would seem, the so-called scientific explanations must yield to a higher level of accounting. We will pursue this aspect further in the next two chapters.

10

How Natural Is Natural Selection?

A recent issue of the influential science magazine *Scientific American* ran an article titled "Scientists and Religion in America." This article reports on a recent survey of contemporary scientists exploring whether or not they believed in a personal God and in immortality. Of all the responses summarized in the article, the one that most caught my attention was that of National Academy of Science member and evolutionary biologist John Avise: "Only natural selection comes close to omnipotence, but even here no intelligence, foresight, ultimate purpose or morality is involved. Natural selection is merely an amoral force, as inevitable and uncaring as gravity."[1] This deliciously bizarre response of Avise's encapsulates a fundamental doctrine of faith for the materialist—that the action of Darwinian-style natural selection really has made God redundant. We must therefore explore this pivotal idea in some depth.

Vitalism Sneaks in Through the Back Door
In the conventional wisdom of neo-Darwinism it is the impersonal process of natural selection that provides the creative, ordering mechanism. It is natural selection that drives the products of chance to the remarkable heights of complexity and sophistication so clearly evident in the living

---

[1]E. J. Larson and L. Witham, "Scientists and Religion in America," *Scientific American,* September 1999, pp. 78-83.

world. Addressing those who would doubt the truth of this central dogma of scientific materialism, Jacques Monod says:

> Even today a good many distinguished minds seem unable to accept or even to understand that from a source of noise natural selection could quite unaided have drawn all the music of the biosphere. Indeed natural selection operates *upon* the products of chance and knows no other nourishment.[2]

So at the very core of the neo-Darwinian worldview is the belief that essentially undirected, random variations in the genetic material of the organism may throw up almost unlimited possibilities for change and therefore evolution. Natural selection is deemed to be the sole agency that creatively exploits and guides this potentially chaotic grab bag of possibilities.

However, this mechanism of selection presupposes that the functional success of a particular organism is to be favored over and against its functional failure. Implicit within the meaning of natural selection is the assumption that "to want to live" in the face of testing external challenges is a paramount biological principle. If a particular innovation that improves an organism's chances of survival is to be exploited or captured by the sieving action of natural selection, then this can happen only if the survival instinct operates as an absolute principle in the natural world.

In fact biology, when it asserts the crucial role of natural selection, is really demanding that we accept a distinctly "prolife" principle that violates completely the rules that should govern a totally material universe. Surely in such a universe things "just happen to be," they "just are." Secret, vitalistic ambitions are no more likely to be found in complex arrangements of atoms in biological systems than in rocks or biscuits or any other form of matter. The moment we advance the notion that things actually want to live, to improve their lot, to go on living in the face of potentially destructive forces, we have transgressed the fundamental assumptions of an impersonal, law-bound universe. Natural selection therefore embodies an idea that is both unnatural and alien to the spirit of a materialistic science.

Tinkerers and Scrutinizers
Charles Darwin believed he had discovered in natural selection the mechanism that would explain what previously had required some form of vitalism or supernatural assistance. He wrote:

---

[2]Jacques Monod, *Chance and Necessity* (London: Collins, 1972), p. 114.

It may metaphorically be said that natural selection is daily and hourly scruti-
nising, throughout the world, the slightest variations; rejecting those that are
bad, preserving and adding up all that are good; silently and insensibly working, whenever and wherever opportunity offers, at the improvement of each
organic being in relation to its organic and inorganic conditions of life.[3]

Darwin was also acutely aware of the potential confusion conveyed by the
expression "natural selection" and sought to reassure his readers that it did
not imply conscious choice or the active power of God. He went as far as
to say that in a literal sense it is false:

Some have even imagined that natural selection induces variability, whereas
it implies only the preservation of such variations as arise and are beneficial
to the being under its conditions of life. . . . In the literal sense of the word,
no doubt, natural selection is a false term.[4]

Darwin clearly rejected any thought that natural selection was anything
more than a purely impersonal process or mechanism. This is of course
precisely what the neo-Darwinist asserts—that it is the purely material
means by which variations in a species are systematically gathered up to
produce a gradual increase in complexity, or evolution.

Those changes in an organism that make it better equipped to face the
rigors of the outside world will confer on it a survival advantage and will
therefore be naturally selected. It will have a competitive edge over its rivals. And given that the living organism has a real interest in surviving,
such an interpretation of natural selection seems, at least on the surface,
perfectly reasonable. But this is by no means the end of the matter, as we
shall see in a moment.

It should be noted here that neo-Darwinism goes further than Darwin
did and gives an even more materialistic definition of natural selection. According to neo-Darwinism, those animals that leave the most offspring are
most likely to survive (as a species) and will therefore be naturally selected. Fitness is thus equated with breeding success, presumably because
if you produce more offspring, there will be a richer pool of variability in
these offspring that will increase the chances of one or some surviving that
are better tuned to meet the challenges of the outside world.

However, it should also be mentioned here that even among evolution-

---

[3]Charles Darwin, *The Origin of Species by Means of Natural Selection,* 6th ed., Everyman's
Library (London: J. M. Dent, 1928), p. 84.
[4]Ibid., p. 81.

ary theorists there remains widespread disagreement as to whether the above definition of natural selection makes much sense. Because one offspring survives instead of another, this may not mean it has greater evolutionary potential. The lucky chicken that survived the hungry fox's nocturnal raid on the poultry coop may well have been suffering from insomnia on that particular night. Survival of the fittest thus becomes "survival of those that survive," which doesn't tell us a great deal.[5]

Most importantly, what is largely ignored in discussions on natural selection is the rather obvious fact I referred to earlier—the living organism actually wants to live. It is not simply a passive bit of rather complex substance that happens to have a biological origin. The living organism wants to be alive in its own special way. We might even ask the materialist, "Why all this talk about the idea of survival and about deficiencies or improvements that threaten or enhance survival?" Or "Why, in an impersonal, purposeless and wholly material universe, should we introduce into the discussion such words as *deficiencies* or *improvements?*" Why does an animal possess a sense of wanting to survive? Why does it strive to reproduce, to pass on its genetic endowment to the next generation? Surely in a completely material world things just are. Why did Darwin need to talk about variations that are "beneficial" or "injurious" to the animal?[6] Isn't he really implying that the organism actually wants to hang on to life in the face of opposition from a potentially hostile environment? It seems that in whichever direction we turn we are confronted by the inescapable fact that there really is a premium on life.

Darwin wrote much about the "struggle for existence" in the living world. Inert matter does not "struggle to be." Struggle is an intrinsic part of being alive, whether as a human being or a lettuce plant. We seek food and drink when we get hungry. We avoid death by whatever means we can. The lettuce plant will, under hot summer conditions, "bolt," or go to seed, thus providing for the potential continuity of the lettuce species through its offspring. Any competent gardener knows the importance of keeping the lettuce patch well watered during hot periods to maintain a

---

[5]For more on the difficulties surrounding the use of the term "natural selection," see the following: Gertrude Himmelfarb, *Darwin and the Darwinian Revolution* (London: Chatto & Windus, 1959), chap. 16; Norman MacBeth, *Darwin Re-tried* (London: Garnestone, 1974), chap. 7; Philip Johnson, *Darwin on Trial* (Downers Grove, Ill.: InterVarsity Press, 1993), chap. 2.

[6]Darwin, *Origin of Species*, p. 81.

supply of lettuce that hasn't turned bitter by bolting.

The neo-Darwinist's claim that natural selection is a completely material process is, I believe, sheer fantasy. However, this conceptual error is cleverly disguised in the images and language materialists employ to narrate their scientific myth.

The theoretical biochemist Stuart Kauffman sees the role of Darwinian evolution, at least in part, as a kind of self-improvement program that through "mutations and natural selection, can improve a biological system through the accumulation of successive minor variants, just as tinkering can improve technology."[7] Here we see an expression like "tinkering" used to convey the idea of a low-grade, haphazard or unthinking input that achieves a creative end. This idea of tinkering, or mindless, random changes, is at the very core of neo-Darwinian thought and therefore deserves closer scrutiny.

Imagine your car has been running a bit rough of late and you have committed your Saturday morning to an engine tune-up (figure 10.1). You know very little about how an internal combustion engine works. Perhaps you have a vague notion that tinkering with the carburetor or the ignition system could be helpful, and so you fiddle around with these parts in the engine compartment. As a kind of crude analogy, we might even liken these rather unskilled adjustments to what happens in the living organism's genetic library when random mutations occur as a consequence of radiation or chemical damage.

Figure 10.1. My unskilled tinkering with the tuning of a car engine is never carried out in a mindless vacuum. (Cartoon by the author.)

However far we wish to push the analogy, there is a small probability

---

[7]Stuart A. Kauffman, "Antichaos and Adaptation," *Scientific American*, August 1991, pp. 64-70.

that your tinkering does improve the running of the engine. It might just happen that you find the mixture adjustment screw and by chance tweak it in the right direction. (Of course the opposite might also occur, and for most amateurs this is a much more likely outcome.) Some might therefore ask, "Isn't this a nice illustration of how useful changes can occur without being directed by any higher influence or cause?" In fact it implies precisely the opposite. Your untrained tinkering is never carried out in a meaningless vacuum. You cannot claim to have improved the tuning of the engine by random adjustment without at the same time recognizing that the tuning has actually improved or worsened. Notice how we said that the mixture adjustment screw might have been *by chance* tweaked in the *right* direction. However chaotic your tinkering might be, the fact is that the exercise requires you to make a personal judgment as to whether the engine begins to run more roughly or more smoothly. This illustrates the crucial role played by an intelligent, discerning mind.

In summary, tinkering, as I have described above, is a perfectly valid, though grossly inefficient, method of improving a system. It is obviously extremely limited in most instances in what it can achieve, but nonetheless it can and should be treated as a workable hypothesis. But most importantly, tinkering to improve something carries with it an all-important *personal* element—the ability to recognize whether or not our tinkering has altered things for better or for worse. It crucially matters that we recognize an improvement (or deterioration) in the system's behavior even if our tinkering is a stab in the dark. We always tinker within a gradient of meaning. Without this our efforts will be in vain—just mindless, chaotic interference with predictably destructive consequences. If the neo-Darwinist is going to use the tinkering analogy to explain the evolution of complex systems in the living world, I cannot see how this personal, nonmaterial dimension can be ignored. But it nearly always is.

Similarly, Darwin's picture of natural selection "scrutinizing," "rejecting" the bad and "preserving" the good, carries the same idea of there being a profoundly important element of intentionality that operates in the living world—the very world he was attempting to explain in purely naturalistic terms. But where does this quality of purpose or intention come from? Few would suggest that it could come from atoms or electrons themselves, unless of course we attribute to them qualities akin to mind or personality. This would be anathema to those scientists committed to their naturalistic presuppositions. I would therefore argue that the very concept of natural selection as defined by the neo-Darwinist is fundamentally flawed and that its persistence in the evolutionary literature only serves to disguise the need to recognize a transcendent dimension that lies beyond the myopic vista of a materialistic science.

This science will of course admit to no such limitation. Its confident belief that reality is ultimately lifeless matter more than compensates for any glaring weakness that might be entailed in a particular mechanistic scenario. "Natural selection" is the materialist's sacred utterance or mantra, an incantation that can tap "magical material powers" capable of performing wondrous feats of creativity and transformation.

This doublespeak on the part of the materialist—in both denying the transcendent and invoking the mystical powers of the sacred utterance—is no more vividly illustrated than in Richard Dawkins's account of eye evolution. We will therefore examine this example in some detail in the next section.

A Different Message from the Mountain

In his book *Climbing Mount Improbable* Dawkins argues that the evolution of biological complexity is achieved by gradual, almost imperceptible steps of improvement.[8] This is embraced in his metaphor of scaling the lofty peak of Mount Improbable. Rather than trying to make an ascent via the impossibly steep cliffs and precipices, evolution takes the easy route up the gentle grassy slopes of gradually increasing complexity. All that is required is that one (that is, the evolutionary "machine") heads for the summit.

In order to produce his hypothetical eye Dawkins draws on the computer-based modeling studies conducted by the Swedish biologists Dan Nilsson and Susanne Pelger.[9] They take as their theoretical starting point a flat, circular patch of pigmented light-sensitive cells (these are virtual, not real) sandwiched between a transparent protective layer and a layer of dark backing pigment. Rather significantly, but understandably, Nilsson and Pelger also state that they "avoid the more inaccessible problem of photoreceptor cell evolution."

In their model, mutation works by producing at random small-percentage changes in the degree of curvature of the "cell" patch, in the diameter

---

[8]Richard Dawkins, *Climbing Mount Improbable* (Harmondsworth, U.K.: Viking, 1996), chap. 5.
[9]Dan Nilsson and Susanne Pelger, "A Pessimistic Estimate of the Time Required for an Eye to Evolve," *Proceedings of the Royal Society of London* 256B (1994): 53-58.

of a light-restricting aperture, in the thickness of the transparent layer, and in the value of the refractive index of a particular region. The computer model is programmed to perform a simple ray-tracing analysis to determine the sharpness of imaging for each configuration. Selection is then made to act on those changes that improve spatial resolution or visual acuity (figure 10.2). In a relatively small number of generations the model is shown to transform from the flat patch, through continuous minor improvements in design, into a two-dimensional, graphical representation of a focused "fish" eye.

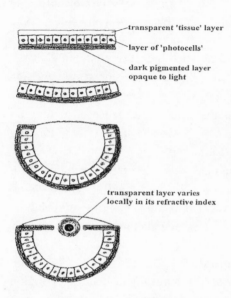

Figure 10.2. Schematic of theoretical eye object after the computer-generated scheme of Nilsson and Pelger (see text). It involves the progressive transformation of an initially flat layer of imaginary, light-sensitive cells sandwiched between a dark backing layer and a transparent covering whose refractive index can be made to vary locally. (Drawing by the author.)

In the context of his own metaphor Dawkins asks the fundamental question "Where can you get to on the mountain if you start from a given base camp and go steadily upwards?" For him the Nilsson-Pelger model nicely answers this question: "Going upwards means mutating, one small step at a time, and only accepting mutations that improve optical performance. So, where do we get to? Pleasingly, through a smooth upward pathway starting from no proper eye at all, we reach a familiar fish eye, complete with lens."[10]

Now leaving aside such nontrivial questions as who or what was required to devise an appropriate computer program in the first place, or whether any such graphic representation can model in even the most simplistic way the development of biological novelty such as an eye,[11] it is cru-

---

[10]Dawkins, *Climbing Mount Improbable,* p. 151.
[11]Again we see illustrated in this model a fundamental category error: the mistaking of an object for something analogous to a living system. The eye—even the most primitive kind—is not simply an appropriately drawn shape or object. It is a dynamic functioning organ responding

cially important to appreciate that Dawkins's attempted explanation for how the eye might have evolved is anything but purely material. His metaphor of climbing the mountain is loaded with intentionality. No climber ever reached the summit of a high and difficult mountain (figures 10.3 and 10.4) without a powerful sense of wanting to get there. The very fact that Dawkins admits to aiming for the summit, or in his own words "only accepting mutations that improve optical performance," is surely the most blatant admission that his version of neo-Darwinism is, despite claims to the contrary, profoundly goal-centered and purposeful. And the laws of physics and chemistry as currently understood today remain powerless to account for these transcendent qualities so obviously consistent with the activity of mind.

How Super Is the Natural?

The problem for biological materialism is even more serious than I have suggested so far. Living organisms possess an amazing lust for life. They are highly innovative going concerns. Their ambition is to live and to go on living. Whether it is the single-celled bacterium or the highly integrated, multicellular, differentiated animal,

Figure 10.3. Real mountain climbing: Whether one is considering Dawkins's metaphorical ascent of Mount Improbable in order to evolve an eye or the scaling of an actual mountain peak, mountain climbing is an activity driven by an essential element of intentionality that transcends the purely material. (Courtesy of Richard Wesley.)

the prolife principle is forever at work. This is the fundamental given for those working in the biological sciences, and we must see this in contrast to the world of, say, the engineer, who is forced to begin from scratch to build up purposeful systems using intelligent design and creativity.

Clearly, with this prolife force driving the natural world, tinkering, in the

via the nervous system to external light stimulation in a most creative and purposeful way. I have already discussed this object-versus-system confusion in chapters three and seven.

Darwinian sense of variations being continuously exploited by the sieving action of unnatural, life-promoting selection, becomes a legitimate mechanism for organic improvement, that is, evolution. But all this poses an enormous problem for neo-Darwinism, for it requires the rejection of the fundamental dogma that ultimate reality is lifeless matter.

Calling Nonsense by Its Name

Quite apart from the enormous scientific problems facing naturalism (I have raised several of the most important ones in earlier chapters), its blatantly dishonest use of language serves to reinforce the poverty of its belief system. I referred earlier to the sacred utterance, the calling down by the materialist of the magical powers of natural selection to both breathe life into lifeless matter and to achieve ever-increasing levels of biological complexity over the eons of time. "Natural selection" is the mantra that is repeatedly chanted by the materialist when special acts of creativity are required of once-lifeless matter.

Figure 10.4. How mountains *aren't* climbed. New Zealander Edmund Hillary and Sherpa Tenzing Norgay reached the summit of Mount Everest at 11:30 a.m. on May 29, 1953, because they really wanted to get there. (Cartoon by the author.)

Many neo-Darwinists have admitted to the semantic problems raised in the use of the term "natural selection." Interestingly the eminent Harvard University zoologist Ernst Mayr has this to say:

> Darwin's choice of the word *selection* was not particularly fortunate. It suggests some agent in nature who, being able to predict the future, selects "the best." This, of course, is not what natural selection does. The term simply refers to the fact that only a few (on the average, two) of all the offspring of a set of parents survive long enough to reproduce. There is no particular

selective force in nature, nor a definite selecting agent. There are many possible causes for the success of the few survivors. Some survival, perhaps a lot of it, is due to stochastic processes, that is, luck. Most of it, though, is due to a superior working of the physiology of the surviving individual, which permits it to cope with the vicissitudes of the environment better than other members of the population. Selection cannot be dissected into an internal and an external portion. What determines the success of an individual is precisely the ability of the internal machinery of the organism's body (including its immune system) to cope with the challenges of the environment. It is not the environment that selects, but the organism that copes with the environment more or less successfully. There is no external selection force.[12]

But if this really is the case, then the term "natural selection" should be removed from the working vocabulary of evolutionary theory. For if Mayr is correct, then we are left with an explanation that, in effect, states that the winning offspring of a reproducing organism is the one better equipped to stand up to the rigors of environmental pressure. But why should "winning" be so important to an organism? Why should it feel it has to take a stand against these hostile forces? Why not simply "go with the flow" and be carried along by the brute forces of an impersonal and wholly material universe?

If there is no nonmaterial selecting principle operating by which the performance of one variant of an organism is judged as being either less or more successful than another variant, as Mayr seems to imply, what then does he mean when he uses such expressions as "superior working" and "the ability . . . to cope"? Surely the only sensible explanation is that the living organism is possessed of a quite *unnatural*[13] will to live. It strives and competes; it is aggressively prolife; and this innate behavior remains unaccounted for by any science that denies a higher principle of purpose in the living world.

So if materialistic science is unwilling to admit to the reality of this vital dimension, then let's call nonsense by its name and rid ourselves of this unnatural idea of natural selection. We should instead use language more in keeping with biological realities and call it "unnatural or purposeful, life-promoting selection" in recognition of the powerful element of intentionality that is so evident in the world of living beings.

---

[12]Ernst Mayr, *One Long Argument: Charles Darwin and the Genesis of Modern Evolutionary Thought* (New York: Penguin, 1991), p. 86.

[13]That is, "unnatural" in the sense of not being explicable in terms of the purely material (impersonal) processes of nature.

11

Biology & Destiny

Each worldview will have its own rules of engagement. These are the primary beliefs and assumptions that give it a degree of internal consistency and cohesion. Naturalistic science is no exception and prides itself in honoring the one supreme commandment—thou shalt not think metaphysically!

Before we explore further the assumptions of naturalism, it is important to recall here the distinction I made at the beginning of chapter eight between the term *evolution* and the neo-Darwinian theory of evolution. The first is purely descriptive and refers to the gradual unfolding over time of biological forms from the simplest creatures to the most complex and to the interconnectedness of all living forms. Neo-Darwinism by contrast claims to provide an explanation for the entire living world within a totally materialistic framework. It is overwhelmingly hostile to any nonmaterial guiding principle, accepting only the raw, undirected working of chance events channeled by the sieving action of natural selection.

In examining this unyielding, naturalistic stance Tomlin offers a suggestion as to why the theory appears to command such commitment:

> There seems to be one very powerful reason. If you can persuade yourself to believe in NS [natural selection], you are thereby released from the obligation to believe in selection for any other reason. Purpose or finality can be ruled out from the start. The specialist can breathe again. Indeed, the faintest hint

of directedness is deemed to constitute a serious breach of scientific etiquette. A taboo has been violated. Even if you find order here and there, or even "apparent purpose," you must not find order or purpose, real or apparent, in the world as a whole. You may search for particular reasons: you must not presume to descry an overall reason.[1]

Tomlin then comments further: "The reason is the extreme reluctance to admit the smallest element of reason, order, or even meaning in the process, because such an admission would oblige them to cross that threshold which leads to the dread realm of metaphysics."[2]

This, then, is the dilemma for naturalism. It needs something more than the purely material, but it dare not admit to this publicly. In private, however, barely hidden within the subtleties of its own images and metaphors, it betrays a desperate need for a guiding hand in order to provide a coherent science of life.

Nature Knows What It Wants

Whatever level of sophistication or complexity we choose to consider, the living world seems to demand some kind of teleological or goal-centered explanation that is entirely at odds with the neo-Darwinian view of life. This view, as I noted at the beginning of this chapter, is one of undirected chance being acted on by another purely material force—natural selection. In the naturalistic scheme of things life has no deeper purpose or meaning. Life, however complex it might appear to be, is nothing more than a fortuitous conglomeration of chemical and physical interactions. But the hard facts of science tell a very different story.

Consider the humble bacterium (figure 11.1). This tiny single-celled organism is a hi-tech factory in miniature. Packed full of complex molecular machinery, this microscopic factory gathers in raw materials from the outside world and, using a cleverly conceived "business plan," draws on its genetic library and proceeds to construct an identikit factory on the "vacant site next door." This is called cell reproduction, and it is a highly focused activity. The respected international agency Habitat for Humanity, using a carefully coordinated construction program, can, I believe, assemble a domestic dwelling in an impressively short period of eight hours. Some bacte-

---

[1]E. W. F. Tomlin, "The Dialogue of Evolution by Natural Selection," *Universities Quarterly* 38, no. 1 (1983-1984): 55.
[2]Ibid., p. 66.

ria will reproduce themselves in just twenty minutes, and for sheer complexity and sophistication beat Habitat for Humanity's constructional feats by a clear mile!

The humble bacterium is possessed of an irrepressible drive to expand its business interests, and under the right conditions will establish several

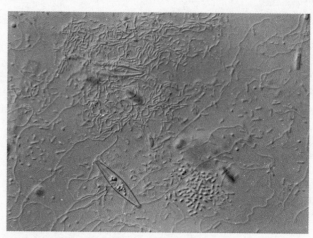

million new microbial factories in a single day. Sadly, this mega-growth mentality can also exact a frightening toll on human health. Anyone who has experienced a bout of food poisoning will know precisely what I mean.

There is another lesson to be learned from our tiny bacterium. Any reader who has been faced with the unpleasant

Figure 11.1 Microbial conquests. In this photograph, taken at about four-hundred-times magnification, multiplying bacteria surround two boat-shaped diatoms (a form of plankton) and are in the process of forming a biofilm. (Photograph by the author.)

task of unblocking a domestic waste pipe will have noticed a wet, slippery coating on its inner surface. This is known as a biofilm and is created by individual bacteria somehow communicating with each other and agreeing to team up to achieve conquests otherwise considered impossible by an individual organism. This microbial collectivization has been given the rather elegant name of "quorum sensing."[3]

This cooperative behavior between bacteria that results in biofilm formation, as well as accounting for the slippery coating inside the waste pipe, also explains the fouling of ships hulls, the formation of plaque on our teeth and certain complications associated with the lung disease cystic fibrosis.

A fascinating example of this quorum sensing is found in some species

---

[3]The interested reader is referred to Tim Thwaites, "Small Talk: Tapping into Bacterial Conversations," *Odyssey* 6, no. 1 (2000): 53-57.

of squid (and other marine animals) that exhibit a phenomenon known as bioluminescence. The squid is a night feeder, and by "lighting up" it is able to extinguish the tell-tale shadow it would otherwise cast on a moonlit night. But how is this achieved? Here a bacterium called *Vibrio fischeri* comes to the rescue.

Vibrio fischeri is a bioluminescent bacterium resident inside the squid's body that actually generates the light the squid needs for its own survival. A single bacterium produces only a miniscule flicker of light and would therefore provide no protective function for the night-cruising squid. At the same time it would be a considerable drain of the bacterium's energy reserves. *Vibrio fischeri* very intelligently keeps its light switched off until it has millions of companions available to "turn on a really good show," and this collective response is orchestrated by group communication (quorum sensing). Purposeful behavior is clearly an unmistakable characteristic of the microbial world.

At the other end of the living spectrum philosopher Margorie Grene explores this idea of organisms or parts of organisms expressing this drive to achieve using examples in nature where teleological language[4] is required because we are confronted with occurrences needing to be explained "for the sake of something." These appear to point to something beyond their own happening or existence. She takes as an example Darwin's own words: "What can be more curious than that the hand of man, formed for grasping, that of a mole for digging, the leg of a horse, the paddle of the porpoise, and the wing of the bat, should all be constructed on the same pattern."[5] Grene insists that this language is clearly teleological in that there is recognized a "pattern" by which a hand, a leg, a fin or a wing is seen to be constructed from its constituent parts. The individual pieces become significant only as parts of a whole. They exist, as natural entities, for the sake of the whole.

Similarly Grene argues that the insect eye and the mammalian eye are constructed on different principles "for seeing." This diversity of structure is not an end in itself but serves a particular end goal, that of achieving sight.

Grene identifies a third and perhaps most important example of goal-

---

[4]In the present context the word *teleology* conveys the important idea of something happening because it contributes to or fulfills an intended goal. It encapsulates the spirit of Aristotle's final cause (see chapter three).

[5]Marjorie Grene, "Time and Teleology," in *The Knower and the Known* (London: Faber & Faber, 1966), pp. 226-52.

centeredness in nature, that observed in an organism's own development. In the lower animals amputation of part of an organ results in a remaking of the organ from a source of tissue that is not involved in the generation of the original organ. Thus when the normal source is not available, the *need* for the organ evokes from neighboring tissues a contribution they would not make under normal circumstances.

It is this type of quite spectacular experimental observation that, Grene argues, provides compelling evidence that in the living world the end, though last in time, is in some sense prior to or causative of the steps that lead to it.[6] Put simply, the living organism seems to know what it wants. In the context of this goal-centeredness so evident in the biological world Grene, who was writing in the 1960s, had these scathing remarks about the conceptual mindset of most biologists of her day:

> The theoretical framework of the biologist's training is centred—implicitly and indirectly if not explicitly and directly—in the theory of evolution by Mendelian micromutations and natural selection. In terms of ultimate beliefs, this means the view that the present population of the earth's surface is derived by a repetition of a few simple mechanisms . . . from unicellular and ultimately from non-living particles of matter. This picture is associated also with an aggregative conception of the organism itself. "Ultimately," one believes, an organism such as a mouse or a frog or a man will be identifiable in terms of material particles and their spatio-temporal relationships. . . . The trained biologist, in other words, works under the aegis of a guiding principle that organisms are aggregates of material particles moved by mechanical, physico-chemical laws. . . . Scientific discourse, accordingly, *qua* scientific must be wholly non- and anti-teleological, and any speech tainted with teleology must remain wholly extraneous to science.[7]

Embryological Feats

Grene's criticism of the reductionist fixation of many biologists of her day could easily apply to the conceptual thinking that prevails in the complex field of developmental biology. One of the great wonders of the living world is the process of embryonic development. Lewis Wolpert, a professor at University College, London, and a world authority on the embryo, describes in his readable book *The Triumph of the Embryo* the astonishing drama of development in which the single fertilized cell transforms into the fully formed animal. In the first chapter of his book Wolpert reveals clearly

---

[6]Ibid., p. 232.
[7]Ibid., p. 234-35.

the materialistic framework of his embryological science: "I will show that there is no 'master builder' in the embryo, no vital force. Each cell has its own developmental programme which makes use of a limited number of processes that have been used again and again, for hundreds of millions of years."[8] Wolpert then provides the reader with a fascinating account of the embryo's developmental journey. It begins with the fertilized cell dividing

repeatedly to give rise to a population of smaller cells arranged as a hollow sphere referred to as the *blastula* (figure 11.2). What follows is a quite remarkable process, called *gastrulation,* in which the blastula is re-

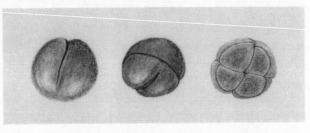

Figure 11.2. Early embryonic development begins with the fertilized cell repeatedly dividing, or "cleaving," to form eventually the hollow blastula as shown in figure 11.3. (Drawing by the author.)

shaped into a form that hints at the final plan of the animal.

In most vertebrate embryos the cell rearrangements that occur during gastrulation are too complex to visualize easily. However, the developing sea urchin embryo, because of both its size and its transparency, has provided scientists with a marvelous microscopic picture of this early shaping phase. The blastula consists of about a thousand cells, and one of the early

Figure 11.3. Gastrulation occurs when one side of the hollow blastula migrates inward, fuses with the opposite side, and eventually forms the animal's gut. (Image by Vivian Ward, University of Auckland.)

events in its gastrulation involves a small group of cells on the outside moving inward to create an infolding that is destined to become the gut of the fully developed animal (figure 11.3). These cells put out strong armlike

---

[8]Lewis Wolpert, *The Triumph of the Embryo* (Oxford: Oxford University Press, 1993), p. 10.

extensions, or filopodia, that make "groping" contact with the opposite inside surface, which also infolds slightly. The major infolding sheet of cells is pulled farther in by these extensions until direct contact between the two groups of cells is established. These eventually fuse and break down to form a channel that becomes the urchin's future mouth, the original site of infolding forming its future anus.

Now what should be obvious to the reader is that the cells know exactly what they are aiming for. They seem to know what to do. Wolpert explains it in the following way:

> If the cells in the embryo "know" where and when to change shape, contract, or move, then it begins to be possible to envisage a programme for the development of form. It becomes possible to think of accounting for all the changes in form of early sea-urchins development in terms of a changing pattern of cell contractions and cell contacts. We can think of this pattern of cell activities as being part of the embryo's developmental programme. It is a programme that does not describe the final form, but a generative programme that contains the instructions for making the shapes. A key feature of a generative programme is that it can be made up of quite simple instructions, yet generate very complex forms.[9]

But notice how Wolpert sees this remarkable shaping process in terms of "quite simple instructions" contained in what he calls a generative program. In one sense he is perfectly correct—a simple command can produce complex changes in the behavior of a system. But this is only because the generative program that provides the shaping instructions is a highly sophisticated information-bearing system. In the previous chapter we saw how this principle was exploited in the algorithmic structure of a knitting pattern where small alterations in the instructions can lead to dramatic changes in the completed garment. Wolpert fails to point out that generative programs don't come cheap—they require a large investment in programmer intelligence and creativity. The reader, instead, is left with the distinct impression that "simple instructions" are sufficient.

Cells with a Mission

In looking more closely at Wolpert's story of the embryo it soon becomes obvious just how important a role rich imagery and metaphor play in his efforts to present a coherent, reductionist explanation. For example, he de-

---

[9]Ibid., p. 17.

scribes how the cells in the blastula wall migrate inward (figure 11.3) and send out their filopodia to make grasping contact with the cells on the opposite side and adhere, as if engaging in a tug of war, thus resulting in a contractile force that draws the cells inward. He then explains: "The winner seems to be determined by how strongly the extensions adhere to the wall, and the cell eventually moves to the site where the attachments are strongest. It is not unlike climbing out of the sea on to a slippery rock. One comes out where one can get the best grip."[10] This is of course the kind of real-life situation that a reader might easily relate to, and on the surface the analogy appears convincing. But is it?

For a start it explains absolutely nothing about the underlying motivation behind the cells actually engaging in this so-called tug of war within the blastula. In my clambering onto a slippery rock from the sea the fundamental driving force is most probably my desire to get to the safety of dry land (figure 11.4). Locating suitable places to gain a foothold is merely a means to a much more important end. But in reading Wolpert's account one detects the insinuation that differences in adhesive strength between cells will serve as the fundamental reason for this critical process of gastrulation.

Figure 11.4. Gaining a foothold on the slippery rock is merely a means to a higher end—reaching the safety of dry land! The materialist's description of embryonic development fails to acknowledge this crucial element of intentionality that dominates the world of living organisms. (Cartoon by the author.)

Wolpert has his cells doing even more than merely groping with their filopodia—they are "always exploring their environments," they "seek stability."[11] Further on in the chapter dealing with pattern formation, he would have the reader imagine "conversations" between cells in which they declare their locations with respect to each other and to some critical refer-

[10]Ibid., p. 15.
[11]Ibid., p. 16.

ence point.[12] This highly anthropomorphized behavior is then reinterpreted as resulting from vaguely defined concentration gradients and so on. Again the rich imagery has done its job for the materialist. The reader is reassured that the seemingly intelligent behavior of the cells is, when all is said and done, just a matter of impersonal gradients and concentrations.

Wolpert seems to want us to believe that the vital process of meaningful cellular communication can be accounted for in purely impersonal, physicochemical terms. But what Wolpert is really describing is "cells with a mission," cells that seem to know what they want in life, and this is hardly the currency of his materialistic claim that in embryological development there is "no master builder, . . . no vital force." The vitalism so utterly scorned by the high priests of biological materialism seems alive and well in Wolpert's embryological world, if only in an unexamined, rhetorical way.

Wolpert then explains direct cell-to-cell adhesion in terms of differences in the affinities between cells. These differences lead to discrete cell groupings and ultimately to distinct tissue structures.[13] Special protein molecules that are embedded in the cell's surface membrane have certain features that stick out and bind selectively to matching molecules on other cells. This binding effect is, in turn, thought to be mediated by the presence of other simple chemical entities such as calcium ions.

So here we have, it would seem, a set of molecular mechanisms for putting cells together and forming new tissue structures under, as always, "the right conditions."[14] But surely the crucial requirement in all this is the precise control of these ions—where and when they should act. What fundamental rules are invoked to control their effect? Calcium ions aren't just sloshing round in any old fashion. Rather, there must be a harmonizing of their presence in the correct concentration with all the other related events that are required to take place. The exquisitely synchronized orchestration of a whole array of biochemical events is of paramount importance. It is easy to gain the impression from reading Wolpert's account that, provided one has on hand a bagful of impersonal physicochemical mechanisms, all is, in principle, explained in purely reductionist terms.

---

[12]Ibid., p. 39.

[13]Ibid., p. 24.

[14]This apparently harmless phrase actually disguises one of the most crucial aspects of living systems—each individual process within the cell comes under the control of boundary conditions that cannot be explained merely in terms of the inanimate laws of physics and chemistry. This concept has already been explored in detail in chapter three.

The dramatic process of "induction" occurs when a portion of tissue, the organizer, signals to another tissue to change its whole pattern of development. Wolpert then asks whether the organizing cell actually instructs the cell in the host tissue in the sense that it tells the cell something it does not already know. He suggests this is not so and uses the analogy of a jukebox to show that a simple selection of a number can provide any one of the tunes in its repertoire. He argues analogously that the cell's own highly complex internal program enables it to respond to quite simple external instructions and that it is the cell's past history that allows new patterns of behavior to emerge in response to simple commands.

This notion that simple inputs can achieve big ends is popular with many reductionists, but it puts a completely wrong slant on the fundamental problem. It obscures the fact that with any achieving system the simpler the input that is to be used to operate that system, the more complex its internal workings have to be. Blaise Pascal (see figure A.12) some three and a half centuries ago saw this "systems" principle with brilliant clarity when, in describing the calculating machine he had invented, he remarked, "To make the movement of my machine's operation the more simple, it had to be composed of a movement the more complex."[15] And so it is with Wolpert's analogy of a jukebox: the reason it can deliver a tune in response to a simple number command from the operator is precisely because it has a richly structured electromechanical system that has been designed to achieve this end.

The same argument applies to that potentially lethal automobile speed control device, the cruise control function. A simple selection of road speed by the driver will cause the engine to maintain this under ever-changing driving conditions. But this response is possible only because the car is equipped with a highly sophisticated computer-controlled electromechanical system specifically designed to achieve this end.

In each of the above examples simple commands are fed into a richly structured, carefully contrived system designed to respond so as to achieve a certain goal. If the living world consists of systems that are vastly more sophisticated than systems created with human ingenuity, it is surely difficult to deny the influence of mind in the former.

Wolpert also attempts to strengthen his reductionist arguments by appealing to the example of a computer program where the "signals are es-

---

[15]Quoted in Morris Bishop, *Pascal: The Life of Genius* (London: Bell, 1937), p. 30.

sentially noughts and ones but the response depends on previous events."
Again this is totally misleading. The present status of a program certainly
depends on the past steps taken in the program, but these are in turn a direct function of the intended goal of the computer programmer who knows
precisely what he or she wants to achieve. This critical element of intentionality appears to be completely ignored by Wolpert, presumably in order
to support his declared faith in biological materialism.

Lewis Wolpert appears to belong to a large community of biological materialists who see the remarkable events of biological development firmly
under the control of genetic programs. In chapter seven of *Triumph of the
Embryo* Wolpert describes the fascinating process of embryological development of the fruit fly *Drosophila,* which begins as a tiny cylindrical egg
and emerges from its larval phase as a fully segmented fly. The larval stage
hints at how the eventual fly body is divided or constructed from individual
segments. Early on in its development the embryo consists of a single cell
containing several thousands of nuclei (the inner body of the living cell
that stores the genetic material). The genes in these nuclei become active
in seven bands or stripes along the body axis, each stripe being specified
by the earlier activity of other genes. Remember that a gene codes for the
formation of a protein (see chapter five).

One of the earliest of these controlling genes to be activated in the embryo is the bicoid gene. At the (future) head or anterior end of the embryo
the cell cytoplasm (the clear fluid within the cell) contains a special signal
molecule that turns on this gene coding for the bicoid protein. Production
of this protein commences when the egg is first laid and forms a concentration gradient, highest at the anterior end and reducing along the axis of the
egg. This protein concentration gradient controls the setting up of the first
stripe pattern and then the position of the boundary between the head and
thorax of the fly.

The remarkable story of the fruit fly's developmental journey as told by
Wolpert is one of beautifully controlled and timed sequences of signaling
to genes at correct "addresses" to switch on the required protein-making
operation, the setting up of concentration gradients that activate certain
proteins at specific concentrations, which in turn produce proteins that activate yet further proteins—all in the interests of producing an end "product," the fully developed animal. This spatial and temporal hierarchy of
gene activity (the genetic program) occurring during embryonic develop-

ment, which is admitted by Wolpert and which is so beautifully and economically "managed" to produce the fully developed animal, is surely evidence of a level of orchestration that transcends the purely material. But right to the end of his book Wolpert holds to his materialism in claiming there is no "master builder."[16]

Biologist Jonathan Wells in a recent article analyzes some of the major problems, both scientific and philosophical, facing modern developmental biology with its fixation on neo-Darwinian materialism. In the face of a growing body of evidence suggesting that much more is needed to account for the developmental process than simply "genetic programs" in which molecules are the only real entities, Wells suggests that much more creative sense will be made of recent discoveries

Figure 11.5. The candle flame eventually "dies." However, we do not invoke a science of disease in order to explain this "death." (Reproduced from E. J. Sullivan, *Line: An Art Study* [London: Chapman & Hall, 1922].)

in embryology where there is "an intellectual environment in which organisms are regarded as designed. If an organism is designed, then the idea for it preceded its existence, and formal and final causes are real. To be sure, one can regard organisms as designed and still treat them as molecules in motion; but one is also liberated, even encouraged, to regard them as much more."[17]

A Distinguished Antireductionist Speaks Some Common Sense

The writings of Michael Polanyi come as a breath of fresh air amid the suffocating "nothing but" atmosphere produced so predictably by biological-mentality ingrained in the thinking of so many materialists. At almost every twist and turn in their story there is the assertion that impersonal material

---

[16]In fact, the very idea of a genetic program controlling the development of the embryo implies a profoundly goal-centered activity. It really is going on a journey of *becoming*. It really does have an agenda it is pursuing. When the materialist then asserts that there is no "master builder" or guiding force, this would appear to contradict rather obviously the idea of such an agenda. Materialists, to be consistent with their presuppositions, should purge the expression "genetic program" from their vocabulary and replace it with "mindless meander"!

[17]Jonathan Wells, "Unseating Naturalism: Recent Insights from Developmental Biology," in *Mere Creation*, ed. William A. Dembski (Downers Grove, Ill.: InterVarsity Press, 1998), chap. 2.

processes alone are all that are needed. Polanyi challenges this reductionist mindset, contending that the powerful antiteleological bias of modern science is largely a consequence of the belief that the world can be reduced to its atomic elements acting blindly in terms of an equilibrium of forces. But this, he argues, is incompatible with our experience of the living world.[18]

Figure 11.6. The tiny paramecium, approximately 0.25 mm in length and found in stagnant waters, is a true achiever despite its apparent simplicity as a single-celled animal. This photograph captures a shoal of these fascinating, slipper-shaped animals in a frenzy of activity. (Photograph by the author.)

Polanyi notes, for example, that we appear to require the category of "achievement" in order to talk about living things. A science of pathology is required in order to understand organisms fully in terms of their success (achievement) or failure, their malfunctioning and their diseases. Conversely, he argues, it would be totally inappropriate to propose a science of pathology in connection with an open physical system such as a thunderstorm or a flame (figure 11.5). Here there is simply no place for such a concept.

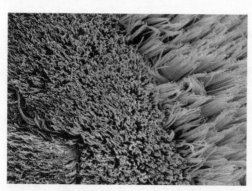

Figure 11.7. The surface of the paramecium's body is covered with a carpet of eyelash-shaped cilia. It uses the synchronized beating of these cilia as a means of propulsion. (Courtesy of Warren Judd.)

Polanyi then describes the behavior of a simple organism such as the paramecium, a tiny single-celled organism found in stagnant waters (figure 11.6 and figure 11.7). It strives to adapt itself to the prevailing conditions, to feed and to reproduce. It possesses mechanisms for the achievement of these ends, and these mechanisms may succeed or fail in any instance. Po-

[18]Michael Polanyi and Harry Prosch, *Meaning* (Chicago: University of Chicago Press, 1975), pp. 161-81.

lanyi contrasts this hard-won achievement (or failure) of the living creature with something like a metal's reaction to acid. Hydrochloric acid can never fail to dissolve zinc (figure 11.8), and it cannot dissolve platinum by mistake. Only living things can fail or succeed. Then in a forceful passage Polanyi summarizes this concept of achievement in the living world:

The fact is, therefore, that every living organism is a meaningful organization of meaningless matter and that it is very highly improbable that these meaningful organizations should all have occurred entirely by chance. Moreover, looking at the general direction the evolutionary development of living organisms has taken, one must in all fairness admit that this direction has been toward more meaningful organizations—more meaningful both in their own structure and in terms of the meanings they are able to achieve. From microscopic one-celled plants, able to do very little more than to provide for their own sustenance and to reproduce, to minute animals, sensitive as individuals to their surroundings and able to learn very rudimentary sustaining habits, to more complex animals, able to do many more things, to the higher mammals, and finally to man, who is able to achieve so many things that he frequently supposes himself to be a god able to achieve all things—this evolutionary history is a panorama of meaningful achievements of almost breathtaking proportions.[19]

Figure 11.8. Hydrochloric acid dissolves the metal zinc while releasing bubbles of hydrogen gas. It cannot fail to do so. This is a consequence of the way the impersonal material laws of chemistry work and cannot be seen in terms of a goal that might or might not be achieved. (Photograph by the author.)

So if it is true that the living world bears an indelible imprint of meaning and purpose, then any science that seeks to explain the nature of life while denying this crucial element because of an overriding commitment to a materialistic ideology will ultimately undermine the integrity of its

---

[19]Ibid., p. 172.

mission. To pretend that science can explain, in an ultimate sense, the entire phenomenon of life is as absurd as imagining that the existence of any man-made machine can be accounted for without regard to its human inventor.

12

Beyond Naturalism

Modern science has given humankind a wonderfully detailed understanding of the physical, chemical and biological systems that operate within the natural world. Much of science's power lies in its ability to formulate and codify laws or patterns of material behavior on which these systems depend.

The knowledge of these laws has in turn given science enormous predictive power and with this the ability both to harness and, moreover, to modify these systems in order to achieve particular technological goals, whether for good or for ill. We see this spectacularly illustrated in such modern achievements as the launching of a space probe, the exploding of a nuclear bomb or the successful development of a new and potent form of therapeutic drug.

It is surely one of the great tragedies of recent human history that the intellectual brilliance and creativity reflected in the achievements of modern science have not always been matched by an equal desire to use these with a comparable degree of moral wisdom.

Destructive Arrogance or Constructive Humililty
The fundamental knowledge provided by modern science has given humankind the ability to exploit the fearsome energy contained within the nucleus of the atom. In doing so it has done some good, but more, it has

brought the world's greatest political egos to the brink of committing mutual assured destruction and has inflicted on the biosphere a frightening
degree of nuclear poisoning that will effectively remain for all time.

Science has not learned from its nuclear transgressions. Using its fundamental knowledge of the biological world it has now set its powerful molecular tools loose on the genome. Much that is said to be good is
promised by the manipulators of the gene but there is an accelerating
sense of unease that the scientists' ability to tamper with the workings of
the gene far outstrips science's knowledge of how the gene really works in
a truly integrative sense in the living organism.

The mechanistic mindset that prevails in biological materialism, with its
reductionist LEGO-like model of gene function, finds it easy to justify this
fundamental interference with the processes of life. Many gene scientists
are surely "rushing in where angels fear to tread."

Of course, if life is nothing more than the blind gropings of impersonal
matter and energy then why shouldn't science have a go at rearranging and
perhaps "improving" things on the shelves of the genetic library of life? The
scientific arrogance all too often displayed by the exponents of biological
materialism was no more vividly illustrated than at a recent meeting of the
British All-Party Parliamentary and Scientific Committee where DNA expert
James D. Watson argued that there is nothing intrinsically wrong with the
idea of scientists "playing god" by modifying the genetic essence of life.
Watson rejected criticisms of genetic engineering by asking, "In all honesty,
if scientists don't play god, who will?"[1]

By contrast the worldview of the theist should encourage a rather more
humble and respectful attitude towards the natural world. For if there is a
deeper meaning to life, if there really is a transcendent dimension that has
shaped and nurtured the amazing edifice of creation over the vast aeons of
time, then we humans, who have been so privileged to explore and comprehend aspects of this creation in such depth, have an enormous respon-
sibility to act with due care.

Historian and theologian Donald Nicholl suggests one slightly unortho-
dox but helpful route back toward a renewed appreciation and respect for
the created world. He describes his own experience of walking from the
top down the steep path to the bottom of the Grand Canyon. As he de-

---

[1]Steve Connor, "Nobel Scientist Happy to 'Play God' with DNA," *The Independent* (London),
May 17, 2000.

scended he observed layer upon layer of fossil-bearing sedimentary deposits formed over millions of years. Noting this remarkable succession of previous life forms frozen in rock he comments:

> Observing the traces of them in this way you feel a true kinship with all those beings, knowing that both they and you trace their existence to that first moment of transcendence when life appeared on this earth. And then you start to reflect that the very eyes with which you are observing these wondrous evidences are themselves the results of millions of years of striving for light, ever since the first pin-hole eye appeared on those primitive marine creatures, the cephalopods. And you are the beneficiary of all that struggle for light, the heir of all that agony. And as you gaze at your hands or think of your ears or of your tongue it takes your breath away to envisage the innumerable strivings that had to be attempted before you could see and touch and hear and taste and speak. Had any breakdown in that series of stirrings occurred it would have destroyed the possibility for you to see and hear and sing. The breakdown was prevented by untiring faithfulness on the part of millions of beings. The mere thought of this makes you realize what an incredibly hard-won privilege it is simply to be a human being; and at the same time it is an awesome responsibility. Every human being has a responsibility towards all those creatures whose agony and groaning has given him birth.[2]

Perhaps more than anything else, Donald Nicholl is emphasizing the integrity of the entire living world, the untiring faithfulness over the eons of time of those vitally creative processes that have served the unfolding drama of creation. He is pointing clearly to a cause that transcends an unfeeling and aimless materialism.

Of Things Science Cannot Speak

I have sought to address several important issues in this book. First, the knowledge and insights gained using the tools of scientific inquiry, however sophisticated they might be, will always be fundamentally limited. Science cannot provide answers to the really big questions concerning meaning and purpose.

Science is a human activity circumscribed or limited by the finiteness of the human participant. All of science is a strictly limited view from the "inside." Science can never sketch for us the "big picture" simply because it is trapped within the very system it is endeavoring to describe and explain.

---

[2]Donald Nicholl, *Holiness* (London: Darton, Longman & Todd, 1987), p. 20.

So scientists who make bold but demeaning pronouncements concerning those most fundamental issues such as the existence of God and human significance on the basis of evidence derived from their own commitment to a materialistic ideology are guilty of speaking from prejudice rather than from real understanding.

My second point is that although science is ultimately limited in the insights it can provide, it does point convincingly to a dimension that transcends the processes and systems in nature that this same science so successfully describes. We have seen that the very activity of science assumes an essential rationality and coherence that lies outside the explanatory power of this science. This is what William Temple refers to as the one "colossal assumption" of science.[3]

Successful science *draws* on a much deeper principle that is not accounted for by science itself. The scientist is a believer in a universe that should make sense. The scientist constantly appeals to this principle in order to conduct his or her experiments. Even the pretentious claim made by a growing number of contemporary cosmologists that they will one day discover a grand "theory of everything" is surely an admission that this universe is magnificently if strangely coherent.

Third, in considering the living world, we find that even the simplest organism demands an explanation that cannot be expressed in terms of only the impersonal processes of nature. Even if we simplistically describe living systems as complex biological machines (they are surely machines but also much more), this compels us to seek explanations for their existence above and beyond the inanimate processes of physics and chemistry. The very machinelike nature of living systems, contrary to what is so often argued by the reductionist, requires a nonnaturalistic or transcendent explanation.

In our consideration of such elemental phenomena as the origin of life or the development of the embryo, we saw that some kind of nonmaterial vital force or drive is required. We find that the entire living world operates within a rich *gradient of meaning*. It is a world that expresses vast amounts of creativity, orchestration, goal-centeredness and ultrasophisticated levels of communication. It is a world driven by an overwhelming "urge" to live and to keep on living. It seeks to "attain," to "achieve," to "improve." This I

---

[3]William Temple, *The Faith and Modern Thought* (London: Macmillan, 1913), p. 9.

have called the "prolife" principle. All of these attributes, it would appear, lie completely outside and beyond the power of science to explain.

The Age-Old Question

Doubtless some, perhaps most, materialists will criticize me for not having so much as acknowledged the problem of suffering and evil in the world, a world which I argue is infused with and dependent on a transcendent presence—God. The exquisite beauty of the living world, its sophistication and variety is, I contend, consistent with a God who revels in the giving of life in all its manifold abundance—a good God. But the materialist will surely accuse me of having conveniently ignored the other side to the story. In the words of Steven Weinberg, "the God of birds and trees would have to be also the God of birth defects and cancer."[4] The American paleontologist Stephen Gould similarly contends that any attempt to "argue that God's nature and benevolence were manifest in the excellent design of organisms and the harmony of ecosystems—in other words, in natural goodness" is hard to justify in the face of such appalling events as Hiroshima and the Holocaust.[5]

In considering the metaphysical shadow cast by the infamous problem of evil, the materialist might be excused, at least superficially, for thinking he or she has a more coherent system of belief than that of the theist. For if the universe is ruled ultimately by the impersonal laws of physics and chemistry, then all suffering, disease and evil are simply an inevitable consequence of the cosmic machine grinding away in accordance with those purely material laws. However unfair certain actions or events might appear to be, in an impersonal universe all things just are.

The problem is that we do not, indeed cannot, function as normal human beings within such a brutally amoral belief system. Philosophical materialism, or atheism, is just too simple-minded. It is a theory fit only for philosophical playboys (and of course playgirls). It has no practical use in a real world where we act as though people matter and where good and bad deeds are simply not equally irrelevant. This should arouse our suspicions.

The fact is that morality, although differing somewhat in detail, has always been universal in humans. As civilized societies we certainly do not dismiss suffering and transgression as merely part of the inevitability of life.

---

[4]Steven Weinberg, *Dreams of a Final Theory* (New York: Pantheon, 1983), p. 250.
[5]Stephen J. Gould, *Bully for Brontosaurus* (New York: W. W. Norton, 1992), p. 323.

Rather, we see them as realities to be confronted and fought against with an energy and dedication that seems quite out of character with the functioning of a supposedly amoral universe. We care about alleviating suffering. We react to evil deeds. We judge them as wrong, so wrong that in some instances we are willing to give all to see them minimized.

In dealing with our own questionable behavior we seek ways to excuse ourselves, or we suggest reasons why others should not judge us so harshly. We function within a universe that makes moral demands on us moment by moment. We experience the "I ought to" moral force in our lives as a daily even hourly experience, challenging us to act in ways often contrary to our most powerful bodily impulses. How we *actually* behave may be very different than how we know we *ought* to behave.

The existence of a moral law impinging on almost every aspect of our behavior, urging us to do right and making us feel uncomfortable when we do wrong, is a fundamental aspect of human experience and relies crucially on the reality of free will. We are constantly faced with choosing to obey or disobey the "inner voice" of this moral law. Our response to this law is fundamentally different from the way we respond to the so-called material laws that act in an impersonal mechanical sense. We cannot say no to gravity but we are free to disobey the moral law.

Judeo-Christian theism therefore holds two fundamental ingredients of reality in constant tension. It asserts the primacy of a transcendent Being, a good God who is the source of a rational material universe that also has an intrinsic moral order. It acknowledges also the existence of human freedom and therefore the potential for both good and evil deeds. Moral choice has consequences that may resonate far beyond our individual actions and lives.

The question, Why do the wicked prosper? is one that was asked repeatedly by the ancient Hebrews. We struggle equally with the problem, Why do the innocent suffer? Those believers in an impersonal, law-bound universe in which reality is ultimately lifeless matter must finally abandon any search for a just solution to these questions because justice, finally, has no basis—indeed, no meaning—in the materialist's worldview.

The Christian theist will admit to the enormous problem of suffering and evil but will not give up searching for an eventual resolution. The Christian theist believes there is yet to be a "moral balancing of the books," a resolution of cosmic proportions that will reveal just how significant are the consequences of human freedom.

Christian theism speaks of this resolution in terms of both the human person and the material creation. It speaks of a creation that is in "bondage to decay" and "groaning in travail" (Romans 8:21-22 RSV). Although words of great perhaps unfathomable mystery, they nonetheless hint at a creation that is in pain, in disequilibrium, and not what it should be. "Nature red in tooth and claw" symbolizes a flawed and dysfunctional creation rather than one as it was intended to be.

Christian theism asserts a crucial causal connection between humans as the apex of creation and all that exists beneath. Our truly significant actions in the moral realm will have both constructive and destructive consequences that flow on into the rest of creation. The imagery contained in the third chapter of Genesis is a powerful statement to this effect. Both we humans and the rest of creation are in need of redemption, which is an implicit declaration that a profound unity exists between the seen (material) and the unseen moral and spiritual dimensions of the cosmos.

Reassembling the Scattered Fragments

We glimpse here a holistic science to be conducted with moral care after the few centuries of Enlightenment travesties. In a way, we may recover and refurbish the essential interconnectedness of the material and spiritual dimensions whose separation was pioneered by Descartes some three and a half centuries ago (see appendix). However, in saying this it should also be stressed that this separation, despite having such disastrous consequences, was essential to the development of a critical science in which no part of the natural world was deemed too sacred for close investigation. The tragedy is that it has been misappropriated and exploited in the interests of materialism far beyond Descartes' original intent which was certainly not to deny the importance of the spiritual.

Some, no doubt, will accuse me of wanting to see science dragged back into a kind of medieval authoritarianism. This is certainly not my wish. Rather, in recognizing a purposeful dimension that transcends the material processes in nature I believe an integrating wholeness can be injected into this same science that necessarily works by dissection and fragmenting analysis. Science need no longer employ the dubious language of circumlocution and doublespeak. Apparent purpose will yield to actual purpose. Genes will no longer be "selfish." They will instead be recognized for what

science has clearly shown them to be—wholly material strings of appropriately sequenced molecules possessing some special chemical properties,
but harnessed in the service of a higher living cause.

So then: for the reader who has followed my arguments this far and who
is willing to step out in a direction signposted by inferences drawn from an
examination of some of the limitations of naturalistic science, there is a
much more exciting journey to be made. It is a journey into a realm that
must both embody and yet transcend those qualities expressed in the material laws that this science so elegantly describes. It is, I believe, a journey
toward the transcendent Divine presence.

Sadly, this is a journey that few scientists today would dream of taking.
And why this extreme reluctance? Perhaps it reflects the age-old problem
that human beings have always struggled with—the craving for power—a
desire to retain control over a mini-universe humanistically and therefore
falsely delineated by an impoverished, naturalistic science—a desire to remain the leader of the expedition rather than be led by the One who might
take the scientist into territory that cannot be charted by the instruments of
his or her own profession.

But for the restless pilgrim who wants to press onwards are there any
maps, albeit imperfectly sketched, that might give guidance on the way?

One widely known and respected thinker who comes immediately to
mind is C. S. Lewis. His enormously popular book *Mere Christianity,* first
published in 1952 following a series of BBC radio talks, is still available in
paperback. Although not writing specifically on the theme of science,
Lewis provides in a highly readable style a philosophical and practical de-
fense of Christian theism and addresses very clearly the problem of evil
which I alluded to a little earlier in this chapter. He presents what I believe
is a compelling case for a personal God who is both immanent in, and
transcendent over, all creation.

Finally, a science whose limits are rightly understood should not lead us
down the pathway to cosmic loneliness and despair. Those practitioners of
this intellectual craft we call modern science have every reason to be inspired and thrilled by a world packed full to the brim with purpose, meaning and wonderful displays of innovation and creativity. At every turn we
see a living world striving to *become,* asserting itself and surviving at times
in the face of massively destructive forces. Here I can do no better than
quote the words of Michael Denton:

> Whether one accepts or rejects the design hypothesis . . . there is no avoiding
> the conclusion that the world *looks* as if it has been uniquely tailored for life:
> it *appears to have been designed*. All reality *appears* to be a vast, coherent,
> teleological whole with life and mankind as its purpose and goal.[6]

This abundant evidence is entirely at odds with a universe judged by the materialist to be brutally meaningless and impersonal.

In this book I have tried to offer the reader a tiny glimpse of the sheer wonder of life. It is my hope that many will shun the temptation to embark on that journey through the arid desert of naturalism, choosing rather to follow the route signposted so clearly by the findings of science, the path that leads to the source of all life—God.

---

[6]Michael J. Denton, *Nature's Destiny: How the Laws of Biology Reveal Purpose in the Universe* (New York: Free Press, 1998), p. 387.

Appendix

Birth of an Idea

Humans are creatures driven by intense curiosity. From ancient times this urge to discover focused not just on the myriad detail of our immediate environment but also on the much larger picture of human existence and its place within the vastness of the cosmos. How was the world created? Why is it the way it is? What is the purpose of life and its ultimate goal?[1]

In medieval thought the earth and its human occupants were the primary focus of cosmology. Medieval scientists looked for the ultimate causes behind natural events. They asked questions about God, the human soul, good and evil, heaven and hell. Humankind was perceived to be at the center of the universe. In one fundamental sense human beings were the very point of the entire order of things.

But about four hundred years ago this worldview was well and truly shattered—shattered in considerable part by the birth of modern science. Physicist Victor Weisskopf describes this fundamental shift in the focus of human curiosity:

> Instead of reaching for the whole truth, people began to examine definable and clearly separable phenomena. They asked not What is matter? and What is life? but How does blood flow in the blood vessels? not How was the world created? but How do the planets move in the sky? In other words, general questions were shunned in favor of limited ones for which it seemed easier to get direct and unambiguous answers.[2]

---

[1]For those readers interested in the historical context in which the birth of modern science took place, this appendix is a brief glimpse of some of the key figures and their ideas that guided this great intellectual journey of the human race.

[2]V. F. Weisskopf, "The Frontiers and Limits of Science," *American Scientist* 65 (1977): 405-11.

The Patriarchs of Modern Science

Two key intellectual figures stand out in the crucial period leading to the birth of modern science—Francis Bacon (1561-1626) and René Descartes (1596-1650).

Bacon (figure A.1), a lawyer, philosopher and Lord Chancellor of England, believed that there had been little real progress in the growth of scientific knowledge since the days of antiquity. He saw the status of science as bogged down in an obsessive preoccupation with final causes. These, he argued, belonged rather to philosophy and religion. Too little attention was given to carefully thought-out experiments. He criticized the accepted methods of experimentation as being "blind and stupid—men did it as though they were schoolboys engaged as it were in sport." Scientists of his day he accused of glancing too hastily at the results of their experiments and then imagining that the rest could be done by sheer contemplation.[3]

Bacon called for "minds washed clean of opinions."[4] He stressed the fundamental importance of properly organized observation and experimentation, the careful recording of results and the need for interaction among investigators in different disciplines. The latter would, he believed, result in a mutual enrichment of the various areas of knowledge. The figure of Francis Bacon stands out in the history of science as archcritic of the Aristotelian tradition in science with its slavish commitment to speculative ideas derived largely from classical antiquity.

Figure A.1. Francis Bacon (1561-1626). He criticized the medieval method of experimentation as "blind and stupid." Engraving by Francis Holl, after an old print by Simon Pass. (Reproduced from J. Spedding, R. L. Ellis and D. D. Heath, eds., *The Works of Francis Bacon* [London: Longman, 1857].)

But it is René Descartes (figure A.2) who has been popularly described as the father of the scientific method. He is widely credited with having created the conceptual framework that made the birth of modern science

---

[3]Herbert Butterfield, *The Origins of Modern Science* (London: Bell, 1968), p. 100.
[4]Ibid., p. 111.

possible. Descartes conceived reality as comprising two fundamentally independent and separate realms—the thinking thing (mind) and the extended thing (matter). Everything in his system is to be explained in terms of this dualism of mind and matter, of the spiritual and the material, and it was to lead eventually to the development of scientific materialism with its implicit or explicit denial of the transcendent. However, this clear distinction between these two realms was also crucial to the emergence of a new way of doing science—a science that was to be founded on careful observation and well-planned experimentation.

Descartes was a catholic in the broad sense of the word. His religious beliefs allowed him to make a clear separation of the material creation from the Creator, and this provided the basis for a new kind of freedom, a new way of looking closely at the wonders of nature without fear of offending the spirits that in the prevailing Aristotelian science inhabited and empowered the material world.

Figure A.2. René Descartes (1596-1650). Against the occult magic and mysticism that shrouded the pursuit of knowledge in his day, Descartes believed that truth was accessible to the human intellect, providing it was rightly directed. An engraving by Edelinck, after the portrait by Franz Hals. (Reproduced from E. S. Haldane, *Descartes: His Life and Times* [London: Murray, 1905].)

Descartes began from first principles to formulate a whole new system of knowledge. He had a personal vision of a complete and certain science of nature. The key to the universe was its mathematical structure. His desire to describe nature mathematically led to his famous discovery of analytical geometry (a fusion of algebra and geometry), and this inspired Descartes's belief that all physical phenomena could be reduced to exact mathematical relationships.

He expressed a degree of confidence in his theory of matter and his laws of motion that today appears ludicrous. For example, in a 1632 letter to the French mathematician Marin Mersenne, Descartes wrote, "I have become bold enough to seek the cause of the position of each fixed star."[5]

In fact Descartes used little rigorous mathematics in his explanations of physical phenomena. Rather, he employed quite simple and commonplace models and mechanisms to explain many aspects of the physical world.[6] He believed that a satisfactory science of nature would avoid any reliance on the occult or the mysterious, and this represented a fundamental break with much of the thinking of his day.

It is, however, incorrect to assume that this rejection of the foundations of Aristotelian science began only with such historically prominent seventeenth-century figures as Descartes. John Philoponus, a sixth-century Greek Christian and professor in the academy of philosophy in Alexandria, was in his day one of the greatest exponents of the works of Aristotle and challenged his cosmology at its most vital points.

In a recent book, *The Roots of Science,* theologian Harold Turner explores the remarkable contributions to both philosophy and modern science made by a number of much earlier thinkers, especially Philoponus. Turner seeks to "dispel the stereotype of a dark and stagnant, anti-scientific period in European history from which the Renaissance and then the birth of modern science delivered us." He writes: "There was in fact much more continuity between what went before and the scientific revolution that followed, than our artificial and in this case ignorant cutting up of history into periods allows for. Copernicus, Galileo, Descartes and the other sixteenth century pioneers of modern science knew and drew upon most of the figures we can name in the so-called Middle Ages; and indeed even further back, for it now transpires that Galileo knew the key work of Philoponus, from a thousand years earlier."[7]

Returning then to Descartes's science, we find that in his analysis of nature he proposes wholly material explanations for such phenomena as light, color, heat and sound largely in terms of the size, shape and movement of particles and their interactions in accordance with principles confirmed by everyday experience. He used the familiar example of the slingshot to account for both planetary motion and the phenomenon of

---

[5]Quoted in S. Gaukroger, *Descartes: An Intellectual Biography* (Oxford: Clarendon, 1995), p. 249.
[6]John Cottingham's book *Descartes* (Oxford: Basil Blackwell, 1986) provides a readable introduction to the philosophy of René Descartes.
[7]Harold Turner, *The Roots of Science: An Investigative Journey Through the World's Religions* (Auckland, N.Z.: DeepSight, 1998), pp. 97-102.

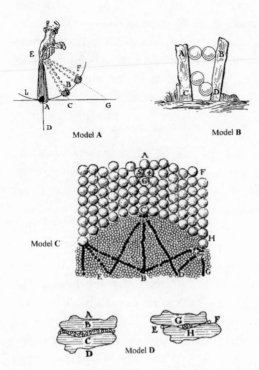

Figure A.3. Simple models employed by Descartes to explain various phenomena in nature. (Reproduced from a facsimile edition of Descartes's *Principia philosophiae* [Paris: Adam & Tannery, 1905].)

light (model A in figure A.3). He explained the differing speeds of revolution of the planets using a simple scheme of spheres progressively constrained in their downward motion by a narrowing set of stocks (model B in figure A.3). He accounted for the "bending," or refracting, of light observed in the tail of a comet with a model comprising large particles resting on much smaller ones (model C in figure A.3). Descartes explained the formation of glass from lime and ashes and the fusion of individual glass particles by means of particles crawling and flowing over one another under the "force" of fire (model D in figure A.3).

Perhaps the most famous model proposed by Descartes was the vortex that he used to account for celestial motion (figure A.4). Here Descartes has the reader imagine a piece of flotsam floating down a river:

> If some straws (or other light bodies) are floating in the eddy of a river, where the water doubles back on itself and forms a vortex as it swirls; we can see that it carries them along and makes them move in circles with it. Further, we can often see that some of these straws rotate about their own centres, and that those which are closer to the centre of the vortex which contains them complete their circle more rapidly than those which are further away from it. Finally, we see that, although these whirlpools always attempt a circular motion, they practically never describe perfect circles. . . . Thus we can easily imagine that all the same things happen to the planets; and this is all we need to explain all their remaining phenomena.[8]

---

[8]Quoted in René Descartes, *Principles of Philosophy,* pt. 3, trans. V. R. Miller and R. P. Miller (1644; reprint, Dordrecht, Holland: Reidel, 1983), p. 96.

So Descartes proposes not merely the vortex as an analogy of celestial motion; rather, for him the mechanism that produces the whirlpool in a river is the same mechanism that operates on the cosmic scale. The "matter" of the heavens is fluid, and it is the motion of this fluid, in Descartes's scheme, that carries all the bodies of the heavens.[9]

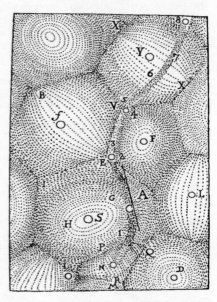

Descartes embarked on a personal journey to set himself free from all the opinions and ideas inherited from the ancient world. He was determined to "doubt everything and start naked once again, without any foothold whatsoever save the consciousness that I who do the doubting must exist even though I may doubt whether I am doubting." Descartes's motive for this radical doubt (figure A.5) was in fact a supremely positive one—that he might discover a firmer basis for truth. In his famous essay "Discourse on Method" Descartes established the fundamental principle of common sense that "all things which we clearly and distinctly conceive are true." [10] As Butterfield notes:

Figure A.4. Descartes's system of vortices used to explain the movement of the heavenly bodies. (Reproduced from a facsimile edition of Descartes's *Principia philosophiae* [Paris: Adam and Tannery, 1905].)

> In the system of Descartes God was another of those clear ideas that are clearer and more precise in the mind than anything seen by the actual eye. Furthermore, everything hung on this existence of a perfect and righteous God. Without Him a man could not trust in anything, could not believe in a geometrical proposition, for He was the guarantee that everything was not an illusion, the senses not a complete hoax, and life not a mere nightmare.[11]

Beginning from this divine reference point, Descartes proposed that the en-

---

[9]Cottingham, *Descartes,* p. 93.

[10]René Descartes, *Essential Works of Descartes,* trans. Lowell Bair (New York: Bantam, 1966), pp. 1-47.

[11]Butterfield, *Origins of Modern Science,* p. 113.

tire universe could be rationally deduced with the exactness of mathematical proof. From just a few fundamental truths that Descartes believed could be established, he was convinced he could reason his way to the very existence of the heavens, the stars and the physical world. Again Butterfield comments:

> The beauty and the unity of the system of Descartes lay in the fact that on the one hand it started from God and worked downwards by a system of reasoning that was claimed to be watertight; while at the same time it worked upwards from below, drawing generalisations or axioms from the experiments.[12]

It appears, however, that Descartes was less concerned about establishing a fact than about its explanation. He considered it more important that his system could provide an explanation, having taken something to be fact. The obvious weakness in Descartes's system was its impoverished experimental base. And as Butterfield has noted, many of Descartes's accepted "facts" were not derived from careful experimentation but were inherited without examination from the scholastic tradition.[13]

Figure A.5. An engraving by Roger Vieillard portraying "Descartes in the Forest of Doubt." He was determined to doubt everything and start "naked" from first principles. (Copyright © ADAGP, Paris, 2000.)

It was certainly an age of strange contradictions. For Descartes, God was essential to his scientific philosophy. In fact, his biographer Father Adrian Baillet wrote, "No philosopher ever had a more profound respect for the Deity than Monsieur Descartes."[14] But Descartes's view of the material world as a perfect mechanical system, functioning in accordance with precise mathematical principles,[15] was probably his most important contribu-

---

[12]Ibid., p. 115.

[13]Ibid.

[14]Quoted in Cottingham, *Descartes*, p. 95.

[15]The idea of nature being likened to a great machine operating with the precision and rationality of a mathematical theorem proved to be a vastly inadequate conceptual framework for the advancement of modern science. The discoveries of the nineteenth century were to

tion to the eventual development of a God-denying scientific materialism.

In his "Discourse on Method" Descartes describes his philosophical calling as having come to him in an oven. History has it that as a late riser he was greatly concerned about keeping warm during his waking hours.[16] He also was living in the midst of a war ("though part of the line lately quiet").[17] It would seem that Descartes had escaped into a baker's oven for physical protection as well as for warmth and solitude. Interestingly, William Temple suggests that perhaps the most disastrous moment in the history of Europe was when René Descartes, having no claims on his time, remained for a whole day "shut up alone in a stove."[18] Temple was of course referring not just to the influence that Descartes's philosophy had on the development of a scientific view of the world, with materialism as its foundation, but also to the much larger picture of Western thought embodied in its religious and ethical systems and in its art, politics and economics.

Descartes's quaint account of his retreat into a "stove" was in one sense a profound metaphor for an entirely new way of establishing truth. He entered his cozy chamber with no thoughts but his own. Beginning with only himself, he proceeded to formulate a radically new interpretation of reality. His action symbolized a breach with that coherent system of thought grounded in the theology and authority of a corrupt medieval church. We might say that the spirit of modernism was born with Descartes's private act of contemplation—the individual becomes the source of ultimate authority and therefore of truth. Temple's chapter "The Cartesian Faux-pas" in *Nature, Man and God* provides an excellent critique of Descartes from this wider perspective, maintaining that relationships, not individualism, are fundamental.

The Italian Giovanni Alfonso Borelli (1608-1679), a contemporary of Descartes and a physiologist, mathematician, astronomer and politician, employed the Cartesian "machine" view in order to explain many aspects of animal movement. Borelli argued that all of the body's physiological

---

show that the important unifying concept of the electromagnetic field required a fundamental break with both the dualism of Descartes and the mechanical model that reached its zenith with the development of Newtonian physics.

[16]Anthony Kenny, "Descartes to Kant," in *The Oxford History of Western Philosophy*, ed. A. Kenny (Oxford: Oxford University Press, 1994), pp. 107-92.

[17]Descartes's own words translated from the French passage quoted in William Temple, *Nature, Man and God* (London: Macmillan, 1951), pp. 63-64.

[18]Ibid., p. 57.

functions, both external and internal, and as diverse as the "cleaning of the blood in the kidneys," muscle action, nutrition, the sensing of pain, shivering and fatigue, could all be explained by mathematical and mechanical laws. He wrote in his famous treatise *De motu animalium*, "As clearly enunciated by divine Plato, Geometry and Arithmetics are two wings by which we ascend to heaven since they enable us to understand the arcanes of Astronomy. We also claim that Geometry and Mechanics are the ladders by which we climb to the wonderful knowledge of the movements of animals."[19] Borelli's mechanical interpretations of the body, and

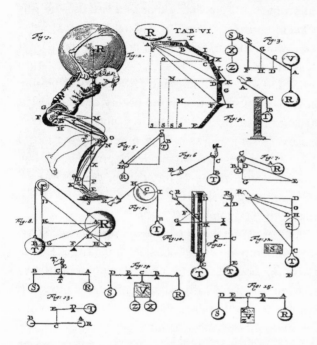

Figure A.6. Giovanni Alfonso Borelli's mechanical analysis of the body showing that a load carried on the neck of a stevedore may require a force to be generated in the extensor muscles of the leg more than forty-four times the carried load. (Reproduced with permission from Giovanni Alfonso Borelli, *De motu animalium [On the Movement of Animals]*, trans. P. Maquet [Berlin: Springer-Verlag, 1989].)

in particular his many splendid drawings (figure A.6), provided a wealth of insight, especially in the field of medical anatomy.

We can think of several other great figures who played profoundly important roles in the rise of modern science. Tycho Brahe (figure A.7), a Dane, was acknowledged to be "a king among astronomers" by one of the most important nineteenth-century mathematical astronomers, Germany's Friedrich Bessel. Tycho was probably the world's greatest naked-eye astronomer, and with his construction of a large quadrant for accurate angu-

---

[19]Giovanni Alfonso Borelli, *On the Movement of Animals*, trans. Paul Maquet (Berlin: Springer-Verlag, 1989), p. 36.

lar measurement of stars he pioneered a whole new era of celestial order.

Tycho also thought very highly of himself. His arrogance had embroiled him in a duel in which he lost part of his nose, and so he wore a replacement fashioned from a silver-gold alloy. One of Tycho's most famous instruments was his great Mural Quadrant (figure A.8) installed in his "castle of the sky" on the island of Hveen near Copenhagen, a forerunner of the great modern observatories. The quadrant consisted of a brass arc with a radius of nearly seven feet and was screwed to the observatory wall. Tycho had filled out the empty space inside the quadrant with a

Figure A.7. Portrait of Tycho Brahe (1546-1601). (Reproduced from J. L. E. Dreyer, *Tycho Brahe* [Edinburgh: Black, 1890].)

mural of himself (complete with metal nose) and the interior of his dwelling. He is represented as pointing up to the heavens, and there at his feet lies a dog, "an emblem of sagacity and fidelity."[20]

One of the most spectacular astronomical observations in Tycho's life was his discovery in 1572 of a new star in the constellation Cassiopeia. This supernova explosion seemed to appear from nowhere, grew even brighter than Venus and could be seen for a time even in broad daylight. By 1574 it had faded almost to invisibility. Apart from the sheer wonder of such an observation, Tycho's new star provided seemingly irrefutable evidence for a universe that was not fixed and unchanging. The observation of a new body in the heavens, and all that it implied, was indeed a frontal assault on a medieval worldview that was grounded in Aristolelian/Ptolemaic cosmology (see next two sections).

Tycho Brahe, with his armillary spheres, large and accurate quadrants and sextants and the many techniques he developed to improve the precision of astronomical measurement, laid the foundation for a revolution in the way the world was to be investigated. Johan Dreyer, the Danish astronomer who became director of the observatory in Armagh, Ireland, in 1882 wrote eloquently of the significance for science of Tycho Brahe's discovery of the new star:

---

[20]For a detailed account of the life and achievements of Tycho Brahe, see J. L. E. Dreyer, *Tycho Brahe* (Edinburgh: Black, 1890).

It roused to unwearied exertions a great astronomer, it caused him to renew astronomy in all its branches by showing the world how little it knew about the heavens; his work became the foundation on which Kepler and Newton built their glorious edifice, and the star of Cassiopeia started astronomical science on the brilliant career which it has pursued ever since, and swept away the mist that obscured the true system of the world.[21]

And so it was to his young German assistant Johannes Kepler (1571-1630) that Tycho Brahe bequeathed both his huge body of hard-won astronomical

data and his belief in the importance of testing theory against carefully collected observations. The brilliant Kepler held a professorship in mathematics and, importantly, possessed a deep faith in the order of God's creation. He was convinced there must be a definite regularity in the movement of the planets and is perhaps most famous for his formulation of the mathematical laws governing planetary motion. Kepler remained deeply fascinated at the thought of spiritual beings having an active role in the workings of the universe.

Figure A.8. Tycho Brahe's famous Mural Quadrant in his "castle of the sky" on the island of Hveen near Copenhagen. (Reproduced from J. L. E. Dreyer, *Tycho Brahe* [Edinburgh: Black, 1890].)

We will discuss the contribution to cosmology made by the great Italian physicist, mathematician and astronomer Galileo Galilei (figure A.9) in the next two sections. For now we might simply note that Galileo wrote as if his own thoughts were in tune with the mind of God. He believed that the very laws he sought to find within the physical world were

---

[21]Ibid., p. 196.

but an expression of the Almighty's thoughts at work within the natural world.

While the scientific and mathematical discoveries of Isaac Newton (figure A.10) were eventually to lay the foundation for the mechanistic, law-bound model of the universe (a view that has come to preoccupy the modern Western mind), Newton himself reflected deeply on the role of the Almighty (figure A.11). In fact Newton was no theological novice. Throughout much of his life he spent a great deal of time in careful study of the Bible. He formulated rules for its interpretation and wrote much about the fulfillment of biblical prophecy and the events of human history. His view of God was certainly of One who transcended the laws of creation.[22]

The French prodigy Blaise Pascal (figure A.12) before the age of eleven "whined for mathematics as another would whine for candy."[23] He published his famous essay on the geometry of conic sections at sixteen, laying the foundation for perspective geometry. He made major contributions to number theory and probability, and solved mathematically the area of the cycloid, the curve described by a point on the rim of a moving wheel.[24]

Pascal's father held an important position as a government administrator of central France. Driven by the sheer drudgery associated with his father's endless calculations of tax levies, Pascal, at the age of nineteen, conceived and subsequently built the first mechanical calculating machine. In his day this invention was judged to be his major

Figure A.9. Portrait of Galileo Galilei (1564-1642) aged about forty years. (Reproduced from J. J. Fahie, *Galileo, His Life and Work* **[London: Murray, 1903].)**

---

[22]For a recent account of Newton's religious beliefs, see John Brooke, "The God of Isaac Newton," in *Let Newton Be! A New Perspective on His Life and Works,* ed. J. Fauvel, R. Flood, M. Shortland and R. Wilson (Oxford: Oxford University Press, 1988), pp. 169-83.

[23]Morris Bishop, *Pascal: The Life of Genius* (London: Bell, 1937), p. 8. For a full account of Pascal's life, this book is an excellent resource.

[24]Galileo had already solved this problem by a practical method of cutting out the figure and weighing.

Figure A.10. Portrait of Isaac Newton (1642-1727) by Robert C. Bell. The eighteenth century has been described as "the age of Newton." (Reproduced from D. Brewster, *Memoirs of the Life, Writings and Discoveries of Sir Isaac Newton* [Edinburgh: Constable, 1855].)

achievement. Today he is perhaps best known for his experiments elucidating the nature of pressure in fluids.

One of the issues that most preoccupied the intellectual world of Pascal's day was the vacuum. Aristotle had denied its existence, and common belief held that "nature abhors a vacuum." The Italian physicist and mathematician Evangelista Torricelli in 1643 discovered the principle of the barometer. He took a tube, closed at one end, and filled it with mercury. With the open end inverted in a bowl of mercury, he demonstrated that the level in the tube sank to a fixed height above the level in the bowl. Torricelli dared to defy the philosophers' abhorrence of the void by arguing that the empty space in the top of the tube was a vacuum created by a balance between the pressure of external air pressing down on the mercury in the bowl and the pressure arising from the height of mercury in the tube.

Inspired by Torricelli, Pascal set out to test the radical vacuum hypothesis experimentally. One of Pascal's less-discussed experiments furnished almost definitive proof: He repeated Torricelli's experiment within another vacuum; that is, he created a vacuum within a vacuum and demonstrated behavior consistent with the hypothesis. Pascal then arranged for a party to take his barometer to the top of the Duy-de-Dome, where, with a decreased weight of air, a drop in height of the mercury column was recorded. These experiments not only enabled him to conclude that "nature has no repugnance for the void"[25] but also led on to important generalizations concerning the behavior of liquids and gases.

Pascal's contribution to the development of modern science was immense. While the science of the seventeenth century was still dominated largely by the principle of authority, Pascal's work on the vacuum was im-

---

[25]Bishop, *Pascal,* p. 65

FOUR
LETTERS
FROM
SIR ISAAC NEWTON
TO
DOCTOR BENTLEY.
CONTAINING
SOME ARGUMENTS
IN
PROOF of a DEITY.

LONDON:
Printed for R. and J. DODSLEY, *Pall-Mall,*
M DCC LVI.

Laftly, I fee nothing extraordinary in the Inclination of the Earth's Axis for proving a Deity, unlefs you will urge it as a Contrivance for Winter and Summer, and for making the Earth habitable towards the Poles; and that the diurnal Rotations of the Sun and Planets, as they could hardly arife from any Caufe purely mechanical, fo by being determined all the fame way with the annual and menftrual Motions, they feem to make up that Harmony in the Syftem, which, as I explain above, was the Effect of Choice rather than Chance.

Figure A.11. An excerpt from Newton's correspondence to Richard Bentley, classicist and master of Trinity College, Cambridge. Isaac Newton reflected deeply on the role of the Almighty. (Reprinted by permission of the publisher from *Isaac Newton's Papers and Letters on Natural Philosophy* **edited by I. Bernard Cohen, Cambridge, Mass.: Harvard University Press, Copyright © 1958, 1978 by the President and Fellows of Harvard College, © renewed 1986 by I. Bernard Cohen.)**

portant to the rise of the scientific method in which ideas and hypotheses were tested against careful reasoning and appropriately devised experiments. His works brought about a further undermining of confidence in the scholastic tradition, which saw Aristotelian authority as the ultimate basis for understanding the physical world. Pascal spoke of pitying "the blindness of those who appeal to authority alone as proof in physical matters, rather than to reasoning or experiment."[26]

He was also a man of deep Christian piety and belonged to the nonorthodox Roman Catholic movement known as the Jansen sect. One of his most popular works was a small book called *Pensées* or *Thoughts on Religion and Other Subjects* in which he reveals the intimacy of his belief in a personal God who alone is the

B. PASCAL.

Figure A.12. A bust of Blaise Pascal (1623-1662) by Pajou. (From *Pascal: His Life and Works* **by Jean Mesnard. London, Harvill Press, 1952.)**

---

[26]Ibid., p. 72.

source of perfect knowledge.

What these pioneers of the new science had begun to create was the idea that nature was a well-oiled cosmic machine, operating with mathematical precision according to immutable laws.[27] And although these great minds had laid the foundation for the eventual development of a God-denying scientific materialism, they saw no conflict between a mechanical cosmos and their own religious convictions. For them God was indeed the Grand Engineer of this machine, having created it and set it in motion like a kind of cosmic Watchmaker. The idea that the Creator then had no further involvement—a now-defunct idea called deism—was firmly rejected, however. God was crucial to the completeness of their worldview, and they saw the soul as being outside the confines of this great mechanical metaphor. But this separation of the observable world from the spiritual was to lead eventually to a radical shift in humankind's perception of itself. Philosopher William Barrett hints at the consequences of this separation:

> For the Christian believer of the 17th century who might be tempted into scientific materialism, there was always a special exception for the Soul. It was not a natural phenomena [sic], like other phenomena; it stood outside of nature. But the effect of this adjustment was to leave the Soul perched precariously on the edge of matter in strange conjunction with its body.[28]

Farewell, Aristotle

In medieval cosmology, before Galileo in 1609 opened wide for us the window of experimental astronomy, the scientific understanding of the world rested on two principal authorities—Aristotle and the Church. Medieval science principally offered a metaphysical explanation of nature rather than a coherent body of knowledge that could both predict and control events in the natural world. Medieval thinking focused largely on the significance and purpose behind natural phenomena. The central issues were those concerned with the nature of God, the human soul, life after death, good and evil.

Aristotle's universe reflected the geocentric (earth-centered) model de-

---

[27]It must be stressed here that the term *law* as used in the context of scientific discovery should not be taken to imply absolute knowledge or understanding. The laws of science represent observable regularities or patterns of behavior of the natural world as determined by science's current ability to measure. These laws should never be given the status of finality or absoluteness as their formulation is dependent on the always finite experience of the human investigator.

[28]William Barrett, *Death of the Soul: From Descartes to the Computer* (Oxford: Oxford University Press, 1987), p. 7.

veloped earlier by the Alexandrian astronomer Claudius Ptolemy. It was divided into sublunary and superlunary realms, the pure celestial moon marking the division between them. Beneath the moon was the earth and all that was changeable and subject to decay. Above it was the unchanging perfection of the heavens, which were conceived of as a series of concentric crystalline shells whose various rotations explained the complex movements of the stars and planets embedded as "pure jewels" within them (figure A.13).

Figure A.13. An engraving from William Cunningham's *The Cosmological Glass,* London, 1559, portraying the Ptolemaic cosmology with its earth-centered view of the universe. Atlas is condemned to support the vault of heaven on his shoulders. (Reproduced from Leonard C. Bruno, *The Landmarks of Science* [Washington, D.C.: Facts on File, 1989]. Courtesy of the Rare Books Collection, Library of Congress, Washington, D.C.)

The earth-centered cosmology in medieval wisdom appeared to explain much that was both obvious to the senses and consistent with prevailing religious thought. All that was heavy, lumpy and brutish was impelled by its very nature to come to rest at this earthly, corruptible center of the universe. An object such as a stone fell because, being brute matter as opposed to undefiled heavenly substance, it was drawn to where it naturally belonged—the earth.

Perhaps the most powerful aspect of this prescientific wisdom was its view of humanity.[29] We humans were at center stage in the cosmic arena. Human significance was at its zenith! But almost overnight, it seemed, this supposedly coherent, authoritative and timeless cosmological system was to be uprooted and discarded as a view totally at odds with the sure facts presented to us by modern science.

---

[29]Bryan Appleyard in his book *Understanding the Present* (London: Picador, 1992), chap. 2, offers an insightful analysis of this dramatic shift from the medieval to the modern scientific worldview.

Galileo's Perspicillum

In light of the firm hold medieval cosmology had on the Western mind, imagine Galileo's shock as he got his first
glimpse of the night sky through his telescope, or as he called it, his perspicillum.
Though quite primitive by modern standards, Galileo's instrument nevertheless
revealed a sight incompatible with prevailing medieval belief. The surface of
the lunar landscape was more like that
of a barren planet (figure A.14), with its
mountaintops and craters (figure A.15),
than that of a pure celestial object. There
were dark spots, or "blemishes," on the
face of the sun. His observations of the
Milky Way revealed a countless array of
faint stars all pointing to a universe that
was vast and perhaps even infinite in its
extent.

Figure A.14. One of Galileo's drawings of the lunar landscape—not the
unblemished celestial object of medieval belief but earthlike with mountains and craters. (Reproduced from
Leonard C. Bruno, *The Landmarks of
Science* [Washington, D.C.: Facts on
File, 1989]. Courtesy of the Rare
Books Collection, Library of Congress, Washington, D.C.)

Galileo's discovery of four of Jupiter's satellites (figure A.16 and figure
A.17) seemed to undermine the Aristotelian system still further. It revealed
the existence of heavenly bodies that weren't revolving directly round the
earth. Wasn't this convincing proof that the earth was not the center of the
universe?

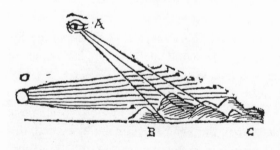

Figure A.15. Galileo's method of obtaining the height
of the lunar mountains. He did this by measuring the
lengths of their shadows—a spectacular example of
the power of the new science with its emphasis on
careful observation. (Reproduced with permission
from Colin Ronan, *Galileo* [London: Weidenfeld &
Nicholson, 1974].)

Galileo's main astro-
nomical discoveries were
completed with his obser-
vation of the phases of
Venus and the rings of
Saturn. Copernicus had
earlier predicted such
phases for both Venus
and Mercury when postu-
lating his much simpler

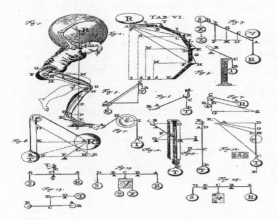

Figure A.16. A portion of Galileo's manuscript recording his observations of Jupiter's satellites. (Reproduced from J. J. Fahie, *Galileo, His Life and Work* [London: Murray, 1903].)

astronomical system in which the planets revolved around the sun (figure A.18) rather than the earth as in Ptolemy's scheme (figure A.13).

The early observations Galileo made of the planet Saturn created for him an inner crisis. From his initial observations he described Saturn as a large central sphere with two smaller ones in close attendance on each side. A later observation indicated that it had the appearance of a single sphere. This threw him into deep self-doubt. Were these apparently conflicting observations really a hallucination, the product of an unstable mind? Were all his amazing discoveries just wild fantasies? In correspondence to Mark Welser, chief magistrate of Augsburg, Galileo reveals his agonizing self-doubt:

> Looking at Saturn within these last few days, I found it solitary without its accustomed stars, and, in short, perfectly round and defined like Jupiter, and such it still remains! Now what can be said of so strange a metamorphosis? Are, perhaps, the two smaller stars consumed like spots on the sun? Have they suddenly vanished and fled? Or has Saturn devoured his own children? Or was the appearance, indeed, fraud and illusion, with which the glasses have mocked me and many others who have observed with me? . . . I cannot resolve what to say in a change so strange, so new, so unex-

Figure A.17. Galileo explains his discovery of Jupiter's satellites to the Grand Duke Cosimo II de Medici. (Reproduced with permission from Colin Ronan, *Galileo* [London: Weidenfeld & Nicholson, 1974].)

pected. The shortness of time, the unexampled occurrence, the weakness of my intellect, the terror of being mistaken, have greatly confounded me.[30]

As it turned out, Galileo had actually observed the rings of Saturn (figure A.19), and these, when viewed at some stages in the planet's orbit around the sun, presented an edge view and were therefore impossible to resolve with a primitive telescope.

This brief account of just some of the remarkable achievements of one of the great intellects of the early seventeenth century serves to illustrate several of the key influences that led to the birth of modern science.

Figure A.18. Copernicus's heliocentric cosmology. Against the prevailing Aristotelian wisdom of his day, Copernicus was to declare that "in the midst of all dwells the sun." (Reproduced with permission from a facsimile edition of the *Complete Works of Nicholas Copernicus*, ed. Pawel Czartoryski [Warsaw: PWN Polish Scientific Publishers, 1972].)

First, experimentation was considered fundamental to the growth of knowledge. Whereas the classical wisdom was essentially speculative and based on tradition and authority, the pioneers of modern science placed a high value on knowledge gleaned from actual measurement and observation.

Second, the early scientists recognized the great importance of mechanical devices in their experimentations, Galileo's tele-

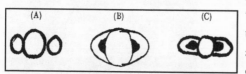

Figure A.19. Galileo's drawings of Saturn. His earliest observation (sketch A) noted that "Saturn was not a single star but three together, which, as it were, touched each other." Galileo's drawings some six years later (sketches B and C) hinted clearly at the familiar ring structure around the planet. (Reproduced from J. J. Fahie, *Galileo, His Life and Work* [London: Murray, 1903].)

---

[30]J. J. Fahie, *Galileo, His Life and Work* (London: Murray, 1903), pp. 110-11.

scope and Tycho Brahe's large quadrant being obvious examples. There was therefore a crucial underpinning of the scientific revolution by technological developments that greatly aided these early experimenters in their endeavor to make accurate observations of the natural world.

A Clockwork Cosmos

Slowly but surely a view of nature, based more on observation and careful experimentation, was beginning to take root in the seventeenth-century mind. Isaac Newton was to show that Kepler's three laws of planetary motion could be deduced from his principle of universal gravitation, thus overturning Descartes's idea of a subtle matter that swirled around in vortices. Newton's laws of mechanics described the behavior of matter in motion, whether it be the movement of the planets in the heavens or the flight of an arrow. These laws provided the early modern scientists with a wholly new kind of power; it was now possible to predict the behavior of many aspects of nature because the same laws were seen to rule everywhere. Isaac Newton's famous optical experiments using a glass prism to split a beam of sunlight revealed the complex nature of light and the origin of color and provided yet another

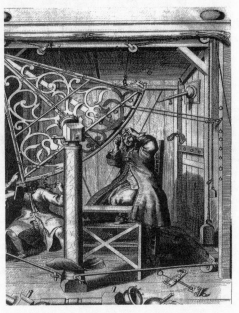

Figure A.20. Hevelius and assistant at work in his observatory. (Reproduced from J. Hevelius, *Machinae coelestis* (1673-1679). Image provided courtesy of the Rare Book Collection, Library of Congress, Washington, D.C.)

spectacular example of the power with which the tools of early modern science could unravel the mysteries of nature.

Thirty-seven years after Galileo made his drawings of the moon, Johannes Hevelius of Danzig (figure A.20) published his *Selenographia*, a masterpiece of astronomical observation. In this meticulously compiled atlas of the moon Hevelius personally engraved some 110 copper plates detailing the lunar features with remarkable accuracy (figure A.21). Hevelius's

Figure A.21. An informal map of the lunar landscape produced by Hevelius. His many engravings combined a rare degree of artistic ability and scientific accuracy. (Reproduced from Johannes Hevelius, *Selenographia sive Lunae descriptio* [1647]. Image provided courtesy of the Rare Books Collection, Library of Congress, Washington, D.C.)

wealth enabled him to build one of Europe's greatest observatories. He explored the heavens with a huge telescope and constructed sophisticated instruments for measuring with great precision the angular distances between pairs of stars.

With Hevelius we see yet another spectacular example of the power of careful observation to shrink ignorance and mystery and to nurture an ever-increasing growth of understanding and mastery of the natural world. Increasingly, the entire universe was viewed as functioning according to elegant mathematical laws, and for many this could only be the expression of a profoundly intelligent and all-powerful God who had devised it all with the precision of a super mathematician-cum-watchmaker.

Figure A.22. Portrait of Michael Faraday by H. Adlard, from a photograph by Claudet. (Reproduced from J. Tyndall, *Faraday as a Discoverer* [London: Longmans, Green, 1894].)

But this new science was also to lay the foundation for a view that would eventually challenge the assumed centrality of human beings within the universe. Theologically, humankind had occupied a preeminent place in the entire order of things. We seemed to be the very point of the cosmos. But the discoveries of these early seventeenth-century scientists were increasingly revealing just how insignificant was humanity's place on one tiny planet no longer at the center of the universe but instead revolving about one of a countless number of equally insignificant suns.

While the pioneers of early modern science had held, almost without exception, strong religious convictions, these were rapidly lost from view in much of the "enlighten-

ment" that surrounded the growth of modern science in the eighteenth and nineteenth centuries. But it must also be remembered that the Enlightenment period had its own remarkable men of deep theistic persuasion. Michael Faraday (1791-1867) was perhaps this period's most famous

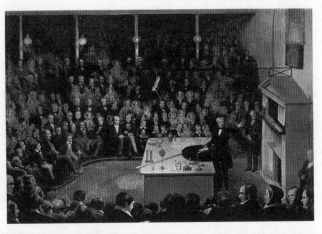

Figure A.23. A Christmas lecture by Michael Faraday at the Royal Institution. He sought to evoke in his audience a sense of wonder for the Creator. (From a painting by Alexander Blaikley. Courtesy of the director of the Royal Institution.)

Figure A.24. James Clerk Maxwell when he was Cavendish Professor at Cambridge University. (Used with permission of the Cavendish Laboratory, University of Cambridge.)

figure (figure A.22) with his discoveries of both electromagnetism and electrochemistry. A devout Christian, Faraday was also renowned for his public lectures on science, which he delivered at the Royal Institution in London (figure A.23). In these lectures he sought to evoke in his audience a profound sense of wonder for God as Creator. Writing about the religious motivation underpinning Faraday's science, Geoffrey Cantor says:

> It must be stressed that Faraday was no secular utilitarian nor did he consider that the primary aim of science was to improve the physical condition of mankind via tech-nology. Instead, the foremost rationale for science was that it displayed the structure of the Creation and therefore glorified the Creator. The justification for science was therefore moral and not utilitarian.[31]

The Scotsman James Clerk Maxwell (1831-1879) was one of the greatest mathematicians and physicists of the nineteenth century (figure A.24). He was also a devout Christian in the Scottish Reformed theological tradition. Maxwell drew on the pioneering experimental research of Michael Faraday. Stimulated by a mathematical paper written by the famous Scottish physicist and engineer William Thomson (later Lord Kelvin), he developed exact mathematical descriptions of electric and magnetic fields and formulated his theory of electromagnetic radiation, which, in unifying magnetism, electricity and light in a single comprehensive theory, brought about a truly remarkable advance in understanding the physical world.

Maxwell's discoveries heralded a new conceptual framework for viewing nature, one that transcended the prevailing Newtonian science founded on the notion of bodies acting instantaneously on each other at a distance and within empty, uniform space and time. In particular, he developed the unifying concept of continuous, space-filling fields of force that were envis-

---

[31]G. N. Cantor, *Michael Faraday: Sandemanian and Scientist* (London: Macmillan, 1991), p. 195.

aged as an intrinsic part of what particles really are.[32] Theologian and philosopher Thomas Torrance says this of Maxwell's thought:

> He severely questioned the analytical, atomistic and rather artificial interpretation of nature in terms of abstract mathematical symbols, necessary as they were in their proper place, for it had the effect not only of dissecting nature but of distorting the real dynamical relations that are all-important in nature's actual behaviour and regular manifestations, and nowhere more than in the electromagnetic field.[33]

Torrance also suggests that this unified relational interpretation of the physical world was possibly motivated by Maxwell's own Christian understanding of personhood in which relationships among individuals rather than persons in isolation are primary. This, he argues, was intrinsic to the theology underpinning Maxwell's philosophical worldview. Interestingly, the contemporary biographer Ivan Tolstoy observes:

> Maxwell's letters, poems and essays show that his life had many strands, all important to him, all running deep—religion, philosophy, love of family, a sense of duty to his fellow men and women. But science provided the day-by-day *framework* within which he ordered his existence, evolved and thought [*sic*]. All his activities were linked; he was strikingly *whole*. His life is full of interesting continuities. A childhood fascination with contrivances, with bell ringers, with the play of light—these grade into adolescent scientific experiments and musings, and almost imperceptibly, into serious, brilliant and ultimately revolutionary work in mechanics, colour theory and electromagnetism. An early sense of wonder and love of nature never left him and, broadening as the years went by, led to an appreciation of philosophy unique amongst his contemporaries, which gave his work on electricity and magnetism its depth. The love of philosophy was linked to a streak of mysticism which found expression in what was, by virtue of his upbringing and early environment, the only avenue open to him—a traditional Christian faith. From this stem his social views, archaic as they seem to us, they are well meant and part of a coherent *Weltanschauung*. It was all one piece.[34]

However, despite this religious dimension that was integral to the thinking of many pioneers of modern science, the spectacular insights into the work-

---

[32]W. J. Neidhardt, "Biblical Humanism: The Tacit Grounding of James Clerk Maxwell's Creativity," *Journal of the American Scientific Affiliation* 41, no. 3 (1989): 137-42.

[33]Thomas Torrance, *Transformation and Convergence in the Frame of Knowledge: Explorations in the Interrelations of Scientific and Theological Enterprise* (Grand Rapids, Mich.: Eerdmans, 1984), pp. 215-42.

[34]Ivan Tolstoy, *James Clerk Maxwell: A Biography* (Edinburgh: Canongate, 1981), p. 159.

ings of nature that this science provided, and the ever-expanding discovery of unifying laws so effective in making sense of diverse and seemingly unrelated phenomena, brought about a growing confidence and belief in the mechanistic model of nature. God's direct hand in the functioning of nature was increasingly assumed to be displaced by the operation of law-bound, impersonal mechanisms. The religious dimension that had so dominated the thinking of those early modern scientists became more and more perceived as a superstitious legacy inherited from prescientific, medieval ideas.

Of course it is an enormous leap from Galileo's first glimpse of the night sky through his perspicillum to the super-sophisticated technologies that have so dramatically shaped our modern world. It is a gigantic leap over the breathtaking achievements of the human mind—achievements that give us great cause to celebrate the amazing power of the scientific method. The body of knowledge derived from this method has been described as scientific materialism and has, as Barrett notes, become

> de facto the dominant mentality of the West in the three and a half centuries that followed. It ruled not so much as an explicit and articulate philosophy, but more as an unspoken attribute, habit and prejudice of mind. And in this unspoken form, it is still regnant today.[35]

Modern Westernized societies are reveling in the technological fruits of the scientific method, the same intellectual activity that produced the philosophy of scientific materialism. As the dissection of nature reaches increasingly spectacular levels of atomization, so we are also witnessing the advance of a deep moral and spiritual malaise penetrating the very fabric of our humanness. Genetic determinism is the scientific flavor of our age. Almost every day yet another form of human behavior or ailment is declared to have its source in a friendly or roguish sequence of DNA molecules. We have forsaken the large integrative picture of the living organism for the reductionist LEGO model of life.

Understanding molecules in motion has become more important than addressing the big questions that relate to purpose and meaning. Personal behavior is increasingly attributed to impersonal molecules, and herein lies what I believe is the absurd myth of scientific materialism. This book has sought to challenge this philosophy by examining the scientific evidence the materialist uses to declare the universe godless. The evidence is found wanting.

---

[35]Barrett, *Death of the Soul,* p. 7.

Permissions

Figure 1.1. Copyright © The Nobel Foundation. Used by permission.

Figure 1.2. Used by permission of Mark Sagar, Gordon Mallinson and Peter Hunter, University of Auckland.

Figure 1.3. St. Paul's Anglican Church, Auckland. Used by permission.

Figure 2.3. Used by permission of the W. B. Saunders Company.

Figures 2.6. 3.15, 6.1. School of Biological Sciences, University of Auckland. Used with permission.

Figures 2.7. 3.2, 3.3b, 3.4, 3.5, 3.8, 4.2, 5.1, 5.5, 5.7, 6.2, 11.3. Used by permission of Vivian Ward, University of Auckland.

Figure 3.1. Used by permission of Elsevier Science and T. A. Bramley.

Figure 3.7. Steve Strove, University of Auckland.

Figure 3.9. © 1959 by J. Gilluly, A. C. Waters, and A. O. Woodford. Used by permission of W. H. Freeman and Company.

Figure 3.11. Used by permission of Cheriton House, Andover, U.K.

Figure 3.13. Roche Diagnostics, GmbH, Germany. Used by permission.

Figure 3.14. Used by permission of J. C. Polanyi.

Figure 3.16. Used by permission of Gotfried Boehnke, University of Auckland.

Figure 3.17. Used by permission of CORBIS/TRANZ.

Figures 4.1. 5.8. *Biochemistry,* 2nd ed., by D. Voet and J. G. Voet. Copyright © 1995. Reprinted by permission of John Wiley & Sons, Inc.

Figure 5.2. © Howard B. Bluestein, University of Oklahoma. Used by permission.

Figure 5.6. Used by permission of the McGraw-Hill Companies.

Figure 7.1. Used by permission of Richard Dawkins.

Figure 8.4. Used by permission of J. M. Dent, London.

Figure 9.4. Special Collections and Archives, Wright State University. Used by permission.

Figure 10.3. Used by permission of Richard Wesley.

Figure 11.7. Used by permission of Warren Judd.

Figure A.5. Used by permission of ADAGP, Paris.

Figure A.6. © Springer-Verlag, 1989. Used by permission.

Figure A.11. © 1958, 1978 by the President and Fellows of Harvard College, © 1986 by I. Bernard Cohen. Used by permission.

Figures A.13, A.14, A.20, A.21. Used by permission of the Rare Books Collection, Library of Congress, Washington, D.C.

Figures A.15, A.17. © Weidenfeld & Nicholson, 1974. Used by permission.

Figure A.18. Used by permission of PWN Polish Scientific Publishers.

Figure A.23. Used by permission of the director of the Royal Institution of Great Britain, London.

Figure A24. Used by permission of the Cavendish Laboratory, University of Cambridge.

All other drawings, photos or figures are either copyrighted by Neil Broom or in the public domain. Every effort has been made to trace and contact all copyright holders for all figures used in this book. The author will be pleased to rectify any ommissions in future editions if notified by copyright holders.

17
mechanistic model
  and God, 218
  of universe, 218
medieval science
  method of, 195
  nature of, 208
megatime
  as magic wand, 73
  cannot substitute for
    creativity, 117, 163
  and materialism, 73
Mendel, Gregor, 132-34,
  136-37
Mersenne, Marin, 196
Midgley, Mary, 29, 79
Miller, Stanley, 73-77, 79,
  81-82, 91, 100-101, 198
mind of God, 18, 204
models
  and false syllogizing,
    105
  can be eye-catching but
    misleading, 107
  LEGO-like, 106
modern science
  birth of, 194, 213
  as a cultural force, 22
  fragmenting analysis,
    32, 191
  and human potential-
    ity, 19
  limited explanatory
    power, 39
  and meaning, 43-44
  need for abstraction, 30
  spirit of success, 19, 41
molecular motor, 49, 61
monkeys and typewriters,
  119
  misleading analogy,
    119, 121
Monod, Jacques, 23-24, 26,
  160
Mullis, Kary, 114-15
mutation, 61, 113, 136-39,
  142, 147, 152, 156, 163,
  165-67
  beneficial, 139
  harmful, 139
natural selection, 61, 107,
  109, 113-14, 116-18, 121,

131, 135-36, 139, 141-44,
147, 152-53, 159, 160-64,
168-71, 174
  contradicts naturalism,
    165
  implies purpose, 160
  sacred utterance for ma-
    terialists, 147, 165, 168
  semantic problems as-
    sociated with, 168
natural theology, 46
naturalism, 16-17, 42, 98,
  103, 117-18, 134, 168,
  170-71, 193
  its metaphysical di-
    lemma, 171
neck-of-giraffe story, 129,
  133
neo-Darwinism, 127-28,
  135, 137, 139-42, 144,
  147, 151-52, 156, 159,
  161, 167-68
  central dogma, 141, 160
  challenges to, 142
  implies disguised pur-
    pose, 107, 163
  the new fundamental-
    ism, 141
  technical meaning of,
    170
Newman, John Henry, 41
Newton, Isaac, 204-7, 213
  laws of mechanics, 213
  nature of light, 213
  theology of, 205
Nicholl, Donald, 186-87
Nilsson, Dan, 165-66
Nobel prize, 18, 20, 23, 25,
  73, 186
nude gene hypothesis, 98-
  99
objectivity in science, 29
Olsen, R. L., 80, 90, 111-12
Oparin, Alexander, 74
Oreskes, Naomi, on mathe-
  matical models, 105
origin of life, 66, 73, 77, 81,
  103-4, 110, 117-18, 135,
  188
  geochemical plausibil-
    ity, 112
  investigator interfer-

    ence in experiments,
    111
  and megatime, 72
  naked gene theory, 98-
    100
  and naturalism, 72
  and popular science, 76
  in primordial broth, 75-
    76
  protein-first hypothesis,
    101
  reductionist ideology,
    78
  RNA-only hypothesis,
    99
  science's unstated as-
    sumptions, 110
  theories based on DNA
    or RNA, 91
  unreality of experi-
    ments, 112
Paley, William, 16
paramecium, 182
Pascal, Blaise, 179, 205-7
  calculating machine,
    205
  contribution to the sci-
    entific method, 206
  experiments with the
    barometer, 206
  on machines, 179
  on mathematics, 205
  religious beliefs, 207
  on the vacuum, 206
Passmore, John, 19-20
Patterson, J. W., 89-90
Pelger, Susanne, 165-66
Philoponus, John, 197
photosynthesis, 21, 35, 38,
  80, 102
  illustrates power of ana-
    lytical method, 38
Polanyi, Michael, 30, 42, 44,
  50-51, 57-58, 61-62, 126,
  181-83
  and hierarchical struc-
    tures, 50
  irreducibility of ma-
    chines, 57
  on knowledge, 42
  on machines, 126
  on objectivity and per-